Words of praise for *Using Data to Close the Achievement Gap*

"This book represents a significant contribution to the national debate around school reform. Ruth Johnson presents a thoughtful, well-documented treatise on how educators, policymakers, and parents can use data to set achievement goals and to measure school progress towards these goals."

Walter Allen, Professor
Department of Sociology, UCLA
Los Angeles, CA

"Dr. Johnson's work provides both the philosophical and practical blueprint for transforming public schools into the learning communities we want and need. Leaders will find the book to be the most useful document to guide and inform their efforts to close the gap and maximize learning for all students."

Joseph Burke, Superintendent of Schools
Springfield Public Schools
Springfield, MA

"From Johnson's penetrating analysis of current research, policies, and practices, and her wealth of experiences working with school districts around the nation, she clearly makes the connection between using data and achieving equitable outcomes as districts and schools struggle to close the achievement gap."

Aukram Burton, Diversity/Multicultural Specialist
Gheens Professional Development Academy
Louisville, KY

"Ruth Johnson's book is an exceptional tool for helping educators understand the importance of using data to guide discussions."

David Hill, Deputy Director
Charles A. Dana Center at UT Austin
Austin, TX

"If the goal of all students reaching high standards is to be met, Using Data to Close the Achievement Gap: How to Measure Equity in Our Schools *should be required reading for all teachers and administrators. It should also be an integral part of the course of study for those preparing to teach in the United States."*

Vinetta C. Jones, Dean
School of Education, Howard University
Washington, D.C.

"In our opinion, this book is the most comprehensive and useful guide that we have found for implementing the school improvement process. The instruments and tools contained in this work are concise and revealing in determining a school's readiness for the reform process."

Kimberly Kinsler and Mae Gamble, Professors
Hunter College of the City University of New York
New York, NY

"Ruth Johnson's work provides guidance for schools that want to use data to explore the many facets that impact student performance and find ways to address issues that impede academic improvement."

Dorothy Knight, Project Director
Charles A. Dana Center at UT Austin
Austin, TX

"With this visionary and user-friendly resource in hand, all educators—teachers, counselors, and administrators—can and must make data part of a lifelong practice to ensure high achievement for all students."

Laurie Olsen, Chief Program Officer
California Tomorrow

"The guidance, tools and protocols Dr. Johnson presents in Using Data to Close the Achievement Gap take the mystery out of the data inquiry process and bring the concept of educational equity into clear focus. Any school or district attempting systemic change that will close the achievement gap should be using this book."

Phyllis Hart, Joyce Germaine Watts, and Vicki Rice
The Achievement Council

Using Data to Close the
ACHIEVEMENT GAP

Using Data to Close the ACHIEVEMENT GAP

How to Measure Equity in Our Schools

Ruth S. Johnson

Foreword by Anne Wheelock

Second Edition of Setting Our Sights: Measuring Equity in School Change

For information:

Corwin Press, Inc.
A Sage Publications Company
2455 Teller Road
Thousand Oaks, California 91320
www.corwinpress.com

Sage Publications Ltd.
6 Bonhill Street
London EC2A 4PU
United Kingdom

Sage Publications India Pvt. Ltd.
M-32 Market
Greater Kailash I
New Delhi 110 048 India

Printed in the United States of America

Library of Congress Cataloging-in-Publication Data

Johnson, Ruth S.
    Using data to close the achievement gap: How to measure equity in our schools / Ruth S. Johnson.
        p. cm.
    Includes bibliographical references and index.
    ISBN 0-7619-4508-3 (C) — ISBN 0-7619-4509-1 (P)
    1. Educational equalization—United States. 2. Educational evaluation—United States. 3. School improvement programs—United States. I. Title.
    LC213.2 .J64 2002
    379.2′6--dc21   2002002766

This book is printed on acid-free paper.

    03   04   05   06   07   7   6   5   4   3

Acquisitions Editor: Rachel Livsey
Editorial Assistant: Phyllis Cappello
Production Editor: Olivia Weber
Typesetter/Designer: Graphicraft Ltd., Hong Kong
Indexer: Kathy Paparchontis
Cover Designer: Tracy E. Miller
Production Artist: Janet Foulger

Contents

Foreword: A Strategy to Challenge Inequality

Anne Wheelock

This book has a message that is as simple as it is welcome: All our schools can organize themselves so that they work for all students. They can be places where all students learn to use their skills in reading, writing, and mathematics to understand and apply enduring ideas in the disciplines. They can become settings that launch all students into the world of postsecondary education and provide them with the learning that allows them to succeed once they get there. All schools can reform themselves to become such places.

The reality that this book confronts and seeks to change is that our schools are not always places where all students experience equal opportunity for success. Instead of expanding opportunity to embrace all students, our schools have sometimes unwittingly but far too often assumed the task of selecting some students to experience the best public education has to offer, allowing others little more than the "leftovers." And this distribution of the most meaningful learning opportunities to those students who already enjoy the greatest advantages in society has both individual and social consequences.

Whereas some students come to think of themselves as "scholars" whose futures are tied to further education, others learn that "school is not for me" and reject their schooling as forcefully as their schools exclude them from the settings that might persuade them otherwise. Dividing the "haves" and the "have nots" further denies all students the experience of full participation in a community of learners that mirrors the real world. In socially diverse schools, this division plays out along economic and racial lines, allowing stereotypes to become entrenched and making it risky for African American, Latino, and Native American students in particular to succeed academically.

The good news is that some schools are ready for reform. No longer content to "get over," these schools share with Ruth Johnson a distinct understanding that schools' own practices often work to squander the talents of young people and that these practices must change. They understand that it is their responsibility to ensure that the time that so many students—especially those who are poor, African

American, Latino, Native American, or our country's newcomers—spend in schools is not wasted. Educators in these schools are already deeply disturbed about the differential treatment students receive at the hands of traditional practice. For those with the will to tackle the thorny issues of low expectations and unequal access to knowledge in their schools and districts, this book provides a strategy to challenge and redress such inequality.

The strategy that Ruth Johnson proposes involves each school and district in a process of self-examination informed by careful analysis of data that describe how opportunities to learn are allocated to all students. What can such a data-based self-assessment do? First, data highlight the gaps between rhetoric and reality. If the school's banners proclaim "All Children Can Learn," a strategy of breaking data down by race and by grade can reveal the extent to which the school's most meaningful learning opportunities realize this belief. Second, data can point to the steps that must be taken to close those gaps. If the school brags that it is preparing all students for postsecondary education, a self-examination can describe how many more students must enroll in the courses that directly lead to success in such settings. Finally, the process of compiling and reflecting on schoolwide data can bond teachers together in a common understanding that they are part of a larger team of professionals responsible for creating a culture of high achievement for all students. Such a process underscores that the success of the whole school depends on making each and every classroom a place where all students experience powerful learning.

For some readers, the benefits of using school data to mobilize efforts to equalize access to valued knowledge and to boost achievement will be obvious. Why, then, are so many schools reluctant to use data to examine their own practice? In part, the job of running a school, which encompasses tasks that are routine and those that are unpredictable, simply leaves little extra time for gathering and analyzing the data that can help schools move toward more potent practice. What's more, the data schools have about their own performance are often limited to standardized test scores compiled long after the test's administration and passed on to the schools themselves only after they are reported in the local newspapers.

Indeed it is frequently "outsiders"—state officials or university researchers, for example—who first gather the data, and other "outsiders"—the local Chamber of Commerce or politicians with an ax to grind—who then use the data, often for purposes that serve neither schools nor their students well. As a result, many educators have come to think of data—whether couched in terms of the numbers of students passing standardized tests or student survey information gathered to determine how students view their teachers and classrooms—as the stuff that bureaucrats in faraway offices use to beat up on schools. In many communities, published reports of student achievement defined by annual test score successes boost the price of real estate. In other communities, such data become the rationale for a steady disinvestment in public education. More recently, policymakers have moved to use selected data in high-stakes accountability schemes to "reward" schools for test score improvements and to "punish" those that do not post gains.

No wonder teachers become cynical about using data to scrutinize their own practices and chart their own course for improved academic effectiveness. Not only do they have little control over which data to collect, they have little say in how the data will be used. Without the time, resources, or experience to make the data work for them and their students, many educators shrug off reports of "indicators" of performance as just one more way to put down schools. Given these circumstances, then, what does motivate educators to collect data on what happens to students in their school, then analyze and apply the data to clarify the steps necessary for improving student achievement?

This book suggests some answers and offers an alternative way to think about using data on schooling. First, imagine an approach that organizes data to describe not only "student outcomes" but also the context of schooling and, in particular, the conditions that Jeannie Oakes of the University of California at Los Angeles highlights as essential for students' achievement: access to meaningful content, press for achievement, and professional teaching practices. Then imagine that this information collection process is harnessed to a commitment to energizing everyone in the school to promote achievement for all students. This is the approach that Ruth Johnson lays out for us.

It is a practical approach, one that Ruth Johnson has used to jump-start schools and districts on the road to equitable reform. But as practical as this model is, it is more than a process for change in individual schools. As the steps outlined in the following pages reveal, this process also represents a new model of accountability for professional practice, one that offers lessons to policymakers as well as practitioners. Distinct from a top-down bureaucratic approach to managing data, this model puts schools themselves in charge of the data collection process. It focuses on gathering data not simply on student "outcomes" but also on the context of teaching and learning, and in particular, it highlights data that describe patterns of student access to knowledge and opportunity to learn. Finally, it compels schools to explain their practices in light of the data they gather and then to use their findings to extend their most challenging opportunities to learn to all students.

In the end, this book, like the data schools work with, is a means to the end of improved student achievement. *Using Data to Close the Achievement Gap* needs to reach every tracked and resegregated school in the country, as well as the various school reform groups. Ruth Johnson invites schools to use data as a lens through which to examine counterproductive and unequal school practices and to remedy those inequalities. She guides schools and districts in developing the skills they need for reform that is focused on the creation of a culture of high standards and equity. Without such a focus, no reforms will ever take. Informed by years of experience, Ruth Johnson sets forward a broad strategy for schools to use and a set of tools to make that strategy work. Finding the resolve to put those tools to use to benefit all students, however, is up to the rest of us.

Anne Wheelock
Author, *Crossing the Tracks: How Untracking
Can Save America's Schools*
Education Policy Researcher

Introduction

During the writing of this book I always had close in mind my own journey to becoming a data user. Once you are struck by the power of data, the story just begins. It leads to deeper levels of discovery—to see familiar things as you have never seen them before. Using data to move the equity agenda forward must become a lifelong habit, a part of practice. It should be a part of the preparation of all educators—teachers, counselors, and administrators.

My journey to becoming a data user began very personally. When I was a student in junior high school, I saw the sorting and tracking system that relegated African American students to the lowest classes. In the seventh grade I wondered why this was happening. I didn't believe we were less capable, but there was something going on that I didn't quite understand . . . or maybe I did. I experienced counselors counseling me to vocational school, but because of other influences in my community, I resisted and went to the Regents High School of New York. However, my brother Ted didn't escape the claws of the system and was sent to a vocational high school to learn to work in a print shop. His aspiration was to be a doctor. Like many African American males who are discounted by schools, the only reason he went to college was because an athletic coach took an interest in steering him back onto an academic path. However, he never became a doctor.

I went into teaching with the belief that all students could learn high-level material. I soon saw that child after child came into kindergarten ready to learn and doing well, but as they moved through the upper grades their learning curve diminished. By first, second, or third grade, many students were already behind. I decided to try to devise ways to ensure that all of my students achieved at grade level. I personally extended learning time for those kids who needed help. They learned.

My personal database that I was beginning to formulate was that it was possible for all kids to learn at grade level and that it was possible to reverse low outcomes for children that others have given up on. That was when I began to wonder seriously about systemic issues. I saw that data were being used for the wrong purposes—as a weapon. Research was coming out that supported belief systems that some groups of kids were less capable than others, but my personal research and experiences—and those of many other individuals—showed otherwise. My students would be tested at the end of the year, and we, the teachers, wouldn't even see those data. There was no way to get any kind of detailed or even summary information about how we were doing as educators. The test scores were used only to sort and label students rather than to give us information about our teaching.

Also, I saw that data were manipulated to bring about the results some people wanted. I saw that very early on, decisions were made about certain students' capabilities. Many who were placed in remedial classes were never getting out. Elaborate systems were set up that provided rationale for sorting students—the sets of formal and informal rules within the schools. When high-stakes testing became more visible, I saw that more kids were placed into special education so that the school would not have to test them and factor in their scores. The group labels persisted when evidence showed otherwise.

So, as an administrator, I set out on my own quest to gather more data and research to show that African American and poor youngsters were just as capable as higher-achieving groups. Working along with other administrators who were willing to take risks, we examined patterns of tracking and opportunities to take mathematics and advanced placement courses. We used the power of data to uncover practices that disenfranchise children and to confront people with the harm they were doing. And we found that we could change people's attitudes and practices.

I continued to read and study about issues of educational practices that disenfranchised certain groups of children. When it came time to choose a topic for my doctoral dissertation, I wanted to spend time researching the academic careers of children from different racial and economic backgrounds. It was important to find out the long-term impacts of initial placements on different groups of children. I found that the initial labels attached to first-grade children when they were placed in high and low groups followed them throughout their elementary and middle school careers. No children from the first-grade low groups were placed in algebra at the middle school level. Ninety percent of those initially placed in the high groups in first grade were in algebra. African American children were most frequently placed initially in low groups and white children in high groups. Few children moved up, and if there was a shift, it was from the middle groups to the low groups. When children's test scores appeared to indicate placements out of lower groups, it made no difference—they were locked in the low groups. Fortunately, I have been able to share and use what I have learned from my research with others. My research also gave me the impetus to continue searching for and developing ways to examine institutional practices.

Nearly 25 years after I began my journey, I continue to be dismayed at how infrequently data are used for finding out about the lives of children. There continues to be little use of vehicles for tracing what happens to young people—especially along racial and economic lines—as they are processed through schools. Once they are labeled, they're gone; they're out of our sights. We're not even looking at outcomes, much less going deeper to find out why. The simplistic answer persists—that socio-economic conditions are to blame, so what can you expect? Many people are in fact aware of data that prove otherwise, but they don't make them public. Others have access to the data and the information, but they don't put them together to look at themselves. There is still tremendous resistance—a conspiracy of silence.

Using what I had learned inside schools and districts, I began to work as an outside change agent. This gave me the chance to refine my practices in using data—and I'm still on that journey to discover new ways of using data. My journey is clearly not based on a propensity for research or crunching numbers. I began with a need to know how to gain information that could be used as a basis for positive change for children. I had to use a strategy that was accepted—I had to speak the same language to meet the opposition on their own terms. I didn't like what I was seeing, so I set out to find compelling data that told what I saw to be true.

I would like to underscore that even though this book focuses primarily on urban schools, the concepts can certainly be applied to rural schools, where so many low-income children and children of color reside. I've found that, in any setting, once you reach caring teachers, principals, and administrators with the power of data, they begin to ask questions and to design their own mirrors of practice and to encourage their colleagues to do the same. That, in the end, is what this book is about. In and of itself this book cannot create an equity agenda—nor can solely learning to manipulate data. The data process must not become another symbolic exercise that does not meaningfully change children's lives. What one has to bring— or to cultivate—is a vision, a passion, and a belief that all children are capable of achieving at academic levels for enrollment in baccalaureate degree–granting institutions.

NEW TO THE SECOND EDITION

Since the first 1996 publication, *Setting Our Sights: Measuring Equity in School Change*, I have been requested by K-16 educators to assist schools, districts, universities, and nonprofit organizations in addressing and examining the major issues affecting the outcomes, policies, and practices that contribute to inequitable outcomes in schools. As I traveled around the country, having conversations and working with districts in the areas addressed in my work, I experienced firsthand what was useful, what needed to be revised, and what additions I needed to include in future work. Many are anxiously awaiting the second edition.

This second edition, entitled *Using Data to Close the Achievement Gap: How to Measure Equity in Our Schools*, has been revised and updated so that it includes information that reflects current research, policies, and practices. All chapters have been revised and reorganized to become more reader friendly. The former Chapters 5 and 7 have been completely reorganized to help users address measurements of equity based on outcomes, policies and practices, programs, and parent and student voice. There are separate chapters on data dialogues (Chapter 5) and on compiling and combining indicators (Chapter 10). An overview of the chapters is provided in Chapter 1.

The literature has been updated to reflect current research, practices, and policies related to equitable K-12 school outcomes and students' future opportunities in higher education and the workforce. Instruments have been added or revised and have integrated standards reform information. The Bibliography and Resource sections have been updated, and Web addresses are included.

Acknowledgments

There are many people I need to thank for their encouragement and contributions toward seeing the book through.

Using Data to Close the Achievement Gap: How to Measure Equity in Our Schools was inspired by many hundreds of dedicated educators in K-12 schools as well as by external change agents throughout the country who are working for equitable school reform and who have used the first edition of my book. I have been invited locally and nationally to speak; to present workshops; and to work with schools, universities, and nonprofit organizations about the information addressed in the book. All reinforced my belief that data are indeed useful in the reform process through their use of equity measures in their schools and districts.

Special thanks are sent to Gary Anderson, a colleague of mine at California State University, Los Angeles. As I was considering a revision of the first edition, entitled *Setting Our Sights: Measuring Equity in School Change*, Gary was so enthusiastic about the possibility that he offered to introduce my book to the publisher of his book, *Studying Your Own School*. His letter and copy of my first edition sent to the acquisitions editor Rachel Livsey at Corwin Press, Inc., resulted in the submission of my revised manuscript for publication.

Anne Wheelock, whose own work to dismantle tracking in schools is an inspiration, honored the book by writing the foreword. I would especially like to acknowledge Diana Alm Liston and Helen Quon, who contributed the section on technology in Chapter 3.

The comments and suggestions of the many busy professionals who took the time to review the manuscript have tremendously enhanced the final book. Patricia Averette, Shan Boggs, Carole Blunt White, Joyce Germaine Watts, Kati Haycock, and Alyssan Slighter generously lent their time and expertise to review and offer edits to the manuscript.

Many contributed to the data displays used in this book. These data were the results of inquiries conducted in schools. Laurell Schenecker and Rochelle Nichols Solomon contributed data. Nora Armenta, Armando Argandoña, and William Glenn contributed elementary school data. Laurice Sommers, a school change consultant for The Achievement Council; middle school teacher Glenn Burri; and high school student Hassani Turner contributed the student revision of the Assessing Institutional Changes in the Academic Culture of Schools instrument. Bill O'Connor contributed data on high school math. Rochelle Nichols Solomon contributed data on course enrollments. Robert Collins contributed the high school master schedules, and Karen Craig contributed high school data and data forms. Lupe Sonnie also contributed high school data forms. Robin Avellar-LaSalle, director of the Principals Exchange, and Vicki Rice of the Achievement Council extensively used the first edition of my book and contributed information and many data displays from their work. Other contributors who designed instruments are cited in the charts and tables throughout the book.

Tracy Ly, who did the production of my first edition, assisted me in this revision. Her expertise in the formatting of the chapters and the design of the graphics was invaluable.

My loved ones—family and friends—have been neglected for many hours and days as I tried to bring this book to life. I thank them for patience and understanding and for hanging in there with me. Special acknowledgments go to my daughters, Shawn Johnson and Catherine Payne.

The following reviewers are also gratefully acknowledged:

Randall B. Lindsey
Visiting Professor
Pepperdine University
Malibu, CA

Gary L. Anderson
Professor
California State University, Los Angeles
Los Angeles, CA

Linda L. Elman
Director
Research and Evaluation
Central Kitsap School District
Silverdale, WA

About the Author

Ruth S. Johnson is Professor of Educational Administration at California State University, Los Angeles. She received her Ed.D. degree in Educational Theory from Rutgers University. Her dissertation was titled *An Exploratory Study of Academic Labeling, Student Achievement and Student Ethnographic Characteristics.*

Dr. Johnson has served in a variety of educational settings in New Jersey and California. At the K-12 level, she has been a classroom teacher, instructional consultant, director of elementary education, an analyst, an assistant superintendent of schools in the areas of curriculum and business, and a superintendent of schools. She was a compensatory education consultant for the New Jersey Department of Education.

Prior to assuming her current position in higher education, Dr. Johnson directed the Southern California Office of the Achievement Council, a nonprofit public interest organization whose mission is to examine outcomes for urban and low-income students and to help schools and districts to build capacity to prepare students to succeed at the highest educational levels, including four-year colleges and universities. Other nonprofit work included directing a teacher initiative for the Los Angeles Annenberg Metropolitan Project (LAAMP).

Dr. Johnson's major scholarly interests and publications focus on processes related to changing the academic culture of urban schools with an emphasis on access and equity. The first edition of this book, *Setting Our Sights: Measuring Equity in School Change*, is being used in schools and colleges nationally. Dr. Johnson makes frequent presentations and serves as a consultant to schools and districts.

This book is dedicated to all the current and future educators and other adults whose mission and work lead them to make schools places where all young people, regardless of background, learn the knowledge and skills to have limitless opportunities in the 21st century. I hope this book will assist them to use data to open eyes; reveal blind spots; give guidance; stimulate dialogue and reflection; challenge inequitable systems; alter policies and practices; and not remain silent in the face of wrongs done to young people.

Setting Our Sights on Student Achievement

1

The Achievement Gap

Framing Our Minds to Set Our Sights

This book is intended to provide a framework and mindset for using data as a lever to create K-12 equitable school reform. It seeks to awaken those who are in a state of day-to-day survival; to offer insights to those who are experiencing a sense of hopelessness about creating fundamental changes for young people who are not academically successful; to encourage those who are already engaged in equity reforms; to help others realize that using standardized testing as the only reform strategy is shortsighted; and to offer ways to assess, challenge, and address inequitable practices so meaningful reform can occur.

Moreover, this book is about how school communities can use data tools and strategies to help defy a scenario where low-income students and students of color remain underachievers. But we cannot expect school communities to meet this challenge without understanding the context in which most find themselves, however strong their desire for improved student outcomes. This chapter describes the critical issues that schools must surmount in order to turn around achievement levels of students. The stages of an equity-focused change process are then outlined, including how the use of data fits into each. Chapters 3 through 11 of this book are built around these stages.

What do I mean by the term *equity*? In the context of this book, I use the term *equity* "as an operational principle for shaping policies and practices which provide high expectations and appropriate resources so that all students achieve at the same rigorous standard—with minimal variance due to race, income, language or gender" (Hart & Germaine-Watts, 1996, p. xx).

THE ACHIEVEMENT GAP

Public education is currently in an era of accountability, high-stakes standardized testing, and standards-based reform. However, there is an absence of meaningful discussion on how to achieve equitable outcomes that do not unfairly penalize the most underserved students. Despite countless school reform efforts during the last two decades of the 20th century, we begin the 21st century with continuing gaps in academic achievement among different groups of students. The gaps in achievement appear by income and by race and ethnicity. Large percentages of low-income, African American, Latino, and Native American students are at the low end of the achievement ladder, and large percentages of middle- and high-income white and Asian students are at the top of the achievement ladder.

The longitudinal results from the National Assessment of Educational Progress (NAEP, a test that is administered nationally to voluntary school districts in grades 4, 8, and 12) indicate a narrowing of the achievement gap among diverse groups in the 1970s and 1980s. This pattern began to reverse in the 1990s, at which time the gap began to widen again (Blank & Gruebel, 1995; Haycock, 1998; Haycock, Jerald, & Huang, 2001; National Center for Education Statistics, 2000; Viadero, 2000).

The College Board's National Task Force on Minority Achievement (1999) offers compelling evidence about the persistent gaps between African American, Latino, and Native American students and their white and Asian counterparts that begin in elementary school and continue through the postsecondary levels of education:

- The gaps are found among these groups regardless of socioeconomic level.
- At second and third grade, African American, Latino, and Native American youngsters are scoring much lower than their white and Asian counterparts are.
- African American, Latino, and Native American 12th graders made up only about in 1 in 10 of those students scoring at the Proficient level on the 1996 NAEP math and science tests, although they represented about one third of the population who took the test. They did somewhat better in the 1998 reading tests, but their scores were not comparable to those of their white and Asian counterparts.
- There are gaps in other measures of achievement, such as grades and class rank.
- Achievement gaps are evident in the Advanced Placement and SAT exams.
- Although college-going rates are increasing for all groups, African American, Latino, and Native American students earn much lower grades than do white and Asian students with similar admission test scores. Data for 1995 show that they represented only 13% of the bachelor's degrees, 11% of the professional degrees, and 6% of the doctoral degrees earned, although they make up 30% of the under-18 population.

The picture is not all bleak. There are some promising indicators that show increasing numbers of students of all backgrounds taking college preparatory courses and Advanced Placement and college entrance tests. These encouraging signs, however, must be supported by systems that provide not only access, but also appropriate preparation and resources for success.

SOME OTHER CONSIDERATIONS

There are other measures of equity related to student achievement that are not receiving the same attention as test scores. The first is the overrepresentation of some groups in special education, and second, the technology divide. These areas have long-term consequences for students' life opportunities and therefore need careful monitoring.

A recent report on special education by the Civil Rights Project at Harvard University (cited in Fine, 2001) found that African American youngsters are more often classified as needing special education, and once they are classified they are not likely to be placed in mainstream classrooms or returned to regular classes. African American students were more often given labels such as *mentally retarded* and were provided with a less rigorous curriculum. U.S. Department of Education data for 1997 cited in the project report found that "Black students were 2.9 times more likely than whites to be identified as having mental retardation. They were 1.9 times more likely to be identified with an emotional problem, and 1.3 times more likely to be identified with a specific learning disability" (Fine, 2001, p. 6). The study indicates that bias plays some role in the overrepresentation of African American students in special education.

Likewise, the technology "divide" has the potential to perpetuate "haves and have nots," not only in the area of hardware, but more importantly by denying large numbers of students exposure to the kinds of software that give students access to high levels of knowledge. Although more students at all income levels and groups have access to computers, low-income students, females, low-achieving students, minority students, students whose primary language is not English, students who live in rural areas, and students with disabilities are not likely to have the same access to computers as higher-income and white students do (Bushweller & Fatemi, 2001; Scoon Reid, 2001). Other contributing factors that I have observed in many urban schools are woefully old school buildings that do not have the space, the up-to-date wiring, or the security equipment. In these schools, computers were gathering dust or still in the boxes.

The other technology "divide" concerns the type of computer programs students use. Kohl (quoted in Scoon Reid, 2001) states,

> Schools with predominantly minority enrollments are more likely to use their state-of-the-art technology for drill, practice, and test-taking skills. Meanwhile, white students in more affluent communities are creating Web sites and multimedia presentations. The computers become nothing much more than trivial workbook and control mechanisms for kids in the heavily minority schools. . . . In other communities, they are instruments used toward the success and the futures of kids. (p. 16)

There is also a gender divide. Young women are not choosing technology majors, and The College Board reported only a small percentage of the almost 20,000 students who took the Advanced Placement exam in computer science were females (Gehring, 2001).

RETHINKING THE ISSUES: CREATING THE CONDITIONS FOR MOVING FORWARD

We must aim to create a nation of high achievers regardless of background. Most Americans seem to believe that the achievement gaps among groups are inevitable—the result of obvious differences in the economic and educational resources that different groups can bring to bear. But this doesn't explain why some schools—indeed, some whole districts—serving poor and minority children achieve much better results than comparable schools and districts do (see Chapter 2). Indeed, if the causes of underachievement rest primarily in families or the students themselves, these results shouldn't be possible. Perhaps it isn't poverty or racial/ethnic background in and of itself, but rather our response to it (Haycock et al., 2001; Howard, 1991; Irvine, 1990; Jones, 1994; Ladson-Billings, 1994).

Explanations of why the gaps exist are often one-dimensional and offer insufficient, or at worst inappropriate, evidence as to how to address the gap problem. The explanations most frequently cited point to the inadequacies in the child's culture and community and the socioeconomic levels of the family. The assumption about the correlation between low income and low achievement is reinforced by a steady stream of data.

Mickelson (2001), Irvine (1990), the College Board's National Task Force on Minority Achievement (1999), and others give evidence to dispute these simplistic explanations. For example, Singham (1998) found that in Shaker Heights, Ohio, a predominantly African American and white middle- and upper-middle-class community, there were large academic achievement disparities at the high school between African American and white students with similar income levels. Despite having a school enrollment of equal numbers of African American and white students, the composition of the general education track was about 95% African American, whereas the composition of Advanced Placement classes was about 90% white.

Explanations must be more complex than simple. Responding to the notion that the reason for underachievement rests solely on the backs of the students and their families, Singham (1998) concluded, "An alternative explanation is that the primary problem lies not in the way black children view education but in the way we teach all children, black, whites, or other" (p. 12).

There is evidence from as early as the 1970s (Edmonds, 1979) and beyond (see references below and in Chapter 2) that describes how schools with large populations of low-income students and students of color mitigate perceived achievement barriers. Some of the major factors are the following:

- High goals, high standards, high expectations, and accountability for adults and students ("Better Balance," 2001; Haycock et al., 2001; Kahle, Meece, & Scantlebury, 2000; Kim et al., 2001; Olson, 2001)
- Whether or not students receive well-qualified and culturally competent teachers (Darling-Hammond, Berry, & Thoreson, 2001; Ferguson, 1997, cited in Haycock, 1998; Haycock, 1998; Kain & Singleton, 1996; Ladson-Billings, 1994; National Commission on Teaching and America's Future, 1996)
- Curriculum content and rigor (Adelman, 1999; Gamoran & Hannigan, 2000; National Center for Education Statistics, 1995; National Commission on the High School Senior Year, 2001; Office of Education Research and Improvement, 1994; Valverde & Schmidt, 1998)
- Continuous inquiry and monitoring through the use of data (Johnson, 1996a; Olsen, 1996; Sandham, 2001a)

High Goals, High Standards, High Expectations, and Accountability for Adults and Students

We are in an era of a standards-based reform agenda embodied in Goals 2000, the Improving America's Schools Act, and other initiatives. Forty-nine states have standards in at least one academic area (Iowa is the exception). There is mounting evidence that clear goals, high standards and expectations for all, and assessments that are aligned to standards can help in the effort to raise student performance in all schools. There are hopeful indicators. Formerly low-achieving schools that have embraced these principles are demonstrating dramatic gains in student achievement. Throughout the 1990s, the states demonstrating the largest gains in mathematics and reading on the NAEP were Connecticut, Kentucky, North Carolina, and Texas. These states have consistently supported standards-based reform since its beginnings.

Other hopeful signs that support standards-based teaching are cited in a multiple-year study of Ohio's National Science Foundation State Systemic Initiative project (Kahle et al., 2000). The study's major findings were as follows:

- Standards-based teaching in science resulted in improved achievement and attitudes in science for African American students in Grades 5 through 9 in urban schools.
- Although females scored higher, there was a strong and "more positive relationship between attitudes and achievement for boys" (p. 1033).
- Students of teachers who participated in standards-based professional development that focused on content knowledge, inquiry, and problem solving scored higher on the science achievement test.
- The gender achievement gap between African American girls and boys was reduced.

We need to continue to push forward. Although 49 states have adopted standards in one or more subjects, many of the assessments are not aligned with the standards, there is still a lot of focus on low-level testing, the curriculum is often inadequate, and teachers are not receiving appropriate professional development (Olson, 2001). At the inception of the standards movement, Winfield and Woodard (1994) strongly urged us to examine inputs, related to whether and which students are afforded "opportunities to learn," using indicators such as content covered, materials used, quality of teaching and learning, and support systems. This message is still timely. Opportunity-to-learn indicators need to be monitored as stringently as test scores and graduation rates are. If they are not, the standards reform movement, like others, will fail many of our young people. Changing content and performance standards without fundamentally transforming educators' practices, processes, and relationships cannot lead to success.

Teacher Quality

There must be an unrelenting focus on improving the quality of teaching. The National Commission on Teaching and America's Future (1996) is emphatic in its message that teacher content knowledge and strategies absolutely affect student achievement, particularly for students in low-achieving, low-income urban and rural schools. Across the nation, students in low-income schools are more likely to be taught by unqualified teachers. Figure 1.1 demonstrates that low-income students are more frequently taught by teachers who lack a minor or major in the content area that they are teaching.

Studies done in Tennessee, Dallas, and Boston also link teacher quality to student achievement. The teacher effectiveness study in Dallas by Jordan, Mendro, and Weerasinghe (cited in Haycock, 1998) shows the three years' cumulative effect on students who were taught by effective or ineffective teachers. Students who began at similar starting points in fourth grade experienced very different outcomes three

Figure 1.1   Classes in Low-Income Schools Are More Often Taught by
Underqualified Teachers

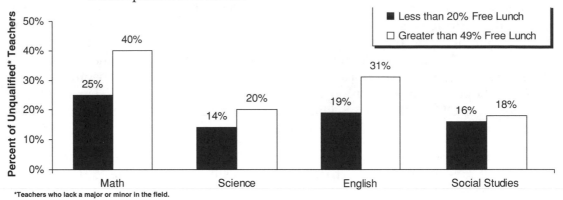

*Teachers who lack a major or minor in the field.

SOURCE: The Education Trust, Inc. *Achievement in America 2000* (Slide 46).

Secondary Source: National Commission on Teaching and America's Future (1996). *What matters most: Teaching for America's future*, p. 16. New York: Author.

Figure 1.2   Effects on Students' Math Scores in Dallas (Grades 3–5)

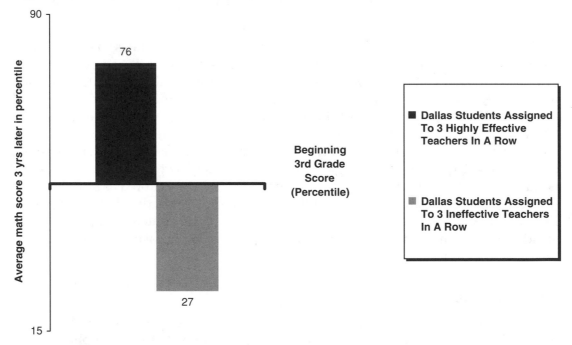

SOURCE: The Education Trust, Inc. *Achievement in America 2000* (Slide 49).

Secondary Source: Jordan, H., Mendro, R., & Weerasinghe, D. (1997). *Teacher effects on longitudinal student achievement.* Paper presented at the CREATE annual meeting, Indianapolis, IN.

years later. Those with three very effective teachers in a row rose to the 76th percentile from the 59th percentile by the end of sixth grade, whereas those with three ineffective teachers had fallen to the 42nd percentile by the end of Grade 6 (see Figure 1.2).

In some cases race is more of a factor than income. Kain and Singleton (1996) found evidence of situations where race played a more prominent role than income. African American students in Texas had less chance of receiving qualified teachers

Figure 1.3   African American Students More Likely to Have Ineffective Teachers: Tennessee

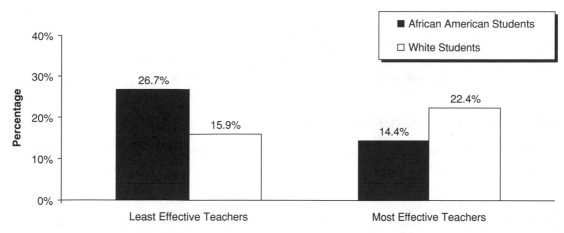

SOURCE: The Education Trust, Inc. *Achievement in America 2000* (Slide 51).

Secondary Source: Sanders, W. L., & Rivers, J. C. (1996). *Cumulative and residual effects of teachers on future student academic achievement*. Knoxville: University of Tennessee Value-Added Research and Assessment Center.

than poor white students did. Sanders's and Rivers's work (cited in Haycock, 1998) in Tennessee shows that African American students were more likely to have an ineffective teacher than white students were (see Figure 1.3).

It is clear that teacher quality has an impact on student achievement. It is also clear that students in low-income schools who need the best are getting the least qualified teachers. Closing the gap requires high-quality teaching and underscores the need for leaders to examine system policies, contracts, and practices that continue to perpetuate conditions of underachievement. It also requires teachers who use culturally relevant approaches to create meaningful learning experiences for students. This approach to instruction builds on rather than "tears down" or devalues a student's background and experiences.

Leadership

Educators look to their leaders for direction and support. But most school districts —particularly urban school districts—are hierarchical systems with honored routines that can be traced back to the early 20th century. These practices inhibit collaboration and true collegiality, resulting in allegiance to institutional norms rather than to student achievement. As a result, schools and districts may inhibit risk taking and stymie individual initiative (Johnson, 1996a; Winfield, Johnson, & Manning, 1993).

If supervisors lack vision and seek only control and containment, they will most certainly not encourage or appreciate any reforms on the part of their staff that might rock the boat. There may be isolated success in some classrooms, but not in entire schools or districts. For reform to take hold, leaders must engage in the process rather than remain outside of the action. Similarly, if leaders offer rhetoric without attending behaviors, educators will become disenchanted.

There has been a continuous stream of literature that has focused on the critical role of leadership in whole school transformation (Barth, 1990; Edmonds, 1979; Elmore, 2000; Evans & Teddlie, 1995; Sergiovanni, 2001). The principal and other leaders in the district must have a vision of change, communicate effectively, lead the instructional path, monitor progress, and support the staff continuously. Fullan (1993) suggests that district administrators are the single most important individuals for setting the expectation for reform within local school districts. He argues that districts need to elevate instruction as a focus, using management to sort out the right choices for curriculum professional development, and so on. It is of critical importance for district administrators to fully understand and be able to implement successful reform strategies (Elmore, 2000; Johnston, 2001; Jones, 1994; Tewell, 1995).

Curriculum Content and Rigor

The evidence continues to build around the necessity for all students to engage and become proficient in rigorous curriculum content and problem-solving skills. There are vast inequities in what gets taught to whom, and many students and their parents are duped into thinking that they are receiving an education that will qualify them for college admission or a "good-paying professional job," when in reality their education may be relegating them to low-paying service positions. In schools that place students in lower curriculum tracks, students are likely to receive watered-down instruction. Chapter 2 will provide a fuller discussion of this area.

Continuous Inquiry and Monitoring Through the Use of Data

The goals, standards, and long-term outcomes for students are important and must be clearly stated so they are measurable. This involves both quantitative and qualitative measures to get authentic information about the school and district culture. Measures are needed to assess the progress of all students—in both the short and long term. The school community must ask the right questions to create a climate of high academic achievement that is good for students and adults. Measuring and monitoring outcomes, program effectiveness, and policies and practices at all levels of the institution should become interwoven into the everyday life of the institution. When policies and practices are analyzed, there is a very high probability that institutional biases and other uncomfortable issues may surface. Surfacing the issues provides the potential for problem solving and improved practices related to student achievement.

STAGES IN THE CHANGE PROCESS: HOW DATA OFFER HELP AND HOPE

Educators who desire broad-scale improvement in student outcomes must embark on a challenging process of changing whole systems—and the cultures within them. This book encourages educators to embrace data as an empowering tool in this work.

The barriers to change—and the conditions that must be created to allow for change to take hold—are significant. But what must give us hope is that many schools have risen and continue to rise to these challenges, using data inquiries at every stage to inform their direction. This section outlines the core stages of the change process that seriously committed schools should anticipate—and around which this book is constructed.

The stages in the change process are presented to assist in visualizing the deep-level work required—they are not necessarily recommended as an implementation model in the strictest sense. They also are not rigid; schools and districts may well enter the stages at different points. Some stages are overlapping and ongoing, and two or three might be active simultaneously. For example, even though monitoring of progress is discussed last in this book, it must be planned and carried out from the beginning of the change process. All of the stages take dedicated time and must be addressed if substantive change is to occur. Finally, although the stages suggested here are fundamental, they are not all-inclusive—educators may identify a number of additional substages within each stage in the reform process.

1. Getting Started: Building the Leadership and Data Teams

Reform begins with individuals within the school, the district, and the community. Sometimes there is an outside catalyst, such as an external review, that identifies the need for major reform. Whatever the reason, individuals must recognize from the beginning the value of an inclusive and equitable reform process and how data can be used as a fundamental tool in the process. Chapter 4 describes the basics of launching the school change leadership team and the data team, and it offers a variety of instruments for teams to assess their internal dynamics and effectiveness as well as to carry out their planning.

The school change leadership team must be committed to initiating and maintaining communication among the entire school community and to building consensus around the change process based on meaningful data. The leadership and data teams must be trained with the proper skills and allowed adequate professional time to collect and analyze data for the school.

2. Killing the Myth/Building Dissatisfaction

Schools are socializing agencies for both educators and students, and the content and context of that socialization are very powerful. As a result of a series of educational practices, educational outcomes are affected. When practices are manifested in low expectations, low-level curricula, and essentially low-level instructional strategies for low-income children, low achievement is the outcome. These can become accepted, institutionalized practices, to which administrators, teachers, parents, and students become accustomed. Thus, the practices go unquestioned and are systematically perpetuated (Haberman, 1991).

Dedicated educators must therefore set about "killing the myth" that low-income children and some racial/ethnic groups are incapable of anything but low outcomes. The school community must review national data on the economic outlook for students who receive an inferior education. They need to see data from schools that have defied the myth that low-income students cannot achieve at high levels. And they need to see the broad discrepancies between rhetoric and actual teaching practices at schools like their own. This is necessary to help build a momentum of dissatisfaction among colleagues that inspires commitment to change. The examples provided in Chapter 2 can be used by school communities for this purpose.

3. Creating a Culture of Inquiry: Assessing Where You Are, Why You Are There, and What Needs to Change

Willingness to ask questions—and to look for the real answers—gets to the heart of how data can stimulate the school change process. School communities and districts need to evaluate the practices and services offered to students and how both are delivered. Creating a "culture of inquiry" involves analyzing relevant data, probing perceptions about why things are as they are, and examining the academic culture, including issues of access, equity, and opportunities to learn. The strategies, a variety of instruments, and the sample data presentations are found in Chapters 5 through 10 to help school communities to

- Measure outcomes
- Assess the academic culture, policies, practices, and programs
- Establish multiple and combination quantitative and qualitative indicators of the school's or district's academic health
- Assess differential expectations and behaviors on the part of staff in providing different groups of students opportunities to learn the curriculum
- Utilize the voices of students and parents to improve access to academic courses and college-going opportunities
- Assess access and equity of achievement opportunities for students using current data sets by disaggregated groups, such as test scores, program placements, course enrollments, and college-going rates by race, ethnicity, language, and gender

4. Creating a Vision and Plan for Your School

Once the school community understands its possibilities and its needs through the inquiry process, it is time to begin envisioning the future. What should institutional practices look like? How will people be behaving and interacting? What types of student outcomes are desired? And what do we want the school to look like in three to five years' time? This planning stage requires long-term intensive collaboration among the implementers of the change. Schoolwide priorities must be identified, responsibilities assigned, resources allocated and reallocated, measures of progress determined, and timelines established. Chapter 11 provides guidance on these issues, including models for school visions and plans.

5. Monitoring Progress

Monitoring must become part of the school culture. Not only do test scores not tell the whole story, they sometimes tell the entirely wrong story and are used unwisely. The quest must be to evaluate whether the reforms are appropriate and whether they are raising the level of student achievement. A plan to monitor the progress of every goal should be devised. In addition to objective indicators of progress, changes in the academic culture of the institution or district need to be monitored. Chapters 6 through 11 provide assistance in looking at both student outcomes and changes in the culture and practices of the school. A wide variety of indicator combinations for monitoring progress are offered.

Before launching into the chapters on the stages of the change process, Chapter 3—"Data in the Reform Process: How and Why"—gives an overview of how school communities can make the shift from unwilling "data providers" to ready and willing "data users" focused on changing outcomes for their students. It describes the fundamental roles data can play in a change process and outlines some basic strategies for collecting, analyzing, and presenting data and creating the data dialogue.

2

Building Dissatisfaction and Killing the Myths

Examining Data as a First Step
Toward Motivating Reform

At a conference on the effects of tracking, a kindergarten teacher was shocked to learn that the student ability groupings she practiced within her own classroom could set the children on a course for life. Students who were taught in low-ability groups and received low-level and watered-down curriculum were on a route to being denied access to college preparatory courses, entrance into four-year colleges, and employment opportunities in higher-level careers that require college degrees. This teacher worked at an inner-city school with a high concentration of low-income African American and Latino children. The practice of teaching only low-level skills was pervasive—children were thought incapable of more challenging lessons or of ever going to college. Yet the teacher and others at the school believed they were doing what was best for "those kids."

But after seeing data on the persistently large gaps in college-going rates between students of different racial groups, as well as the dismal economic opportunities for students who do not go to college, the teacher began to worry. When she saw additional data from a high school in her district showing the gaps between students' own career aspirations and the actual courses in which they were placed, the teacher began questioning most of her own basic assumptions.

In the following weeks, the teacher contacted some of the schools she had learned about at the conference, schools that were challenging the status quo and raising the achievement levels of their students. She soon became determined to change her own school's practices, which she now considered devastating. She asked for assistance from her principal, lamenting, "I can't stand to think of all the children we are destroying."

At the school's next professional development meeting, the teacher made a presentation on the data she had gathered at the conference and informed her colleagues what she was learning about tracking. A core group of teachers became deeply concerned. Together, they spent the next few months reading the research, visiting schools, and looking at more data. They began to design strategies to change grouping practices and the content they were delivering to students. Eventually, they adopted a supportive approach based on the theme "College Begins in Kindergarten." This core group of teachers eventually expanded to become a school leadership team, engaging the entire school community in a reform process.

Overview

This chapter suggests ways to use data to dispel myths about who can learn different levels of content and to build dissatisfaction among the school community about the low educational outcomes for many students. The data include national educational and economic trends, as well as portraits of real schools that have—and have not—offered their students the fullest educational opportunities. Reviewing such data is a vitally important step, because unless the school community is deeply dissatisfied with the status quo and determined to do better, any reforms will be marginal and short-lived.

Data can provide tremendous food for thought in schools where low expectations lead to low results for large numbers of young people—most often low-income students of color. These are the first kinds of data schools should examine to absorb the troubling implications of tracking and other status quo practices that have been outlined in Chapter 1. Data begin to illustrate the gaps between words and actual behaviors in many schools. They can also serve as an introduction to the power of data for educators seeking to build a case in their own school communities for fundamental systemic reform.

When to Use

Data on societal trends and differential educational opportunities are useful at two different stages in the school reform process, depending on the awareness of educators in the setting: (a) in schools and districts that have already decided to embark on fundamental reforms in academic outcomes for students, and (b) to provide a jolt to schools and districts that do not realize that they need to change current practices.

These data have often helped to set the stage for the direction of reform. By highlighting inequities and false assumptions about young people, they provide a context for discussing institutional practices that affect outcomes before the staff tackles looking at its own local data.

These and other data need to be continually updated as new reports emerge. Publications and related Web sites include *Education Week*, a national weekly newspaper; *The Conditions of Education*, which is issued periodically by the National Center for Education Statistics (1993); and publications of the U.S. Department of Education. Nonprofit organizations such as The Education Trust in Washington, D.C., and The College Board in New York publish information about many of the latest research reports and books in education and are useful data sources (see Bibliography and Resources for Equitable School Reform, which includes Web sites for more information).

Stop! Before You Start

At some time during the data review process the school staff should begin a discussion about the ways in which assumptions about "what is" can lead to institutional racism. Understanding the ways institutions function helps in looking at the broader context of why things are the way they are. The definition by Cummins (1989) is compelling:

> Institutionalized racism can be defined as ideologies and structures which are used to systematically legitimize unequal division of power and resources between groups which are defined on the basis of race. . . . The term "racism" is being used here in a broad sense to include discrimination against both ethnic and racial minorities. The discrimination is brought about both by the ways particular institutions (e.g., schools) are organized or structured and by the (usually) implicit assumptions that legitimize that organization. There is usually no intent to discriminate on the part of educators; however, their interactions with minority students are mediated by a system of unquestioned assumptions that reflect the values and priorities of the dominant middle class culture. It is in these interactions that minority students are educationally disabled. (p. 52)

The school community should also read and view the important resources listed here. It might be useful to have a very skilled external facilitator, experienced in issues of educational equity and school reform, to assist with the process (see Chapter 1). The staff will need at least a two-hour block to review and discuss some of the readings and videos, preferably in both small and large groups. A reminder: Don't rush this process or squeeze it in between agenda items at a faculty meeting. The optimal environment is off-site, where the school community is free of distractions. Each group should have a facilitator and a recorder. Some suggested guidelines for questions are the following:

- What information was new to you?
- Did this information cause you to rethink some of your assumptions? Which ones?
- Did this information validate some of your assumptions? Which ones?
- What are the implications for our school and our students?
- What are the challenges?

Readings (see Reference section for full citations):

Answers in the Tool Box: Academic Intensity, Attendance Patterns, and Bachelor's Degree Attainment (Adelman, 1999)

Changing the Odds: Factors Increasing Access to College (Pelavin & Kane, 1990)

Crossing the Tracks: How "Untracking" Can Save American Schools (Wheelock, 1992)

"Do We Have the Will to Educate All Children?" (Hilliard, 1991)

Educate America: A Call for Equity in School Reform (National Coalition of Educational Equity Advocates, 1994)

Measuring What Counts: A Conceptual Guide for Mathematics Assessment (Mathematical Sciences Education Board and National Research Council, 1993)

From Gatekeeper to Advocate: Transforming the Role of the School Counselor (Hart & Jacobi, 1992)

Keeping Track: How Schools Structure Inequality (Oakes, 1985)

Locked In/Locked Out (Dentzer & Wheelock, 1990)

"The Pedagogy of Poverty Versus Good Teaching" (Haberman, 1991)

Savage Inequalities (Kozol, 1990)

The Work of Nations (Reich, 1991)

Thinking K-16, all volumes

Education Trust Web site (www.edtrust.org)

THE BROADER PICTURE: SOCIETAL IMPLICATIONS OF UNDEREDUCATING CERTAIN POPULATIONS

After the staff has spent time grappling with the implications of institutional racism and reading some of the suggested literature, they should begin examining the real-life results of inequitable institutional practices. The first set of "bottom-line" data presented in this chapter calls on a variety of sources to display the intrinsic links between education and life opportunities. What will be the future career opportunities for students who do not attend four-year colleges? Are students of color being educated to fulfill the workforce opportunities of the 21st century? Data that help answer these questions widen the viewing lens of members of the school community, who often don't have opportunities to discuss the connection between educational practices and broader societal issues.

We must be mindful of long-term outcomes for our students in all our practices. Data such as those that follow can begin to plant the seeds for this mindset. In the following pages, only a few examples are offered.

Educational Attainment Counts: Annual Earnings by Level of Education

Figure 2.1 clearly shows that those with the least amount of education are at the bottom of the income ladder. The link to levels of education and future earnings is apparent. These data need to be shared with parents and students, as well as pro-

Figure 2.1 Mean Yearly Earnings Potential as Related to Educational Level

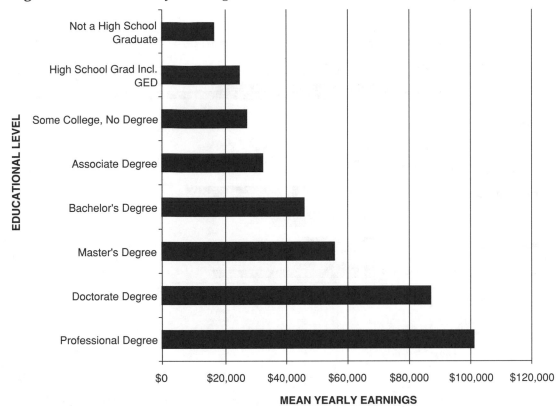

SOURCE: U.S. Census Bureau, 1999 Data. Internet Release Data: December 19, 2000.

fessional staff. All can weigh the longer-term consequences of minimal and maximum educational attainment. As more information is examined, such data will highlight the impact of differing educational practices on different groups in our society.

The Employment Picture Is Changing

The shift in U.S. society from low-skilled to higher-skilled jobs will require greater education. Johnston and Packer (1987) used a "skill rating" mechanism (related to language, math, and reasoning skills) to identify the educational attainment needed for new and existing jobs and concluded that the new jobs that young people might hope to fill will require higher levels of skills and education. They reported that the most rapid increase in the job market would be in professional, technical, and sales employment and that 41% of job growth will require the highest levels of education. They state, "Of the fastest-growing job categories, all but one, service occupations require more than the median level of education for all jobs. Of those growing more slowly than average, not one requires more than the median education" (Johnston & Packer, 1987, p. xxi).

Similarly, the Bureau of Labor Statistics (2001) reports that 70% of the 30 fastest-growing jobs will require post-high school education and that 40% of new jobs will require at least an associate college degree (see Figure 2.2).

Figure 2.2   Fastest-Growing Occupations in the 21st Century (in thousands of jobs)

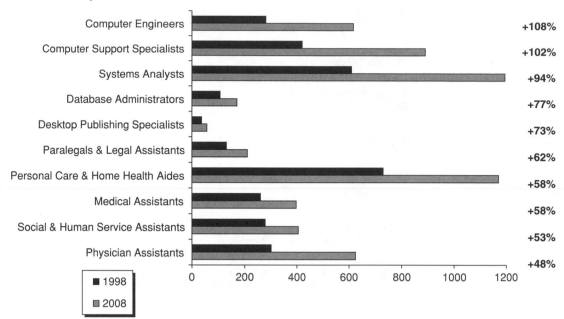

SOURCE: Bureau of Labor Statistics, 1999.

A recent National Science Foundation report by the Committee on Equal Opportunities in Science and Engineering (2000) provides evidence that the fields of science, mathematics, engineering, and technology (SMET) are showing a 51% growth rate. All of these fast-growing fields require a strong background in the areas of science, mathematics, engineering, and technology (see Table 2.1).

The Color and Gender of the Labor Force Is Rapidly Changing: Most New Entrants to the Labor Force Will Be Nonwhite, Female, or Immigrants

The U.S. Bureau of Labor Statistics (2001) indicates that although white men currently constitute the largest share (40%) of the workforce, their labor force share is declining as today's ethnically diverse youth population grows older. The Bureau projects that by 2008 the vast majority (70%) of new entrants to the labor force will be nonwhites and women (see Figure 2.3).

Table 2.1   Projected Employment and Labor Force Growth 1998–2008

SMET employment	+51%
Total employment	+14%
Total civilian labor force	+12%

SOURCES: Fullerton, H. N. (1999, November). Labor force projections for 2008: Steady growth and changing composition. *Monthly Labor Review*. Braddock, D. (1999, November). Occupational employment projections to 2008. *Monthly Labor Review*.

Figure 2.3   Most New Entrants to the Labor Force Will Be Nonwhite and Women

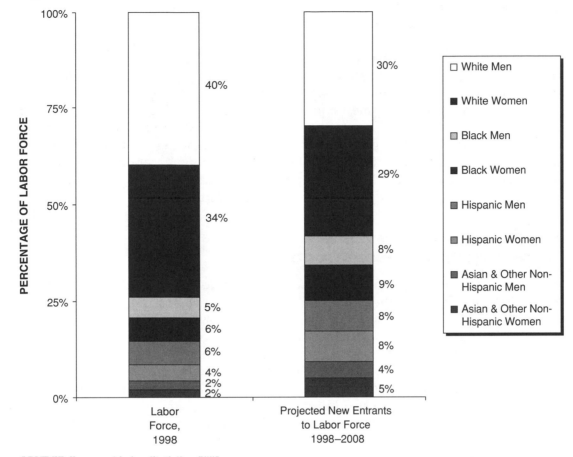

SOURCE: Bureau of Labor Statistics, 2001.

Who Stands to Lose the Most From Low Levels of Education? Black Men and Latinos Face the Greatest Difficulties in the Emerging Job Market

Although the projections show increased representation of minority groups in the labor force by 2008, African American and Latino males will fill an even smaller proportion of the jobs available than they do currently unless education levels improve dramatically. As later data will show, this outcome is likely if the educational practices and outcomes of the vast majority of schools in this nation continue to be perpetuated. The underrepresentation of African Americans and Latinos in higher-level education will shut the door to the higher occupational levels.

Schools Make a Difference: The Stakes of Tracking African American, Latino, and Low-Income Students

It is a myth that educators cause no harm to young people by deciding for them which kind of career or academic preparation they should follow. Historically, African American, Latino, and low-income students are more likely to be found in vocational tracks or in lower-level curriculum tracks as a result of beliefs that these students are more "suited" for lower-level servitude occupations (Jones, 1999). Their higher-income and white counterparts are more frequently enrolled in the higher-level college preparatory tracks.

Figure 2.4 (a, b, c, and d) illustrates that this sorting pattern is not being reversed in any significant manner. Not only does this assume that these young people are not capable or deserving of careers requiring higher levels of education, but, as the previous data show, the typical "vocations" they are prepared for are becoming less and less relevant in the actual labor market. The majority of job opportunities that provide above-poverty-level incomes require higher-order thinking skills—a trend that is only growing. But as the figures show, the more low-level vocational education courses students take, the lower they score on tests of reading aptitude—an essential skill for critical thinking. Students with fewer than four vocational credits score far higher in reading on the National Assessment of Educational Progress (NAEP) test than do students with eight or more vocational credits.

The Emperor's New Clothes and Other Myths: Misrepresented Course Content

Even when students in low-income schools are enrolled in courses with college preparatory and honors labels, there is a danger that the course content may be watered down. This brings to mind the children's fairy tale "The Emperor's New Clothes." The emperor was fooled into thinking that he had received a beautiful new wardrobe of clothes and paraded through town on that assumption. The people laughed because the emperor did not have new clothes but was parading in his undergarments. This was a horrible shock to the emperor, and he found out that the very people he trusted had misled him.

When low-level content is misrepresented as being on grade level or college preparatory when it is in fact below grade level or remedial, we are setting students up for academic ridicule by making them less academically competitive (Adelman, 1999; College Board's National Task Force on Minority Achievement, 1999). Abt Associates (1993, cited in Education Trust, 2001) found that when test scores are compared to grades students receive, an A in a low-income school would be a C in a high-income school. Similarly, when comparing SAT9 test score results in an urban high school, The Principals Exchange in California found that students in a low-income urban high school who were receiving A–C grades had large percentages of students scoring below the 50th percentile on both the reading and math tests (see Figure 2.5, page 22).

These types of practices cheat and mislead students. More powerful than quantitative data is the voice of a student who experienced this course content misrepresentation firsthand. She represents the voices of many students.

Melony Swasey, an African American female student, was in a college preparatory program and had received a "top ten" academic rank in her senior year. She left her urban high school for a year and attended a semisuburban high school. She discovered that the students in her new school were challenged by a more rigorous college preparatory curriculum. This shocking experience caused her to realize that she should expect more of her school and herself. She states,

I have realized that many of the clubs and classes that Kennedy offers bear respectable names or titles, but don't carry the weight or the full challenge that they should. In the supposedly challenging classes that I have, we aren't

Figure 2.4 The Stakes of Tracking African American, Latino, and Low-Income Students Into Vocational Education

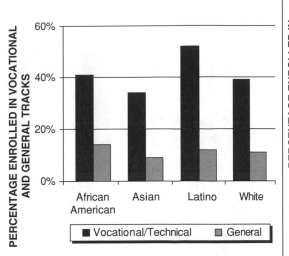

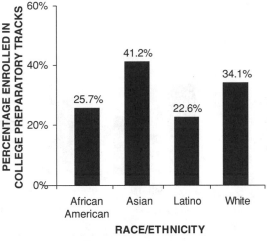

SOURCE: The Education Trust, Inc.

Secondary Source: U.S. Department of Education National Center for Education Statistics. National Education Longitudinal Study of 1988: Second Follow-Up, 1992 in: *A Profile of the American High School Senior in 1992* (p. 36). Washington, DC: U.S. Department of Education, June 1995.

SOURCE: The Education Trust, Inc.: *Achievement in America 2000*.

Secondary Source: U.S. Department of Education, National Center for Education Statistics. National Education Longitudinal Study of 1988: "First Follow-Up Student Study."

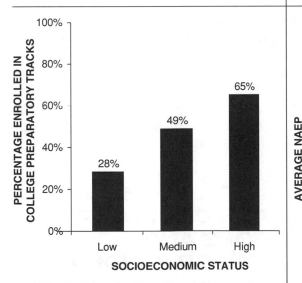

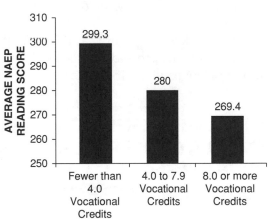

SOURCE: The Education Trust, Inc.: *Achievement in America 2000*.

Secondary Source: U.S. Department of Education National Center for Education Statistics. National Education Longitudinal Study of 1988: Second Follow-Up, 1992 in: *A Profile of the American High School Senior in 1992* (p. 36). Washington, DC: U.S. Department of Education, June 1995.

SOURCE: The Education Trust, Inc.: *Achievement in America 2000*.

Secondary Source: U.S. Department of Education, National Center for Education Statistics. *Vocational Course-Taking & Achievement: An Analysis of H.S. Transcripts and 1990 NAEP Assessment Sources* (p. 20). Washington, DC: U.S. Department of Education, May 1995.

Figure 2.5 Number of Students on "Grade Level": Comparison of Grade Point Averages and SAT9 Performance

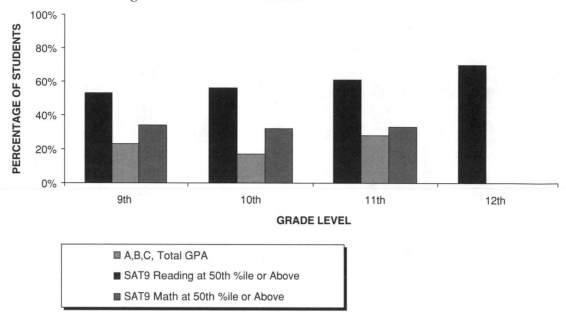

SOURCE: An urban high school. Courtesy of The Principals Exchange, Whittier, CA.

working at the capacity of students in those same classes on a national level. . . . I believe, because of our inadequate preparation, many of us will naively go out as confident soldiers and be knocked down before we even reach the front lines. (Swasey, 1996–1997, pp. 5–6)

She also makes the point that this is a cycle that includes parents who may lack the educational background as well as the students who have been socialized to a "pedagogy of poverty" (Haberman, 1991).

SIMILAR ASPIRATIONS, UNEQUAL CHANCES: DATA TO DISPEL MYTHS AND DEMONSTRATE DIFFERENTIAL EXPECTATIONS AND LEARNING OPPORTUNITIES FOR STUDENTS

The data shown thus far demonstrate the implications of continuing to undereducate large numbers of low-income students and students of color. But how do we move the school community to realize that these outcomes are not inevitable? The following types of data and graphs can be used to help educators reflect upon their assumptions and myths about the capabilities of students who are African American, Latino, Native American, and low-income. These data can powerfully dispel negative images and give hope for the possibility of fundamental reform.

The data also explore how institutionalized schooling practices contribute to different future opportunities for students, as documented previously in this chapter.

Although these powerful data are disturbing, they help educators understand that these issues are not unique to their school but are perpetuated nationally. This allows schools to begin to look more critically at patterns and practices in their own setting in the context of the big picture.

These "myth-killing" data must be presented when the school community has a lengthy period of time to discuss the compelling stories they tell—and their implications for reform. The culture of the school is the best determiner of timing. Most may be used at the beginning of a school reform process as well as at multiple stages whenever change agents feel they can have maximal impact. There will need to be many rich and sometimes uncomfortable dialogues. Information will need to be presented in a variety of formats until there are common understandings about the need for equitable reform. Sometimes it is effective to work with a small group that is representative of the school district, asking them to help shape the presentation strategy and design discussion questions. Boards of education have also been active participants. At all times when presenting such data, the focus must be on moving the reform process forward. Then this becomes a constructive rather than destructive process. The information must also be discussed with parent, student, and community groups.

WHO HAS THE OPPORTUNITY TO GO TO COLLEGE?

Who Goes to Four-Year Colleges? The Gaps

Figure 2.6 shows major educational junctures—kindergarten enrollment, high school graduation, completion of at least some college, and the attainment of a bachelor's degree by age 24—and the percentage of each racial and ethnic group that achieves each level. Dramatically different schooling experiences and outcomes for African American, Asian, Latino, and white youngsters are revealed. Compared to Asian and white students, African American and Latino students are lost at far higher levels at every juncture after kindergarten.

When these data are presented to school and district personnel, many are startled, others are numb, and some are not surprised, having come to expect these dismal inequities and outcomes. Most would agree that these are unacceptable outcomes, particularly in a nation where the emerging majority in public schools are students of color and at a time when the workforce is requiring higher levels of education for well-paying jobs. A similar analysis can be accomplished at the local district level. Do district and school results mirror those of the nation? What practices contribute to these kinds of results? What are the implications if reforms do or do not occur?

"Nobody Ever Asked Me Whether I Wanted to Go to College": Exploding Myths About College Aspirations

In urban schools, over and over again, low-income, African American, Latino, and Native American students say, "Nobody ever asked me if I wanted to go to

Figure 2.6   Who Goes to Four-Year Colleges?

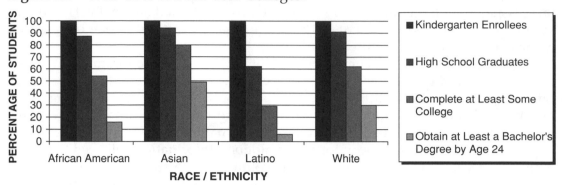

SOURCE: The Education Trust Inc. *Achievement in America 2001.*

Secondary Source: U.S. Census Bureau. (2000). *Current population reports: Educational attainment in the United States* (Detailed Tables No. 2).

college." But the conversations also reveal that these young people in fact have dreams for careers that require a college education—and many assume they will go to college.

Figures 2.7 and 2.8 translate this reality into hard data, demonstrating certain students' and parents' aspirations for the future—versus the actual academic preparation the students were receiving, which would affect whether their dreams could come true. Figure 2.7 presents data from a school district on parents' and students' expectations together with actual two-year and four-year college attendance information. Clearly, students and parents had far greater aspirations to attend four-year colleges than their actual enrollment rates reflect. When personnel in the district were asked about the reasons for the low college enrollment of African American and Latino students compared to other groups, the most frequent response was that these students and their parents had low expectations for college, particularly four-year colleges (i.e., baccalaureate degree-granting institutions). Because of these unchecked assumptions, staff members were steering students into courses that blocked them from going to four-year colleges. These and other data helped set the stage for challenging beliefs about the aspirations of students and their families and assessing implications for change in practices.

Similarly, Figure 2.8 (page 26) explodes the myth that students of color do not have high goals. It shows statewide data for California on career aspirations, college expectations, and course enrollment patterns of students in different groups. Most compelling is the revelation that there are not large gaps among the subgroups in their career aspirations that require college or in their expectations to attend college. However, there is a huge gap in the students' actual enrollment in college preparatory courses; far smaller proportions of African American and Latino students are enrolled in the college preparatory courses needed to attain their goals.

All too often, low-income students and parents are unaware of the consequences related to whether or not students enroll in and complete higher-level course work. A lot of the discrepancies in course taking can probably be attributed to this reason. Students and parents in these groups are receiving little help from the schools in learning the necessary steps to enroll and succeed in a bachelor's degree-granting institution.

Figure 2.7   Comparison of Students' and Parents' Expectations for College Enrollment to Percentage of June High School Graduates Enrolled in College

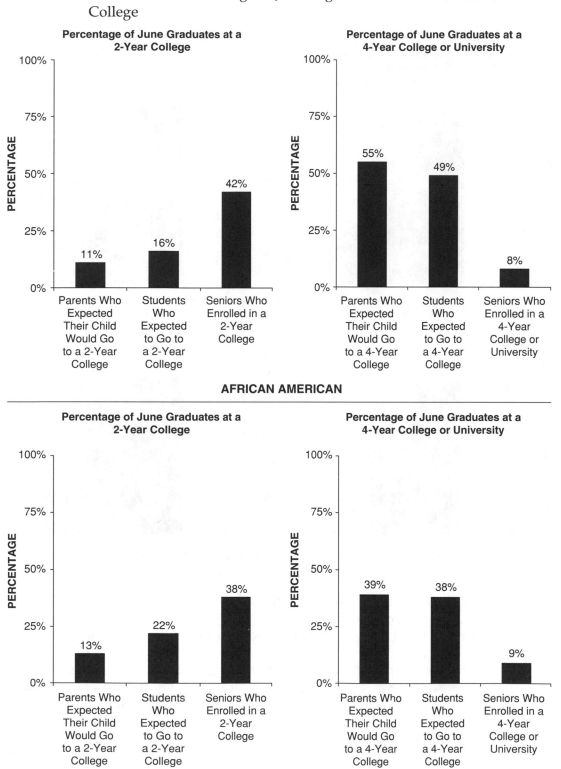

SOURCE: An urban school district.

Figure 2.8 Career Aspirations, College Expectations, and Course Selection

Regardless of race, students have high goals, but some students are steered away from their goals.

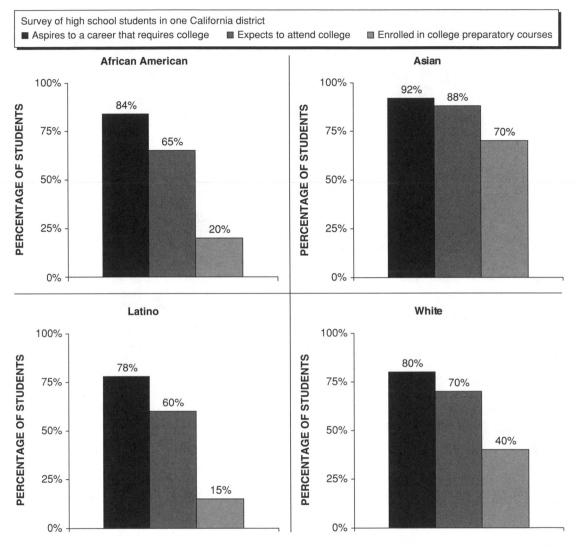

SOURCE: California Department of Education, 1990, Sacramento, CA; The Achievement Council, Los Angeles, CA.

The results from a survey of K-12 students and their parents by the National Action Council for Minorities in Engineering (Leitman, Bins, & Unni, 1995) highlight how uninformed some groups are. Some representative findings are the following:

- Over half of all students plan to drop math and science at the first opportunity. In discussing mathematics, 63% of African American, 60% of Latino, and 58% of American Indian students express this intention, in contrast to less than half of the white students surveyed.
- More than half of white students understand the need for advanced mathematics skills compared to 33% of African American, Latino, and Native American students.
- African American and Native American students had the least amount of understanding about the implications of not taking courses such as algebra. Parents tend to make decisions based on their personal experiences.

- Two in five students reported discouragement by teachers and counselors from taking higher-level courses. More males; American Indian students; and older African American, Latino, and Native American students express discouragement by counselors and teachers from pursuing mathematics and science courses. Most parents are unaware of the discouragement their children are experiencing. There are serious implications when parents leave it to their uninformed youngsters to make decisions about course taking.
- African American, Latino, and Native American students report limited offerings as a reason for not pursuing higher-level coursework.

Understanding the need to inform both parents and students about the consequences of their decisions requires a serious effort on the part of schools. Woefully uninformed students too often are making decisions that have long-range consequences. Schools and districts that want to stay informed about their students' and parents' knowledge bases could conduct similar surveys.

How Many Well-Qualified Students Don't Get Placed in Algebra? Exploding Myths About Fairness

When school personnel are asked about the reasons for the disproportionately low enrollment of African American and Latino students in courses like algebra that would prepare them for college, they typically respond that placement is based on test scores. They believe their system is bias-free and based on merit. But an examination of actual school practices reveals interesting differences. For example, in one school district, a look at algebra placements for students who scored in the top quartile on standardized mathematics tests revealed very different placement practices for different groups. Proportionally, Asian and white students had higher placement rates than did African American or Latino students, even when achievement on tests indicated that the placements should be similar. The educators in the district were most startled by these data because they exposed systemic biases. Use of these data, as represented in Figure 2.9, helped to accelerate changes in practices. Over and over, there are cases reported of low-income students and students of color who are not placed in higher-level classes regardless of how they achieve (Spring, 2000).

CHANGING PRACTICES AND ACHIEVEMENT PATTERNS: EXPLODING MYTHS THAT PERPETUATE UNDERACHIEVEMENT

Around the country, there are schools and districts that are proving that their patterns of low achievement can be changed—that low-income and minority students can achieve at high levels when they are expected to and are provided the appropriate opportunities and resources for achievement at high levels. Data from these schools, districts, and states are critically important in convincing educators and community members that reform is possible. Here are several examples:

1. The January 11, 2001, issue of *Education Week* reported on districts and states that were defying the usual achievement patterns. Figure 2.10a shows overall gains in Kent County, Maryland, where achievement increased contrary to the trends

Figure 2.9   Middle School Students' Performance on Standardized Tests and Course Placement by Ethnicity: How Many Well-Qualified Students Don't Get Placed in Algebra?

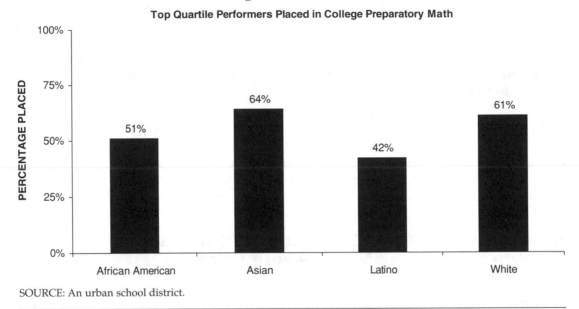

SOURCE: An urban school district.

Figure 2.10a   Raising the Bar and Closing the Gap in Kent County, Maryland

Student achievement in the county is on the rise, as measured by the Maryland state assessment. More students are scoring "satisfactory" or higher on the assessment than in any other county, and the performance gap between black and white students is closing.

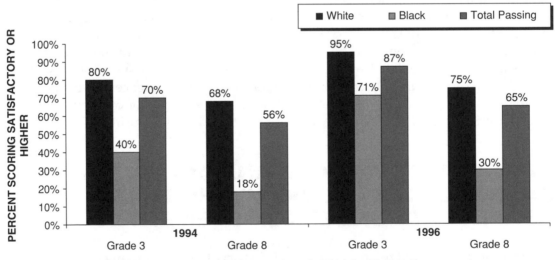

SOURCE: Sandham, J. L. (2001c, January 11). The personal touch. *Education Week*, p. 61.

Secondary source: Maryland School Performance Assessment Program, 1999.

noted in Chapter 1. Most notable is that as the scores improved, the achievement gap between black and white students decreased.

2. Figure 2.10b illustrates data on low-income students in San Benito County, Texas, where low-income students showed greater score increases than students of other income levels did.

Figure 2.10b   Improving the Performance of All Students in San Benito, Texas

Between 1994 and 1998, the percentage of students in San Benito passing the Texas Assessment of Academic Skills increased. The passing rates for low-income students improved at the fastest rate.

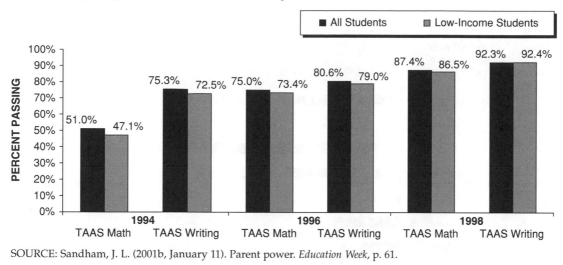

SOURCE: Sandham, J. L. (2001b, January 11). Parent power. *Education Week*, p. 61.

Secondary source: Texas Assessment of Academic Skills, 1999.

3. Figures 2.11a and 2.11b display top-ranked elementary schools in Kentucky in reading and science achievement. The highest scoring of the top 10 schools has high proportions of students receiving free or reduced-price lunches. In fact, the highest-scoring school in science had 94% of their students receiving free or reduced-price lunches, and 4 of the top 10 scoring schools in reading and 5 of the top 10 scoring in science had 50% or more of their students receiving free or reduced-price lunches.

A Rigorous Curriculum Enhances Opportunities and Choices for All Students

A national report by the College Board, *Changing the Odds: Factors Increasing Access to College* (Pelavin & Kane, 1990), looked at the relationship between enrollment in college-level courses and college-going rates and whether African American, Latino, and white students participated equally in those courses related to college going. The authors found that low-income African American and Latino students did not enroll in geometry and foreign languages and did not aspire to a bachelor's degree at the same rates as white students did. However, when they had the opportunity to enroll and completed the courses, the likelihood of college enrollment increased, and the gap between minority students and whites decreased. A more recent report by the College Board (2001) gives a similar message: "Students who took challenging courses such as pre-calculus, calculus, and physics had significantly higher average SAT scores than those students who did not take rigorous coursework. This was true for students regardless of racial or ethnic group" (p. 4).

Figure 2.12 shows a clear and simple story: Regardless of race, students who are afforded the opportunity to study higher-level math score higher on the NAEP math test. With the completion of each math level, from general math to calculus,

Figures 2.11a and 2.11b Kentucky Schools Beating the Odds

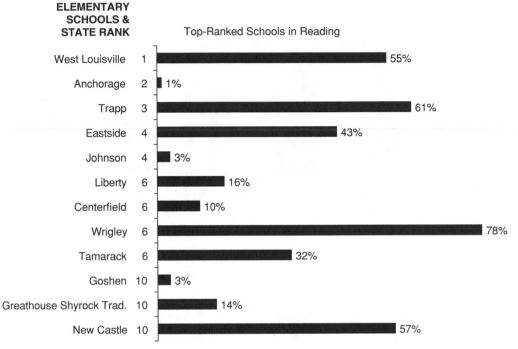

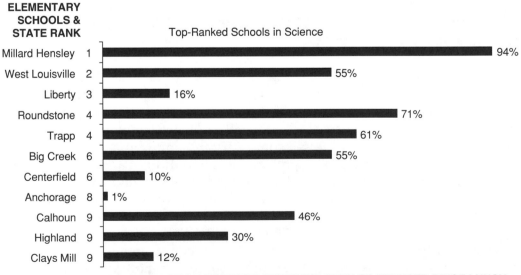

SOURCE: Boser, U. (2001, January 11). Meeting the challenge. *Education Week*, p. 19.

Secondary Source: Prichard Committee for Academic Excellence. (1999). *Kentucky elementary performance and poverty.*

Figure 2.12 A Rigorous Math Curriculum Improves Scores for All Students

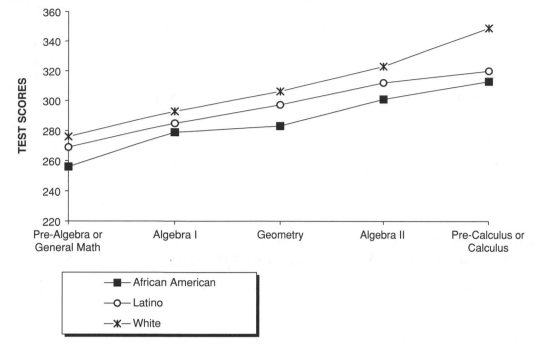

SOURCE: The Education Trust, Inc. *Achievement in America 2000.*

Secondary Source: National Center for Educational Statistics. (1994). *National Assessment of Educational Progress, 1992 Mathematics Trend Assessment, NAEP 1992 Trends in Academic Progress* (p. 113). Washington, DC: U.S. Department of Education.

students' test scores rise incrementally. Why not offer all students the chance to succeed in higher-level math courses?

Adelman (1999) researched curriculum intensity and course quality. Adelman looked at units in six academic areas, including the higher area of mathematics studied, remedial work in English and math, and Advanced Placement courses. A scale with 40 gradations measured curriculum intensity and quality. The consequences of curriculum intensity of courses students take in high school have effects not just on access to a four-year college, but on successful completion of a bachelor's degree. Some major findings are the following:

- "The impact of a high school curriculum of high academic intensity and quality on degree completion is far more pronounced for African American and Latino students than any other precollege indicator of academic resources. The impact for African American and Latino students is also much greater than it is for white students.
- "The correlation of curriculum with bachelor's degree attainment is also higher (.54) than test scores (.48) or class rank/GPA (.44).
- "Of all pre-college curricula, the highest level of mathematics one studies in secondary school has the strongest continuing influence [on] bachelor degree completion. Finishing a course beyond the level of Algebra 2 for example, trigonometry or pre-calculus, more than doubles the odds that a student who enters postsecondary education will complete a bachelor's degree.

- "Academic Resources (the composite of high school curriculum, test scores, and class rank) produces a much steeper curve toward bachelor's degree completion than does socioeconomic status." (Adelman, 1999, p. vii)

More data supporting the contention that higher-level coursework improves academic achievement of all students were found by Gamoran and Hannigan (2000) in analysis of data from more than 12,500 students in the National Assessment of Educational Progress Study. They looked at students at different achievement levels who took algebra. They found that all students benefited, even lower-achieving students. The lower-achieving students had smaller test gains, but there were gains. The gains were also seen in schools with diverse populations. Educators need to rethink the gatekeeping practices that consistently shut students with low test scores out of algebra.

What Happens When Opportunities Are Opened Up for More Students to Take College Preparatory Courses?

After six years of implementation in seven districts, the College Board's Equity 2000 Program had more students passing algebra and geometry than students taking the classes prior to the first year of the program (Jones, 2001). The National Science Foundation Urban Systemic Initiative, a large-scale initiative in 22 large urban districts, is reporting promising results. They report increased enrollments in mathematics gatekeeping courses (algebra, geometry) and in higher-level mathematics and science courses and a reduced disparity of enrollments among African American, Latino, and white students. Gains in assessment outcomes and achievement gaps have been achieved among racial and ethnic groups (Kim & Systemic Research, Inc., 2001).

Figure 2.13 makes a powerful case for all students to have access to higher-level courses and for educators to challenge systems that lock students out of these courses. New York City made a concerted effort to dramatically increase the opportunities for students to take regents-level science courses. For all racial/ethnic groups, the numbers of students who passed in 1995 well exceeded the numbers who were even enrolled in 1994.

Discussion and Cautionary Notes

The push to higher-level standards and expectations for low-income students and students of color who traditionally have not achieved will meet with resistance in many quarters. The sources of resistance may be educators, parents, or the community. Many will argue that not everyone needs to go to college. For example, they will discuss individuals they know who make more money than college graduates.

This is about preparing all students for the college option rather than using determinist practices that certify who is or who isn't "college material." It is about educators, students, and parents understanding the consequences of underpreparation. It is about pointing out how and why some groups are underprepared. Ultimately, it's about transforming the expectations and behaviors currently present in many schools and systems so that there are high-level options for all students. There is sufficient evidence that schools can be transformed from lower-achieving to higher-achieving places of learning.

Figure 2.13 New York City 9th Graders Taking and Passing College Preparatory Science

Grade 9 Students	1994				1995			
	African American	Asian	Latino	White	African American	Asian	Latino	White
# Taking	7,698	2,871	4,281	5,578	17,664	5,119	15,602	9,596
# Passing	6,254	2,766	3,276	5,454	12,776	4,752	10,297	8,281
% Passing	81.24%	96.34%	76.52%	97.62%	72.33%	92.83%	66.00%	86.40%

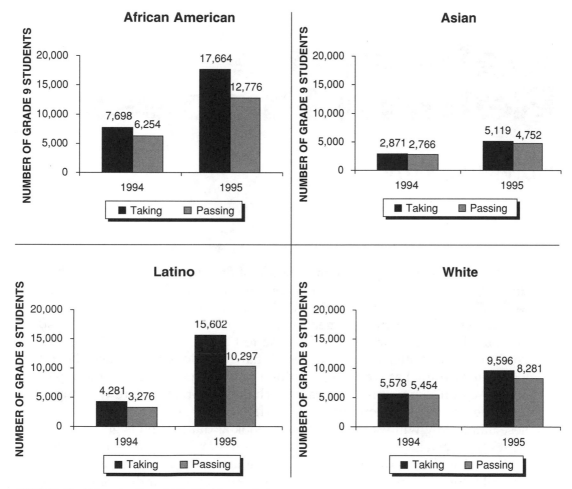

SOURCE: The Education Trust 2001, Washington, DC.

Secondary Source: New York City Chancellor's Office. (1995). *Annual report on the mathematics and science initiative in high schools*.

When asked what they would want for their own children, most educators inevitably say they expect the highest levels of education. Do other people's children deserve any less?

The data offered here should not be used in isolation from a comprehensive reform strategy. Once the hard issues are raised, there must be a long-range, data-informed process to transform school practices and outcomes.

3

Data in the Reform Process

How and Why

At several meetings about the use of data in their schools, teachers and administrators in some urban schools expressed some common complaints that are heard over and over in K-12 schools and districts. There were statements such as, "All we get are test scores and criticism. Tomatoes start flying when the test scores come out. We get the scores six months after we give the test: What good does that do us? The test doesn't measure what we teach! We don't know what all of these numbers mean. We don't know how to measure whether the reforms are working or not." There were other concerns and questions, such as, "Where did you get these data? How will we find the time to look at data? Who is going to collect it? The teachers should get the test scores first. Who is going to help us?"

After listening to the teachers' and administrators' concerns about data, the facilitators who would work with them in using data at their sites developed professional development and successful strategies that addressed the concerns, that moved them beyond looking only at test scores to addressing policies and practices, and that engaged the teachers and administrators in the process. Over a period of two years, teachers, counselors, administrators, and parents came to understand the power of data to make improvement in the achievement of all groups of students. They began to "own" the data and to take leadership in the use of data at their sites. Some results included upgrading curriculum, strategically focusing on students' academic needs, highlighting institutional barriers and discrimination, revising the report cards to align with standards, designing and implementing computer systems to retrieve student-level and teacher-level data, and creating a data culture.

Overview

When schools are asked how they use data, the answer is usually, "We don't, and we just provide what is requested." Most frequently schools provide data to external requesters, such as the state, the district, or funders. Rarely are those from the school who provide the data sure of who will see them or how they will be used. This "data provider" role allows others to define the criteria of progress upon which the school or district will be judged. Because this often results in a public image that school-level educators believe is unfair, many such educators consider data the enemy.

McLaughlin (1996) characterizes this as "the evaluation food chain." He describes it in this way:

> Local educators—teachers, guidance counselors, administrators and staff— live at the bottom of what can be termed the "evaluation food chain." At the top of the chain, federal and state legislators demand data on initiatives they fund, compelling federal and state program officers to require data from the technical assistance providers, state departments, districts, professional development organizations, and others who receive the funding. These service providers, in turn, require that those they serve who work in classrooms, schools and districts provide them with data in exchange for offering continued service to these local clients. At every stage in this food chain, someone is seeking to scrape together whatever data they can to feed the "beast" which threatens to devour them, their programs, and their jobs. The response to such demands for high-stakes accountability data typically is, "Give them the data they want and maybe they will leave us alone." (p. 3)

Beyond providing data, schools also receive piles of numerical data from the district office. Typically, these are stored in someone's office. They are rarely used in decision making, nor are they shared with the entire school community. Sometimes educators are afraid of showing the data, because they may be perceived negatively. Other times educators are simply plagued by a kind of phobia that suggests that you must be a statistician or mathematician to understand or work with data. Being overwhelmed and having "data overload" are also conditions that plague some schools and districts.

But as these fears are overcome and as the school community begins using data together as part of the daily business of improving their school, educators can make the transition from being data providers to being data users. As one educator said, "It wasn't my love for numbers, but my passion for children that led me to study and use school and district data. Data providers let others do all the thinking; I became a data user."

Under the microscope, institutional behaviors often paint a very different picture about what really is happening compared to what we say we believe or want for students. Data can be a foundation for schoolwide examination of these patterns. Properly used, data can be a compelling means of launching, sustaining, and institutionalizing a reform effort. This chapter describes key roles for data throughout the reform process and then offers a review of some of the basics for school communities to become users of data.

KEY ROLES FOR DATA

These are just some of the major uses for data. School communities can probably identify many other ways to utilize data to improve their schools.

1. Improving the Quality of Criteria Used in Problem Solving and Decision Making

Data can help schools and districts to make better decisions in the interest of children. Schools and districts can better understand what is happening to diverse groups of students and whether inequities exist in their schooling. Rather than certifying students as slow or fast, parents as caring or uncaring, and teachers and administrators as capable or incapable, well-grounded information can help us identify strategies that are working, solve problems, and determine the best use of resources.

Careful analysis of data helps us to dig deeper. Often, perceptions of what is working are based on weak indicators, such as whether people "like" an idea or program director, rather than on whether the practice is leading to higher student achievement. Examining the impact of school or district practices can provide a sounder basis for decision making and can crystallize what needs to happen next.

2. Describing Institutional Processes, Practices, and Progress in Schools and Districts

Traditionally, the sole measures used to describe school improvement are standardized test scores. If scores go up, schools are deemed improved. Yet in many low-performing schools a seesaw effect can be seen, with scores going up one year and down the next. What are we to conclude? Sometimes these tests measure only very basic skills and only represent a small fraction of a school's students. More important, the scores typically offer minimal clues about whether the school is changing its normative culture so that higher achievement for all children becomes institutionalized.

We need to transform the way we think about education and the measures of institutional progress. Our indicators of progress must be connected to short- or long-term higher-learning outcomes for all students. In schools where educators are changing practices—by, for example, guaranteeing access to higher-level curriculum for all students—baseline information and progress need to be documented. Similarly, if teachers are encouraging students to develop higher-order thinking skills, progress on how this is being implemented in the classroom needs to be measured, along with the impact on student achievement. Just saying "we are doing it" is not good enough.

3. Examining Institutional Belief Systems, Underlying Assumptions, and Behaviors

Data can help to expose how certain educational practices reflect our institutional belief systems. For example, many schools claim to place students in high- or low-level courses based on academic merit. But upon reviewing test and course placement by race, we often find that schools have placed students based on assumptions about their abilities, rather than on any data. Frequently, African American and Latino students who score in the top quartiles on standardized tests are not programmed into higher-level courses at the same rate as are comparably scoring Asian and white students. Similarly, data comparing who gets placed in gifted courses versus special education or low-level courses show compellingly how access to knowledge is unequally rationed on a daily basis.

4. Mobilizing the School or District Community for Action

Data can be strategically used to mobilize parents, educators, and the community at large. Schools should create opportunities for these groups to help collect, analyze, and represent data—especially student outcome data. This builds ownership of the process and understanding of the power and credibility of data. It also helps to create a sense of urgency to make appropriate reforms for young people.

It must not be assumed that parents and young people cannot collect, analyze, and represent data. Their voices are critical. Data presented by a collaboration of stakeholders can lead to a richer dialogue about factors that contribute to good or poor outcomes, as well as about what roles different stakeholders can play to improve the future.

5. Monitoring Implementation of Reforms

The excitement about a new endeavor can cause schools and districts to rush to implement reforms with no forethought as to how they will measure whether the reforms are working or not. It is important that we resist this temptation and devote time up front to thinking very carefully about how to measure the results of the reforms we are planning. A data-informed monitoring process allows for midcourse corrections, reinforces positive directions, and rewards success.

Monitoring students as they progress through the system tells us about their progress or lack of progress and about what teachers, curriculum, and program interventions they may have experienced. From this information schools can describe conditions and patterns for individuals or groups of students. Using this information, practices and policies can be examined in terms of whether they enhance or inhibit student progress.

6. Accountability

Nationally, the public is demanding greater accountability from schools. At the local level, students, parents, and communities also require information regarding the school's educational intentions and progress. Internal and external accountability systems require data. A school or district needs a plan for collecting, analyzing, and representing data that will answer both external and internal questions. It is also important that there be a plan for rewarding efforts that lead to high-level outcomes for all students.

ASSESSING DATA USE AND ACCESS

Schools and districts need to assess where they are and how they use data relative to the six uses just described. I usually have educators who are beginning the process chart their most frequent uses of data. Accountability is usually number 1, and there is very little use of data for other purposes. There are other issues that also need to be assessed so that educators don't run blindly into the data user process. These issues are addressed by the assessment tools on the following pages.

STAGES OF THE DATA USER PROCESS

The data team (described further in Chapter 4) and school community can think in terms of the following stages as they embark on their journey to become data users:

1. Begin the inquiry, identify objectives, and define questions: What do we need to know?

2. Determine what types of data are needed to answer the question(s), how the data will be collected, and who will be responsible for collection.

3. Collect and disaggregate the data.

4. Determine how the data will be summarized, analyzed, and interpreted.

5. Determine how the data will be represented.

6. Determine with what audiences the data will be shared and the appropriate presentations.

7. Provide a framework for the data dialogue; design appropriate solutions and an action plan.

Cautionary Note

When measuring equity, there are various ways to represent the data. Equity achievement measurements are used to measure achievement gaps among different groups. It is important to measure the gap from the desired standard for all groups. The goal is to have all students reach the standards. Some will achieve higher. When we measure groups only relative to each other, we run the risk of lowering the expectation for achievement. For instance, if the highest group has a median test score at the 40th percentile, and the other groups are lower, we may set the goal to close the gap with the 40th percentile as the goal. The other cautionary note in measuring gaps is the direction of the closing: Gaps can narrow when achievement declines in groups at the top or when there is a shift in students out of the highest percentile groups.

1. Identify Objectives and Define Questions: What Do You Need to Know?

Data collection strategies will emanate from questions asked. The chapters of this book are shaped around the stages of the reform process and the kinds of questions the school community might need to answer along the way. A culture of inquiry allows educators to ask: What are our attitudes about the abilities of our students? How do we determine what "grade level" means at our school? What percentage of each racial, ethnic, gender, and language group is reading on grade level? What

(text continues on page 42)

Assessment 1: How Do You Use Data?

Please check one:

Improving the quality of criteria used in problem solving and decision making
Always _____   Sometimes _____   Never _____

Describing institutional processes, practices, and progress in your school or district
Always _____   Sometimes _____   Never _____

Examining institutional belief systems, underlying assumptions, and behaviors
Always _____   Sometimes _____   Never _____

Mobilizing the school or district community for action
Always _____   Sometimes _____   Never _____

Accountability
Always _____   Sometimes _____   Never _____

Assessment 2: Why Data?

1. What do you perceive as the most compelling reasons for data use at your site?

2a. How do you currently use data?

2b. What kind of impact results from your use of data?

3. What do you perceive as your major issues and roadblocks around engaging in data use?

4. What are the major issues about gathering data related to access and equity?

5. What strengths do you bring to the table around data use?

6. What kinds of professional development do you need to become a more effective user of data?

Assessment 3: Assessing Data Use in Your School or District

Check one: Elementary _____ Middle _____ High _____ District _____

Please answer yes or no to the following questions:

1a. Can you answer to your satisfaction to what extent different groups of students are achieving high standards?

Yes _____   No _____

1b. Can you answer to your satisfaction how different groups of students are achieving by using more than one type of indicator?

Yes _____   No _____

2. Can you answer to your satisfaction how effective your practices are in serving different groups of students?

Yes _____   No _____

3a. Does your school collect data about diverse groups of students' access to different levels of curriculum?

Yes _____   No _____

3b. Is there dialogue or reform resulting from the information?

Yes _____   No _____

4. Have you made an attempt to piece together some data to answer a concern but found that they weren't the right data to answer what you are really asking?

Yes _____   No _____

5. Do you believe that your work is having an impact on students, but you don't have the data to support this belief to others?

Yes _____   No _____

6. Have you used any assessment data about your students that are helpful to better serve your students?

Yes _____   No _____

SOURCE: Revised with permission from p. 110 of Olsen, L., & Jamarillo, A. (1999). *Turning the tides of exclusion: A guide for educators and advocates for immigrant students.* Oakland, CA: California Tomorrow.

Assessment 4: How Much Access Do People in Your School Have to Data? A Survey to Measure the Extent and Quality of Data Access and Use

Name: (Optional) _____

Check one: Elementary ____ Middle ____ High ____ District ____

Directions: Please read each sentence and then circle the answer that is closest to how you feel about that statement.

	Strongly Agree	Agree	Disagree	Strongly Disagree	Don't Know
1. I have a good sense of all the types of data that our school collects about our students.	1	2	3	4	5
2. I have a good sense of what data on students are available to teachers and staff.	1	2	3	4	5
3. I know where to go or whom to ask if I want certain information about my students.	1	2	3	4	5
4. I frequently want to know achievement or background information about my students.	1	2	3	4	5
5. I have found it easy to find the information I want on students from the data gathered by my school or district.	1	2	3	4	5
6. I have gathered data on my students. (for teachers)	1	2	3	4	5
7. I have gathered data on the students in the whole school.	1	2	3	4	5
8. If the school does not collect the information I want, I feel comfortable designing ways to gather that information myself.	1	2	3	4	5

SOURCE: Revised with permission from p. 164 of Olsen, L., & Jamarillo, A. (1999). *Turning the tides of exclusion: A guide for educators and advocates for immigrant students*. Oakland, CA: California Tomorrow.

percentage is below? Are there different patterns for students who have been in the school consistently for three or more years? Are there patterns related to certain instructional approaches? What has been the effect of our staff development? Are we meeting the goals and objectives of different projects?

Many times, as school communities begin to discuss these questions, they find that they are not in clear agreement about meanings. Goals like "every child will read on grade level" sound good, but how does the school community define grade level? Shouldn't some students be reading above grade level? When do we need to achieve this? Does everyone buy in to this goal? As you begin the data process, you will need to spend time defining issues to guide the process.

Questions to be explored with data can be generated by the data and leadership teams (see Chapter 4) and presented to others for comments, additions, or revisions. The teams will also benefit from directly soliciting questions from the school community to help people feel that their issues are being addressed. However, limitations and timelines should be set so that the process is not overwhelmed by too many questions early on.

In fact, to limit the scope of questions, you might employ a 1–5 ranking system to prioritize. Always ask, "How well do these questions focus on our objectives and student achievement? How much do we value this information, and how useful is it in decision making? How hard is it to collect?" Some information can be interesting but not particularly useful, such as, "Did the teacher teach reading at 10 o'clock or 11 o'clock in the morning?" It is more critical to find out about quality and effectiveness for all kids. Therefore, questions related to what the teacher taught, how well, and to whom are more important.

After the initial data are gathered, other questions will very likely be suggested, and as the progress evolves you will dig deeper and deeper. This should become a continuous process of inquiry.

The data and leadership teams must ensure that the strategies are focused, systemic, and purposeful, or else the process can deteriorate. Meaningful dialogue around the questions that will be explored is critical in order to build consensus. The discussion on assessing the improvement of college preparation and college-going rates in Chapter 9 can be adapted to help this process stay focused. Appropriate literature should be read and discussed (see the References section and the Bibliography).

2. The Data Collection Process

Once you have established what you need to find out, you will begin to figure out what type of data you need to collect. Data should be viewed as sources of authentic information that can reveal needed direction for reform. Quantitative as well as qualitative information should be sought (see Chapters 5 through 10). Data should be gathered on outcomes, programs, policies, and practices. Where, when, how, and from whom become the questions. Data collection forms such as those illustrated in Chapters 6 through 10 are helpful. Also during this stage, data users should seek out technological support to help with recording information so it can subsequently be summarized and analyzed. The data team needs to decide which computer programs will be used in order to save valuable time later in the process.

Based on their work in schools and districts, Olsen and Jaramillo (1999) suggest some elements of a district data system that will greatly facilitate the process. They propose a system that has the following characteristics:

- Integrates or links databases: all electronic databases can communicate or interface with one another and share data
- Allows disaggregation of all measure[s] of achievement and participation by race/ethnicity, gender, language status (English Only, Limited English Proficient, Fluent English
- Produces reliable, credible data that [are] updated in a timely fashion and available at key decision points in a school year
- Is easily accessible to school sites, administrators and teachers; such access involves providing training as needed and creating a user-friendly system with the appropriate hardware and software
- Responds to inquiries easily: new reports can be produced in a timely fashion to help school personnel find the answers to their questions about student achievement or equity issues
- Maintains student information longitudinally, so student histories can be traced K-12 without having to resort to individual cumulative files
- Links data to policies and standards set [by] the district and schools, so progress towards attaining those standards can be measured (p. 165)

Most school districts have lots of quantitative information. First, you must determine if the information already exists internally in school or district reports; externally in sources such as accreditation reports, state reports, and Web sites; or in research by other agencies or advocacy groups. If the information exists, find out how to get it to your site.

If you wish to generate qualitative data about, for example, how teachers determine grade levels, what approaches are used with different students, or what and how much content is taught, you might conduct interviews, administer questionnaires, observe classrooms, and keep logs. You may have existing questionnaires that can be revised, or you may need to design your own. Find help if you need it (see Chapters 5, 7, 9, and 10).

Whenever possible, at least two or three kinds of evidence should be collected. Triangulation (the use of three indicators) strengthens your analysis. For example, if you are looking at implementation of new pedagogy, you may use the following techniques: (a) teachers complete a questionnaire; (b) teaching approaches are observed by peers, administrators, or outside observers; and (c) the data team and others analyze grades and samples of student work. If you are examining student achievement patterns, then grades, test scores, performance assessments, textbook tests, and actual student work should all be weighed to present as comprehensive a picture as possible. Time and funding considerations must be taken into account, but the more comprehensive the data, the stronger the decision-making process.

Schools and districts have other information that should not be overlooked when inquiring about equity issues. These data, which Crawford and Dougherty (2000) describe as "artifacts," are readily available in schools but are not often viewed as rich sources of data. Examples such as student and teacher schedules, calendars, time allocations, master schedules, plan books, course syllabi, and counselor advisement information can be analyzed to learn about policies and procedures that affect student achievement and welfare. How these artifacts can be used will be described in Chapter 7.

3. Disaggregation: Critical, but Proceed With Caution

Wherever possible, data should be disaggregated by race/ethnicity and gender, because equity and access to opportunities are of central focus. Most of the data representations in this book are disaggregated by racial/ethnic groups; in some cases, they are disaggregated by gender or economic status. For the most part, this book uses the following broad categories: African American, Asian, Latino, and white. Data on Native American students is unfortunately less prevalent, but the book tries to include examples for this population where possible. Some schools and districts do not even know the size or nature of their Native American student population; it is imperative that data on these students be collected and disaggregated.

Often schools with racial or ethnic groups that appear to be homogeneous see no reason to disaggregate their data by student groups. Comments such as "My school is 100% Latino or African American" are frequently heard in settings where there is racial, ethnic, or income isolation. However, groups are not monolithic, and there is a need to find out if there are patterns that emerge for different groups that are beneficial to some or harmful to others. Variations would very likely be found by disaggregating recent immigrant Latino ethnic groups from second-generation, third-generation, or longer groups of the same national-ethnic heritage. With Pan-African groups, it has been reported by Ogbu and Matute-Bianchi (1990) that immigrants from the West Indies achieve more successfully than African Americans do. For the reasons mentioned, all schools, including those with what appears to be a homogeneous racial/ethnic student population, should not assume that there is no need to disaggregate information. It is worth the extra effort to look at within-group student achievement patterns so that appropriate strategies can be designed and implemented.

The example of Figure 3.1 demystifies the assumption that all Asians are high achievers. There are varying achievement patterns within all of these groups. *The Schools We Need Now* (California Tomorrow, 1995) describes the variability of achievement within the Asian group:

> The Asian community is very diverse in itself, including Asian Americans whose ancestors go back 10 or more generations in the U.S., and immigrant groups from a range of economic and educational backgrounds. Schools are finding that Asian students from very low-income families, mainly children from refugee families from such countries as Cambodia and Laos, are much more likely to drop out of school than students whose families are doing better economically and/or whose parents went to college. In fact, the dropout statistics for these students, if they were to be split out, might reach as high as for African American and Latino students. And the future prospects for these young people will also be as troubling. (p. 9)

Figure 3.1 shows that some groups of Asian students, Hmongs and Cambodians in this case, are achieving lower grade point averages (GPAs) than are other Asian groups, such as Chinese and Japanese students. The more aware educators can become of the unique experiences and backgrounds of different groups—as well as of individual students—the more informed and useful the data analysis will be.

Some people are concerned that disaggregation can perpetuate stereotypes and reinforce negative stereotypes. The achievement data on African Americans, Latinos, and Native Americans frequently paint a picture of low achievement, and the

Figure 3.1 High School GPA (Males): Disaggregation for Asian Groups

Race/Ethnicity	June 2000	June 2001	June 2002
Cambodian	1.67	1.79	1.80
Chinese	3.52	3.90	3.82
Hmong	1.80	2.15	2.00
Japanese	3.70	3.95	3.75
Korean	3.31	3.50	3.73
Lao	1.9	2.00	2.50
Vietnamese	3.40	3.60	3.83
All Asian Males	**2.76**	**2.98**	**3.06**

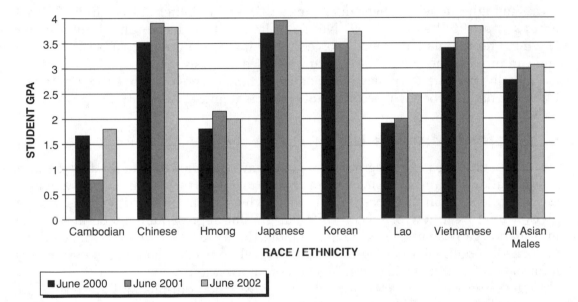

NOTE: Sample data based on 4.0 scale.

unstated or stated response is, "This is the way it has always been, and no matter what we do it remains the same. So why bother, it won't make any difference to try." However, in order to confront the types of institutional bias issues that are affecting different groups of students, it is necessary to disaggregate data. Some policies and practices are causing more harm to some students than to others. Research and other strategies can be used in ways that dispel and confront myths and assumptions about predictable status for groups. This issue is addressed in several chapters of this book, particularly Chapter 2.

4. Recording, Summarizing, Analyzing, and Interpreting Data

Once you have collected a variety of kinds of information, you will need a system to record and summarize the data. Forms should be set up after you determine methods of collection and instruments. Samples of data collection formats appear in

Chapters 6 through 10. Other samples can be found in evaluation manuals, or you can develop your own. For quantitative recording, you can use a computer spreadsheet program. This will enable you to save a great deal of time in doing calculations, summarizing, and making the various types of representations that are discussed in the next section. However, lack of technology should not stop progress; considerable data can be collected by hand and computed with a calculator.

You will need to decide ways to summarize and analyze your data in search of relationships. For the most part, you will use simple statistical procedures such as percentages and numbers of incidence. Be careful using percentages with small numbers, because small changes in small numbers record big percentage changes. Ask yourself, "Which data are worth combining?" (see Chapter 10). Do you want to compare courses taken with scores on tests? What about computer usage for different groups of students? Which groups of students get the most qualified teachers? How do grades compare to test scores? How do different reading approaches relate to test scores? What do the findings tell you? Are there differential opportunities for access to high-quality teachers and courses that lead to better options in life? What groups appear to be doing well? Not so well? What might be some implications? Having a representative group involved in the interpretation gives a better balance and can provide the potential to minimize biased analysis.

Initially, the data team may need some coaching on how to make these data pictures. Eventually, they will become quite proficient and at ease with the process.

5. Representing the Data

Tables, graphs, and pictographs are good ways to organize data for analysis and interpretation of patterns. Some data may need to be represented anecdotally, in narratives, videos, or in their existing formats, such as a master schedule. This section gives a brief overview of several different graphic representations. Because more information can usually be included in a table, there are times when the data will be presented in both tables and graphs. Graphs will be used to show either summary information from the table or a subsection of information.

Tables present summary information in rows and columns and are useful for identifying patterns. The sample Table 3.1 shows the major items that are identified on tables: (a) the title should be a summary of what the table represents, and (b) headings in the columns and the rows describe the categories listed. Usually, a total column or a row with summary statistics is included. Examples are presented here.

The data in Table 3.1 can also be represented on bar graphs such as those shown in Figures 3.2 and 3.3. Figure 3.2 uses a single bar to show summary data for two

Table 3.1   School "X" Percentage of School Days Attended for Females and Males, 2000–2002

Attendance	Females	Males	Total
2000–2001	91%	87%	89%
2001–2002	95%	89%	92%

NOTE: Sample data.

Figure 3.2 School "X" Percentage of School Days Attended, 2000–2002

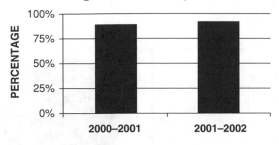

Figure 3.3 School "X" Percentage of School Days Attended for Females and Males

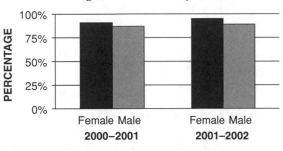

NOTE: Sample data.

years. The information was taken from the "Total" column of Table 3.1. Figure 3.3 uses double bars for each year to show disaggregated attendance data by males and females. This presents a clearer picture of whether or not there are patterns by gender. Many of the graphs in this book use multiple bars. Some use data from two different sources to show combination data patterns. Examples are found throughout the book that show patterns between students' course placements and test scores by race and ethnicity, and so forth.

Each bar graph needs a title, and the vertical and horizontal axes must be labeled. The horizontal axis is labeled by the categories to be compared. The vertical axis describes the scale, such as numbers, percentage, and so forth. Bar graphs can also be displayed with the bars running horizontally, in which case the labels are reversed. A legend is needed if each category is not labeled. Sometimes the bars are patterned or screened to show disaggregated groups (see Figure 3.3).

Circle graphs or pie charts are useful for representing proportions of a whole. They can quite dramatically show shifts in proportions between two points in time through presentations such as those in Figure 3.4, which shows the shifts in the racial and ethnic composition of an elementary school from 1992 to 2002. The circle graph always needs a title and a legend, and the percentages demonstrated for each group in the pie wedges must appear.

Line graphs are one of the most common tools for showing trends over a period of time. The line graph shown in Figure 3.5 illustrates drop-out percentages for five years for several groups. The data have been disaggregated by racial and ethnic groups, and the rates are compared to a state average. The patterns on the graph show that although the rate has dropped for all groups, gaps still remain between groups. Line graphs also need a title, and the horizontal and vertical axes should be labeled. A legend may be needed, or indicators such as those on the graph in Figure

Figure 3.4   1992–2002 Racial and Ethnic Composition of School "Z"

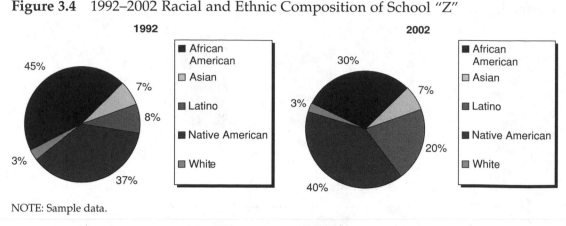

NOTE: Sample data.

Figure 3.5   Need to Improve High School Drop-Out Rates

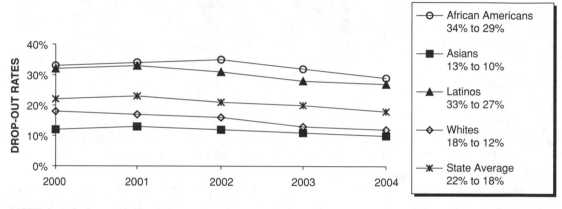

NOTE: Sample data.

3.5 can be used. Some of these considerations depend on the audience, presentation mode, and presentation space.

Pictographs are a creative and fun way of graphing material to capture the attention of people who might otherwise be bored by traditional presentations. The pictographs used by *USA Today* are good examples of data illustration to check out. The sample here, Figure 3.6, depicts the number of students in a first-grade cohort group who graduate from sixth grade. This is essentially similar to the bar graph, but it uses pictures instead of bars.

Some common ways that data are represented include looking at groups disaggregated by race, ethnicity, gender, language, income, and so forth. These data may be represented by indicating the following: (a) Show comparisons of the proportion of each group that are represented in a curriculum area, a program, a test range, college-eligible and college-enrolled students, and so forth. It should be noted when the group is not represented at all in a particular area. For instance, I recently reviewed data in one school with an African American and Latino population that reported no students in gifted programs. (b) Show comparisons of whether gaps are closing over time between and among groups in the areas measured. It is important to use consistent measures and to make comparisons at similar points in time. (c) Show how cohorts of different groups achieve as they move from grade to grade and level to level.

Figure 3.6   What Happened to Our First Graders in Elementary School?

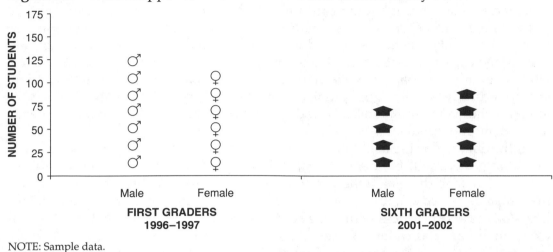

NOTE: Sample data.

6. Determine Audiences of Presentations

When choosing how to present your data, consider the audience. Data presentations need to be audience friendly, and the presenters must have clear goals related to what they expect the presentation to accomplish. Are the data being used to give a status report, to influence the direction of change, to dispel myths and test assumptions, to monitor progress, to examine the effects of practices and programs, or for some other reason? Review the section "Key Roles for Data" at the beginning of this chapter as a guide for determining purposes for your presentations.

- Knowing your audience is important in determining the kinds and amount of information you will present.
- How sophisticated in terms of data is the audience? How much data do you want to provide at any one time?
- How much time do you have?
- Do you want audience participation in charting graphs and so forth?
- Will you need to have a glossary of terms? Will your audience be dataphobic?
- How will they respond to equity-related issues?
- What information do they already have related to equity and reform? Are some members likely to take issue with the findings?
- Are you prepared to respond?

Be sure to know the sources of your data, the time when it was collected, and who collected and summarized the information. Make sure that the data have been checked for accuracy.

7. Structure the Data Dialogue

Handing out and presenting data without a plan for structuring meaningful dialogue can be dangerous and counterproductive. One of the most important goals of data is to stimulate dialogue in the school community. Whenever data are presented, time—and ideally facilitation as well—must be invested for the dialogue. Inevitably, some of the discoveries that the school and district make regarding their beliefs, practices, and outcomes will be painful. The school community must be prepared to work through some hard times. Self-knowledge is the first step toward self-improvement. There will be conflict and debate, and some members of the school community will not be pleased with the data process. The knowledge, beliefs, values, and experiences that we bring to the table influence how data are interpreted. Others can interpret one person's analysis of the data picture very differently. Without opportunity for dialogue, problems and misunderstandings can fester. In the long run, the question should be: How can we use the data to build a common agenda for student improvement?

If the data regarding achievement of various groups of students are particularly disturbing, there will be lots of finger pointing, and the familiar excuses will be heard about why things are the way they are. The responsibility for poor achievement may be placed solely on students and parents and the conditions in which they live. Policies and practices within the school or district may be skirted, and there is likely to be an abdication of the school's responsibility for outcomes. Without thoughtful dialogue, the same old tired solutions continue to occur, such as adding on more programs rather than fixing core problems.

Chapter 5 will provide a framework for guiding the conversations about data findings and will offer some suggestions on ways to design solutions that authentically address the issues related to the data.

USING TECHNOLOGY TO MAKE STRONG PRESENTATIONS

Information is power—but only if it is understood and accepted. How you present your data will determine how they are interpreted and processed. The advertising world has been aware of this for years. In the 1990s, high-tech, computer-generated, interactive commercials and programs have become the "messengers" of choice. The public has become used to messages that are fast-paced, colorful, and above all active.

Information should be presented with as much clarity and life as possible. Data users should not let the lack of the following kinds of presentation technologies stop them from sharing data and the stories they tell with their school community. However, if resources can be secured, some data users may eventually wish to experiment with these presentation strategies.

The presentation of data can take several forms. Slides, overhead transparencies, and interactive multimedia presentations are now commonplace. Several software packages are available for both Macintosh and Windows-based machines to assist with the creation of custom presentations. Software programs such as PowerPoint®, Persuasion®, Freelance®, and Impact® make the job of designing presentations much easier. Each includes templates or predesigned presentations. The backgrounds, fonts, graphs, and graphics of each template can be manipulated to suit individual tastes and styles.

The Microsoft Office suite of applications such as Word and Excel not only is capable of creating attractive text but also has built-in clip arts, drawing, and graphing-charting tools.

Remember the following guidelines when designing your own presentation:

- If a presentation is to be made to an audience of over 100 people, use slides.
- The maximum distance that a slide can be clearly seen is eight times the height of the projected image.
- The slide page has a ratio of 2:3.
- Slides use RGB (red-green-blue) color. You can mix and match colors any way you wish, and the computer software will convert it to RGB color in the end.
- Light text on a dark background shows up best. Slides use projected rather than reflected light, so high contrast makes the slides easier to see and read. White backgrounds drown out almost everything placed on them. If you include scanned images, lower the brightness and heighten the contrast if possible.
- Use contrasting colors when presenting graphs. Colors of the same tone or hue are difficult to distinguish from greater distances. Remember that there is always the possibility that someone in your audience may be color-blind.
- When choosing text or content for slides or transparencies, use a maximum of 10 lines per slide and a maximum of five or six words per line. Do not put the entire text of your presentation on the slide or transparency.
- Only the basic concepts or points are written on a slide. The slide show is intended to provide an outline of what is to be presented. It is easier to remember. The presenter's role is to express and articulate the concepts behind the presentation. In this way, the audience will be paying attention to the significant points in the presentation rather than trying to read slides.
- Use active words and phrases. Keep sentences short. Slides are used as a visual aid. Use the slide to reinforce what you are saying. Do not read the information off the slide.
- Use larger type fonts: 24 points or larger for titles and 18 points or larger for text.
- If transparencies are used, place the material in the upper portion of the transparency. People in the back row cannot always see the bottom portion of a transparency.
- Both slides and transparencies should be created in landscape (wide) rather than portrait (tall) formats.

With each of the previously mentioned software packages, your presentation can be processed in a variety of ways. The most common software package used is PowerPoint. With its animation capabilities it is more welcomed by today's audience. Overhead transparencies can be created, or slides can be projected on a screen. A finished PowerPoint presentation can also be delivered over the Internet or sent to the intended audience along with a viewer.

A well-designed presentation can make the presenter appear confident and knowledgeable. Dynamic presentations have an impact on the viewer and the viewer's opinions. With the assistance of computer software, the only limit to your presentations is your imagination.

Discussion and Cautionary Notes

Data users should be patient with themselves and others. It takes time to become proficient with data; it is a continuous learning process. Don't hesitate to ask for help. You will find your new knowledge to be worth the investment. Ideally, the information in the remaining chapters of this book should help you along the way. The Bibliography lists further resources that can help.

One of the most important goals of data is to stimulate dialogue in the school community.

At all times, accuracy must be a priority when using data. Check and recheck calculations. It is more important to take the extra time to triple-check numbers collected and calculated than to conduct analysis or make presentations that are wrong. Incorrect data can create false impressions and misguided plans.

In the end, if you become a skilled data user, you will be better grounded to be proactive for children among negative and hostile audiences. Without the power of data, you leave others to define the realities of reform.

4

Building Leadership and Data Teams

The desegregated school district had high median test scores and a relatively high state ranking. Therefore, many in the school community were uncomfortable when the superintendent and the board put forces in motion to focus on issues of equity. This would involve disaggregating data to examine the achievement of diverse groups of students in the district. At an after-school meeting, someone made a comment that reflected the sentiment of some others: "Disaggregating data is racist. I don't see color, I only see children." Many did not want to discuss these sensitive issues. However, the superintendent and the board prevailed in directing an initiative in which there would be a focus on equity and standards reform. Perceptions and assumptions about how and why different groups were achieving at different levels would be confronted. School leadership and data teams would play a central role in leading, creating, implementing, and monitoring the reforms.

Over the next year, the school teams had extensive professional development, and the school created inquiries that would be broader in scope than accountability reports were. They asked questions such as the following: What impact does the district have on all groups of students, from the time they enter until the time they leave? If students succeed, what are the reasons? If students don't succeed, what are the reasons? The teams played a major role in moving the schools and district toward a data-user culture. In data presentations and dialogues, the schools and district came to grips with how the policies and practices in the system influence the achievement of students. The teams uncovered information about the achievement gaps at all levels in the districts. Two groups of students, African American and Latino, were performing at lower levels of achievement than white and Asian students were. This information had not shown up when looking at aggregate data. A group of elementary teachers traced cohort groups from kindergarten through fifth grade and found similar patterns. Another data team evaluated program interventions.

The teams read current literature and understood the need to look at institutional barriers rather than placing blame on students and parents. The school communities designed solutions based on their research and data. They designed ways to use more than one type of assessment to measure growth, to improve instructional practices, to improve standards in evaluating student work, to communicate better with parents, to use qualitative and quantitative data to answer inquiries, and to set up a student-level database to monitor student progress and institutional interventions and practices. Schools can now store and easily access data on students. The staff can now analyze data in more complex ways. Two years ago, they were using calculators and going through cumulative folders, and many were computerphobic.

Equity issues are being addressed. There is more participation of underrepresented groups in Advanced Placement classes; standards have not been lowered, and the achievement gap is closing. They have instituted an advanced learning program at the middle school level for underperforming students, and teachers are focused on standards and convene in groups to talk about student work. Schools are focused on students and are continually asking what they need to know to teach and support students. A school and district culture that uses relevant data to focus on the achievement of all groups of students has evolved.

Overview

Nobody can bring about schoolwide reform alone. Experience suggests that it will take a lot of hard work from a very committed core of individuals. And even then, reform is not ensured. Collaborating in teams creates a shared vision and shared responsibility. Thus, there is more potential to penetrate cultures that negatively affect student opportunities (Anderson, Herr, & Sigrid Nihlen, 1994; Johnson, 1996b; Olsen & Jaramillo, 1999).

It is important for those who wish to launch a long-term, successful reform movement to quickly identify a small group to lead the effort. Soon after, a data team will be required. Depending on the circumstances of the school, the initial teamwork may be gradual or rapid.

ESTABLISHING THE NEED: A FIRST STEP FOR HIGHLY RESISTANT SCHOOLS

In schools where the culture is resistant to reform—where staff are more likely to blame parents and students than to accept their share of responsibility—it may be necessary to establish an informal leadership team to work to build consensus about the need for reform and to push the movement forward. If so, the "leader" will want to identify a group of like-minded staff, parents, and community members to strategize about reform.

This early leadership group will want to think hard about their approach. They will need to ask questions like the following: What will it take to convince at least a significant number of our colleagues and fellow community members that our school can do better? What data can we present to make our case? Should we visit more successful schools that share similar students? Do we need pressure from outside—from parents and the community?

Sometimes an informal leadership team will meet for months, searching for an opportune moment to move. Such moments can appear at any time—in the form of a new directive from the board or the superintendent, a new state-mandated planning process, an accreditation visit, or even a story in the local paper. In some cases, the group may have to create the moment themselves by challenging the stand taken by their more resistant colleagues. The goal of the team is to be prepared to seize a moment to start a schoolwide discussion of improving teaching and learning. Meanwhile, the reform process is not at a standstill, because the leadership group is getting ready.

CREATING THE TEAM: THE FIRST STEP IN MOST SCHOOLS

There are many opportunities each year for a principal or site council to engage a school community in reviewing student outcomes, deciding whether they are satisfactory, and choosing a course of action if they are not. Some common opportunities include the need to prepare a Title I or "school improvement" plan, the arrival of a school "report card" from the state or district, the school accreditation review, or the announcement of a new national or state report on educational outcomes. Any of these—or similar—events can become an excellent time to pull together the school community and take a good hard look at how students are doing.

Usually, just a little bit of data will be sufficient to prompt educators and parents in an urban school to conclude that there is a need for a reform effort. Some combination of national data—describing, for example, the continued achievement gap separating minority and low-income students from other students, the low rate of college entry and success, and the economic impact of underachievement—and local or school data can launch the dialogue. At the high school level, for example, the school community might examine the rate at which students in different groups are assigned to classes like algebra or chemistry. At the elementary level, the community might examine differences in reading success or grade retention by race.

The point of all this is critical: to convince at least a substantial segment of the school community that they and their students can do better—and that the community must begin a quest to figure out how. A representative leadership team is then appointed or even elected to guide the inquiry process.

THE ROLE OF THE LEADERSHIP TEAM

The leadership team is a group of individuals charged with steering the effort to increase student achievement by engaging all constituencies of the school community over several years. Because most schools already have a number of committees, councils, and teams working on a variety of functions, it is important that the distinct role and expectations of the school reform leadership team be delineated clearly from the beginning. What guidelines will be used in deciding who should serve on the leadership team? How will the diversity of the school community be represented? What resources will be devoted to helping team members acquire the knowledge and skills needed to guide and manage the process of reform while continuing to carry out their existing responsibilities? How long must team members commit to serve, and what incentives or rewards might they anticipate?

Creating a team structure that can function over the long term to accomplish reform is not a one-step operation. Like the system it aims to reform, a leadership team for school reform must develop over the long haul through a complex process. The leadership team must be dynamic and must expect its inevitable share of ups and downs, particularly if the team represents a cross section of a school community with a healthy diversity.

An equity agenda poses some especially complex issues for a team. The deeply held personal beliefs of members will most certainly have an impact, as will dominant assumptions and theories about whether all students can learn at the highest standards and should have access to an academically challenging course of study. Throughout the process of planning and working for school reform, team members need opportunities to build trust and to explore their own feelings and perceptions on these issues if they are to risk breaking the "code of silence" and engaging their peers in honest dialogue on issues of race, culture, and class as they relate to student achievement.

Learning to work collaboratively must be a priority challenge for the team, especially in a school community that is fragmented or where decision making has traditionally been directed from the top down. The team must learn to recognize and manage political and interpersonal dynamics if it is to become a unified and viable body that can provide leadership for whole-school reform. Opportunities for team building, trust building, enhancing communication skills, and reaching consensus regarding mission are critical in the early stages of team formation.

Team development has been cleverly described by Tuckman (1965) as involving four stages: (a) forming, (b) storming, (c) norming, and (d) performing. Although this may not exactly describe every team's evolution, most will be close.

STRUCTURING THE LEADERSHIP TEAM'S WORK

No leadership team can function effectively without a certain degree of structure. A series of decisions must be made early in the team's formation together to ensure that members establish a structure that is workable and sustainable. Here are some questions that should be addressed early on:

- How frequently should meetings be held?
- Where will we meet?
- How will agendas be set?
- What ground rules will apply?
- Who will conduct or facilitate the meetings?
- Should minutes be kept, and if so, by whom?
- Will these responsibilities rotate?

- Is there a need for subcommittees?
- How will the participation of the larger school community be arranged?
- How will the work be monitored, rewarded, and improved?
- Who should be on the team?
- What is the system to ensure accountability?

Job descriptions are useful for prospective team members to formulate and review prior to making a commitment to serve on the leadership team.

TEAM DEVELOPMENT

This book offers a variety of instruments to help teams develop their strategies on how to build and sustain a successful team process. These instruments help teams reflect on composition, internal dynamics, relationship to the broader school community, potential for effectiveness, and real accomplishments. The instruments can be helpful for team members to review at the outset of their work together to begin visualizing the kind of team they wish to strive for and challenges they will face.

For example, leadership team members often inspire one another during planning retreats together, but once away from the energy of the team they can easily become reabsorbed in the milieu of business as usual. Teams must consciously build in activities, check-ins, and supports to sustain the momentum of their reform plans. The opinions of others in the school community are an important source of information as to how well the team is carrying out its role. Team members may regularly review written evaluation forms that colleagues have completed at the end of workshops conducted by the team. These ratings and comments by colleagues should be incorporated into the team's self-assessment. However, along with outside feedback, the team should also take time for introspection. Some teams may informally "spot-check" themselves. For example, team members might use the last couple of minutes of their meetings to assess the productivity of the session or to give feedback to the facilitator. Also, it is important to set aside time occasionally for more structured and in-depth self-examination, the results of which should indicate reason to celebrate as well as room for improvement. It may be a good idea for the team to plan an off-site activity, such as dinner together, in recognition of its achievements.

A final caution regarding team functioning. Resistance from school colleagues can set in early if they perceive the team as an elite clique with special privileges, or if they see team members as "deputies" of the school administration. Where a school community is deeply divided into factions, certain constituencies may view team members as having "sold out" or collaborated with the "opposition forces." School staff sometimes complain that teams seem to return from off-site planning sessions "enlightened," knowing all the answers and ready to "bestow their wisdom" upon everyone else. This feeling by colleagues that the team intends to impose rather than propose a plan for systemic reform does not lay good groundwork for collaboration. At the extremes, team members may burst on the scene with overwhelming exuberance or, at the other end, perhaps trying to not appear privileged, may creep back close-lipped as though they've been on a clandestine mission! The existing school culture is an important factor for the team to take into account in thinking about how it will define its character, formulate relationships, and set about the reform work.

THE DATA TEAM: CORE TO THE SCHOOL'S SUCCESS IN USING DATA TO ACHIEVE REFORM

The leadership team must convince the school or district community of the merits of using quantitative and qualitative data as a strategic tool to guide the reform process. Then careful consideration must be given to how to do so in a way that ensures that data use becomes a part of the school's culture. Those new to using data on a routine basis often wonder, "Where do I begin? What should I collect? What do I do with all of this stuff now that I have it?" The whole process can be overwhelming.

Someone—or ideally a group of people—must be assigned clear responsibility for the data process. Otherwise, it usually fizzles out. Sometimes the leadership team assumes this responsibility or forms an expanded subcommittee to serve as the data team. If there are separate teams, someone from the leadership team should be on the data team to make sure they are working in collaboration and vice versa. The role of the data team is to lead the process and to keep the data strategy percolating as integral in the reform process. There may be more than one team. In a large setting such as a high school, there may be several strands of inquiry. Data or inquiry teams should be representative of the school community so that different voices can be present in the entire process. They should be made up of motivated individuals who are willing to stretch their development over the long haul. They will need to be organized, meet regularly, develop leadership, and take seriously their responsibility to learn and to report to other leaders and the broader school community. The data will need to be supported with the types of resources discussed next.

Resources.   Budgets must reflect a priority for data, with funds reallocated accordingly. Financial support must be planned for the time and professional development of the data team, as well as for computer hardware and software. Equally critical, members of the data team must have adequate time within their work schedules to effectively organize the school's data inquiries and strategies. The work is too demanding to expect any staff to carry it out in occasional volunteer hours.

Professional Development.   Professional development is essential to building the capacity of the organization as a user of data and enhancing the skills of data organizers. Key people will need to go to workshops, read relevant literature, and work with consultants who have expertise in using data at the school level for organizational reform. Chapter 3 in this book, on the role of data in the reform process, can be of help. Data users will be best equipped if they have an opportunity to learn how to use technology (see Chapter 3).

Evaluating the Need for an External Resource Person.   The school or district may need assistance at various points in the process regarding how to identify, collect, analyze, and represent data. It is important at the outset to identify what kinds of assistance might be needed and to locate where those resources exist. Do you need the services of researchers, experts in research design, or interviewers? What are some of the basics in gathering, analyzing, and presenting data? How do you combine data?

Assessing Technological Capabilities and Needs. The data process can be powerfully expedited with appropriate technology. Many schools are not aware of all the existing information and services that are available within their own district. What types of hardware, databases, and software capacity exist at the school district level? Who at the school or district can assist with gathering and representing the data? Getting to know the resources and the people responsible for this area in the district is essential (see Chapter 3).

To learn more about effective team development, the school community will benefit from reading and discussing literature such as "Building Teams to Rebuild Schools" (Maeroff, 1993), *The New Meaning of Educational Reform* (Fullan & Stiegelbauer, 1991), and "Developing Data Mentors" (Nichols & Singer, 2000), as well as the information and case studies from data teams in the field that can be found in this book. The staff will need at least two hourlong blocks to read and discuss in both small and large groups. Don't rush this process or squeeze it in between agenda items at a faculty meeting.

PLANNING FOR TEAM SUCCESS: TEAM SELF-ASSESSMENT OF STRENGTHS AND NEEDS

Throughout the leadership and data teams' work for school reform, members will benefit from periodically conducting an honest assessment of their individual and collective strengths and needs. The teams should have established mechanisms for ensuring that their efforts are best serving the school reform effort as a whole.

Following a professional development session on data teams, a school data team developed some questions for data teams in their district to consider when assessing a team's readiness and knowledge for a data presentation to their school staff. Figure 4.1 is an example. Data teams may want to develop their own questions that are relevant to their sites.

Figure 4.2 (page 61), Team Self-Assessment of Strengths and Needs, is a more comprehensive instrument that can serve as one of several team-building and -sustaining exercises, and it can form the basis for the team's plan for internal capacity building needed to fulfill its role.

When to Use

Figure 4.2 can be a very useful instrument early in the reform effort for individual and group self-reflection that will help team members become acquainted, identify the constituencies they represent, recognize gaps in the team's composition, clarify their respective roles, and sharpen their understanding of the team's function. This baseline knowledge is needed from the beginning as the team is forming and can be an important factor as it establishes its credibility with the larger school community. A team that has launched its work together off-site may need to conduct this assessment before returning to the school so that, from the beginning, all members are prepared to describe the team and answer questions from colleagues. The instrument also can be used to update the team's profile as new members are added.

Figure 4.1   Questions for Data Teams to Consider

1. Will the data presentation take place during a regular meeting of faculty, or does the team need to create a special block of time (such as a pupil-free day)? 　　Regular meeting _____　　　　　　　　Special time_____ *Comments:* _____
2. Should all team members participate actively? 　　Yes _____　　　　　　　No _____ *Comments:* _____
3. How important is it for the team to achieve and project a solid commitment to its role and the process? 　　Important _____　　　　　　　　Not important _____ *Comments:* _____
4. Are there unresolved tensions within the team? If so, how will these be dealt with? 　　Yes _____　　　　　　　No _____ *Comments:* _____
5. Is there literature that can be shared, and, if so, will time be structured for participants to read and discuss? 　　Yes _____　　　　　　　No _____ *Comments:* _____
6. Do summaries of our findings need to be prepared in lay language for parents? 　　Yes _____　　　　　　　No _____ *Comments:* _____
7. Is translation necessary? 　　Yes _____　　　　　　　No _____ *Comments:* _____
8. If the team developed a plan to initiate the reform process, do we view it as provisional and open to input and approval of the wider school community? 　　Yes _____　　　　　　　No _____ *Comments:* _____
9. What role in decision-making does our team have in relationship to other authoritative bodies on campus? *Comments:* _____
10. Will authority and ownership for the reform process rest with the team alone? 　　Yes _____　　　　　　　No _____ *Comments:* _____

Administering the Instrument

The instrument in Figure 4.2 gives team members the chance to reflect on their own potential contribution to the team, as well as the team's combined strengths and weaknesses. Individuals should first fill in only the column marked "Team," then report and discuss their opinions with one another. Then team members should fold under the "Team" column so they can reflect on what they each bring to the team. After sharing these thoughts with one another, the team members should come to some general agreements as to what actions need to be taken to strengthen the team. The team should also remember to take a moment to celebrate its identified strengths.

Figure 4.2 Team Self-Assessment of Strengths and Needs

A. RATING

Directions: Working independently, in the sections below use the 1–5 scale to rate each item in reference to the team's performance or to your individual performance as a team member. Use the "TEAM" column first. Then fold this column under and use the "SELF" column.

NEED				STRENGTH
Immediate Need	Somewhat Need	On the Way	Somewhat a Strength	Great Strength
1	2	3	4	5

STRUCTURE AND LOGISTICS	TEAM
Representation	_____
Size	_____
Clear focus on improving student achievement	_____
Where the team fits in the organization of the school	_____
Clear delineation of:	
• team's leadership role, function	_____
• team's responsibilities, rights, authority	_____
• each team member's role, responsibilities	_____
Team meetings:	
• schedule—adherence to	_____
• location	_____
• formats and agenda	_____
System for accountability:	
• internally	_____
• with school community	_____
Other	_____
Other	_____

RELATIONSHIPS AND INTERACTION	SELF	TEAM
Team-building trust	_____	_____
Commitments—long-term	_____	_____
Group dynamics—communication skills, participation, inclusion/exclusion, power-sharing, interdependence	_____	_____
Group diversity factors—race, ethnicity, occupation, language, gender, schooling, age, work styles, behavioral styles	_____	_____
Candor, risk-taking, energy, enthusiasm, humor	_____	_____
Meeting agendas—setting and following	_____	_____
Meeting facilitation	_____	_____
Ground rules—shared responsibility for respecting differences	_____	_____

(continued)

Data Analysis and Presentation

Once the team has agreed on the results of its self-assessment, this information should be presented to the school community for feedback. In this way, the team introduces or reinforces practices of introspection and accountability as norms within the culture of the school community. The instrument in Figure 4.2 can be administered periodically—possibly at yearly intervals.

Figure 4.2   Continued

RELATIONSHIPS AND INTERACTION	SELF	TEAM
Decision making: collaboration, consensus-building, synergy	_____	_____
Problem solving	_____	_____
Collecting and using data for multiple purposes	_____	_____
Using research and professional literature	_____	_____
Strategic planning, *implementation, evaluation	_____	_____
Following through according to time-task sequence	_____	_____
Engaging the school community	_____	_____
Using tension creatively and constructively	_____	_____
Receiving and offering feedback:		
• internally	_____	_____
• with school community	_____	_____
Evaluating individual and team	_____	_____
Other	_____	_____
Other	_____	_____

*Includes vision/mission, principles, assessment, goals/objectives, strategies/tasks, resource identification/alignment, roles/responsibilities, timelines

B.   PRIORITIES FOR DEVELOPMENT

STRUCTURE AND LOGISTICS

TEAM

1.

2.

RELATIONSHIPS AND INTERACTION

SELF	TEAM
1.	1.
2.	2.

PROCESS

SELF	TEAM
1.	1.
2.	2.

SOURCE: Designed by Joyce Germaine Watts.

Discussion and Cautionary Notes

If the Team Self-Assessment of Strengths and Needs instrument is used early in the team's work together, the team members may be unaccustomed to the candor and sensitivity required when giving and receiving feedback. Consider the need for a facilitator.

ASSESSING PERSPECTIVES OF TEAM EFFECTIVENESS

As reform proceeds, a leadership team should pause periodically to appreciate its growth and accomplishments and also to note areas where it needs to increase its capacity to lead the reform process. The exercise in collective self-reflection can take various forms. Figure 4.3, Perspectives of Team Effectiveness, is another very effective tool to help organize the team's thoughts and guide its discussion. It can be used in conjunction with reflective writing or other open-ended exercises to gain a more complete picture of how team members feel about the group's level of functioning and success.

Perspectives of Team Effectiveness is a springboard for a fuller discussion of some factors that may have hindered or enhanced the team's performance. To allow for the active participation of all team members, it may be advisable to invite an outside facilitator to guide the meeting. Ideally, the team will have established an atmosphere of trust where opinions can be shared honestly, sensitively, and constructively. The team may want to use certain items, such as "communication and interaction" or "roles and responsibilities," for individual members to rate how they personally enhanced or hindered the team's work, as well as to assess the effectiveness of the team as a whole.

When to Use

This instrument can be used very effectively after teams have been working for about a year. However, the decision of when to collect and analyze this information should be made based on the team's needs to reflect on its functioning. Probably semiannually or annually should be sufficient.

Administering the Instrument

The team needs to set aside ample time to complete this instrument, analyze the information, and discuss implications for the future. Both the team and school community should engage in this experience. The perceptions of the team's functioning may be similar or different based on roles, interaction patterns, and outcomes.

The instrument should be filled out individually, and then the data need to be summarized. The team members might choose to fill out the instrument, summarize their responses, and discuss implications in one session. Involving the larger school community will probably require two phases, because it will take longer to tally and summarize the data. The team-only administration can become baseline data to be compared to the whole-school tally.

Data Analysis and Presentation

The findings of this instrument can be summarized and displayed graphically. The data should be disaggregated by the team's perspectives and others' perspectives. There needs to be content analysis of the comments; the team may select members or an outsider to do this. Because the focus is on the team's functioning, an objective outside facilitator may be useful.

After collecting and discussing the findings, the team needs to present what reforms will take place in its functioning.

(text continues on page 67)

Figure 4.3 Perspectives of Team Effectiveness

Your team has been a working unit aimed at realizing the vision and goals to raise student achievement. The items below are intended to help the team look at how well it functioned and to suggest areas for increasing the team's capacity to move the reform process.

Using the scale, rate each aspect of your team according to how you believe it influenced the team's effectiveness. Consider the impact within the team as well as within the school.

RATING:
Hindered Our   -----1   --2--   --3--   --4--   5----   Enhanced Our
Effectiveness   Effectiveness

ASPECT:

SIZE/COMPOSITION	1	2	3	4	5

Items to consider in rating: What factors were considered in deciding to expand/not expand the teams? If new members were added, how were they oriented and brought up-to-date? Are all members committed to the long-term?	• Team not representative	• Team very representative
	• New members not oriented	• New members fully oriented and brought up-to-date
	• Not committed	• Committed for the long term

Comments: _____

INTEGRATION OF TEAM EFFORTS	1	2	3	4	5

Items to consider in rating: What has been done to link the efforts and data with other related committees or groups at the school? Does the staff view the work of these teams as interrelated components of the same improvement process?	• No linkage to other school teams, committees and/or groups	• Strong integration of related teams/committees/ groups.
	• Staff does not see the team's work as interrelated	• Staff views the work of the team as totally interrelated to other improvement processes

Comments: _____

COMMUNICATION & INTERACTION	1	2	3	4	5

Items to consider in rating: Do all team members contribute fully to discussions or are there factors that inhibit participation? To what degree do team members feel they can express divergent opinions openly? Has the team dealt with any factors that may undermine cohesiveness?	• Certain members dominate	• All members contribute fully
	• Lack of openness	• Divergent opinions expressed openly
	• Hidden agendas	• Deal with factors that undermine cohesiveness
	• Staff views team as elitist	• Staff views team as collaborative and supportive

Comments: _____

Figure 4.3 Continued

ASPECT:	RATING: Hindered Our Effectiveness -----1 --2-- --3-- --4-- 5---- Enhanced Our Effectiveness				
ROLES & RESPONSIBILITIES	1	2	3	4	5
Items to consider in rating: How were roles and responsibilities decided upon? How did team members provide feedback to each other on task performance?	• Unclear about roles and responsibilities				• Clearly defined roles and responsibilities
	• Roles and responsibilities developed by exclusive few				• Roles and responsibilities developed collaboratively
	• Team members do not receive feedback				• Team members receive feedback on a regular basis
Comments: _____					
MEETING LOGISTICS	1	2	3	4	5
Items to consider in rating: How often did the team meet? Were meeting days and times convenient for team members? Were attendance and location concerns dealt with?	• Team does not meet				• Team meets twice a month
	• Times and days are inconvenient				• Times and days convenient for team members
	• Attendance sporadic				• Attendance consistently high
	• Inadequate location for meetings				• Excellent location for meetings
Comments: _____					
STRUCTURE/FOCUS OF MEETINGS	1	2	3	4	5
Items to consider in rating: How were the format and topics for meetings determined? To what extent were meetings focused on implementation of the team's plan?	• No format or agenda				• Well-designed format and agenda
	• No communication flow for team/school community				• Well-implemented communication flow for team/school community
	• No accountability				• Effective system of accountability
	• Focus on routines				• Strategic planning, focus on implementation and evaluation
	• No focus on student achievement				• Strong student achievement focus
Comments: _____					

(continued)

Figure 4.3   Continued

ASPECT:	RATING: Hindered Our -----1 --2-- --3-- --4-- 5---- Enhanced Our Effectiveness Effectiveness				
DECISION MAKING	1	2	3	4	5
Items to consider in rating: To what extent were decisions informed using current literature and data? Does the team monitor the effectiveness of the decisions? Were decisions arrived at through collaboration consensus? How do team members resolve differences? Did all members support the decisions of the team?	• No grounding in current literature				• Decisions well-grounded in current literature on reform, access and equity, forces affecting schools and students, families, communities, etc.
	• No use of data				• Extensive use of data
	• No problem solving				• Hightly skilled problem solving
	• No risk-taking				• No fear of taking risks
	• No conflict resolution				• Dealt with conflicts creatively and constructively
	• No monitoring				• Consistent and continual monitoring using data
Comments: _____					
BUY-IN	1	2	3	4	5
Items to consider in rating: What feedback is there to indicate commitment from the larger school community to the vision, goals, and strategies? What is the level of staff and parent participation in the work initiated by the team?	• Team works in isolation				• Team regularly interfaces with the school community (staff and parents)
	• No feedback and/or buy-in from larger school community				• Extensive feedback and buy-in from school community
Comments: _____					

SOURCE: Designed by Joyce Germaine Watts and Ruth S. Johnson.

Discussion and Cautionary Notes

The team must realize that they may receive some harsh criticism and try not to assume a defensive posture. It is important to listen and look at the patterns that surface. Isolated remarks should be considered, but the collective nature of the remarks is also important. How much emphasis the team puts on addressing an issue raised should reflect whether it could make a significant difference in outcomes. The team cannot always please everyone, but it has to be open and accountable to the school community. Evidence that the team is willing to look at its functioning serves as a model. At some point, others in the school community will need to reflect on how their behavior enhances or inhibits the student achievement agenda.

Developing other rubrics for these instruments is encouraged. The team should hold on to the outcomes of this instrument each year as a record of the phases it goes through. The team can also read the literature to get a sense of some of the developmental stages of teamwork to expect.

PLANNING FOR TEAM LEADERSHIP DEVELOPMENT

Based on the team's assessment of its strengths, needs, and effectiveness, a design for team leadership development should be created. This can set forth a process not only to ensure that all members of the team are contributing productively, but also to support their continued growth as individuals and as a unit. In the team members' enthusiasm to advance the larger plans they have developed, they must not lose sight of their own needs.

When to Use or Develop Forms

Ideally, an outline plan for team leadership development should be drafted hand in hand with the Team Self-Assessment of Strengths and Needs (Figure 4.2) and the Perspectives of Team Effectiveness (Figure 4.3). In fact, each time either of those assessments is conducted, the Plan for Data Team Leadership Development form (Figure 4.4) should be revisited in order to make sure current needs are being addressed. This way, the evolving plan can itself be used as a monitoring form to record progress over time.

Administering the Form

The team should have about 60 to 90 minutes of uninterrupted time to complete this process—and not at the end of the day when members are likely to be tired. Each member of the team fills out the form individually to ensure full participation. Using chart paper, an overhead, or large-screen computer projections, record each member's ideas. The aim is to get the group thinking and not to let anyone dominate the discussion. Arrive at consensus after some discussion about what needs to happen, priorities, timelines, resource implications, monitoring what the team decides to do, and responsible persons. Someone needs to assume responsibility for recording and disseminating the agreed-upon plan.

Figure 4.4 Plan for Data Team Leadership Development

Date _____	
In order to achieve our goals for improved student achievement, we plan to use the following strategies for continuing to develop our ability to work effectively as a team in the use of data.	
STRATEGY #1	**Integration of Team Efforts**
	• Structure for team to meet on monthly basis. • When (days and time) responsible for making it happen. • Analyze data from all school plans and initiatives; report results.
STRATEGY #2	**Roles and Responsibilities**
	• Shared decision making, working with other groups within the school, e.g., councils, advisers. • Develop a job description for team members and share with staff.
STRATEGY #3	**Buy-In**
	• Establishing staff buy-in by personal interactions. • School and grade level meetings with team members to share and receive feedback, report progress, written communications. • Presentation and discussion of useful and compelling data.

An alternative method might be to have team members work in small groups focusing on a particular strategy, with each group then sharing with the whole team. The team will then arrive at consensus.

Data Analysis and Presentation

Data on implementation of the team plan should be maintained. Over time, an analysis of what the team learned did or did not work will contain valuable information for all engaged in this process. A survey or some type of evaluation instrument might be developed to gather the data to be analyzed. The team might want an outsider to give them feedback on their progress. By reporting to the staff, the team can model accountability and how feedback helps them make midcourse corrections.

Discussion and Cautionary Notes

It is assumed that the team has read and discussed the suggested literature on building teams. This is important to developing a sound plan. If the team has not read the literature, delay this experience until members have done so, or else use a two-phase process whereby members come up with their own ideas, then expand or revise these based on what they learn from the literature.

II

Inquiring About Equity

5

Talking About Data

The leadership and data teams had spent a considerable amount of time collecting and disaggregating data and preparing a presentation for their colleagues about the achievement gap in their schools. They were excited about their work and felt that the faculty would be eager to see and address the issues related to the data. The teams, along with the principal, presented their findings at the monthly faculty meeting. Achievement gap patterns were apparent. On every indicator of achievement there were disparities by race, ethnicity, and income. Poor, African American, Latino, and Native American students did less well on standardized tests than their middle-income, white, and Asian peers did. They were disproportionately placed in lower-level groupings and special education, and they also were consistently on lists for disciplinary infractions. However, all groups in the school had similar attendance rates.

After the presentation, the teams asked the faculty to examine and discuss the data in small groups and to propose some solutions to improve student achievement and to close the gap. The teams had allotted about 30 minutes for discussion. This was the first time the staff had looked at such comprehensive disaggregated data, and most of the faculty members were clearly uncomfortable with the information. Instead of breaking into groups, some challenged data accuracy, others said that the achievement disparity had to do with poverty and that there was enough research to prove it, and still others claimed that the parents did not care and that the kids were uncooperative.

Others had silver bullet solutions such as this or that program or creating another remedial course. Some resented the fact that the data were disaggregated and felt that doing so was racist. They claimed that they did not see color and that this presentation was divisive. There were others, however, who saw the data as confirming their assumptions about what was happening to different groups in the school. They were glad that there would be an opportunity to have dialogue around these patterns and to pose some solutions. They had heard about schools with similar demographics that were significantly closing the gap, and they believed that the data picture in their school could change.

Unfortunately, the faculty was not able to begin the data dialogue because the time for the faculty meeting had ended, so they would have to take this up at another time. The teams were disappointed and frustrated because they often were not able to address the challenges posed by their colleagues at this meeting, and they had no idea as to when they could schedule a follow-up meeting.

Overview

This scenario is not that uncommon when schools begin to use data to examine equity issues related to student achievement. Many school teams present disaggregated data and are stumped by the comments and questions of their colleagues after their presentations. I am often asked the question, "How do you get people in the school community to move from constantly blaming the parents, the kids, and the neighborhood for the low achievement to reflecting on their practices and the institutional policies and practices as a major source of the problem?"

Handing out and presenting data without a plan for structuring meaningful dialogue can be dangerous and counterproductive. One of the most important goals of data is to stimulate dialogue in the school community. Whenever data are presented time, and ideally facilitation, must be invested. Inevitably, some of the discoveries that the school and district make regarding their beliefs, practices, and outcomes will be painful. How do we begin to have conversations that can result in some deeper reforms that make a difference for students?

Dialogue will be essential to identify how different stakeholders in the school or district community perceive success. Some may want to eliminate all remedial groupings, some may want all children placed in algebra, and others may be satisfied with incremental increases. These perceptions have an impact on how the changes are implemented and can also affect the levels of commitment to the change. Although these discussions can produce some conflict, the problem solving that ensues can be healthy for the process. If this open dialogue does not occur—or is not allowed to occur—problems from differential expectations will surface later in ways that may not be possible to mediate.

WHY THE NEED FOR DIALOGUE

The central purpose for all of the data activities is to improve learning opportunities and outcomes for students. Without deeper discussions that look at institutional conditions that are barriers to learning, superficial changes or avoidance will continue. Looking at disaggregated data will bring discomfort for many, and identifying inequities by race and class causes a complex array of emotions from anger to denial. Perceptions from past experiences are hard to penetrate.

Probing questions and dialogue can provide an early opportunity for school and district staff to assess and understand the beliefs and values that drive norms of behavior in the school culture (see Chapter 2). Such assessment forces consideration of basic factors that often makes reform value-laden and frustrating. This critical stage of planning for reform is often bypassed because it requires such exceptionally personal risk taking. Discussion of why curriculum reform is needed or who will benefit from a nontracked curriculum requires courageous dialogue because it will expose personal beliefs about human capacity for learning. Ultimately this dialogue can expose a very broad range of expectations and practices behind the often-quoted phrase "all students can learn."

Looking at students by race, class, and language group can at times generate statements such as "I only see children, not color, and disaggregating data is racist!" Even though these statements may have a confrontational tone, they must be addressed to move the equity agenda forward. The skilled leadership of the data team or an external facilitator is needed to address the issue of why we need to look at different groups of students if we are to address the achievement gap.

In looking at data that measure equity, conversations around race, ethnicity, and class need to occur. Many are uncomfortable with these issues and will use code words such as "the students who are bused in" or "the kids in basic math" (when these groups include only students of color) rather than describing such students by their race or ethnic background. There may be fears of accusations of prejudice, but these discussions must occur when patterns emerge that show that some groups are having very different academic or other experiences in schools that create long-term harmful effects.

Additionally, I have found that putting the conditions of schooling in a historical context helps. It will be necessary to bring some perspectives that are unfamiliar to many, including the citation of historical and social forces that are at the root of some inequitable policies and practices in schools. It is important that appropriate literature, such as those in the References and Bibliography sections of this book, be discussed and linked to the issues that the group is probing. It is particularly useful to include data and literature that indicate how negative conditions for students can be reversed. Literature that not only provides explanatory information but also offers hope and meaningful solutions is useful to motivate the group to move forward.

Usually educators have no idea that many of the practices and policies we take for granted have legacies. Many of these policies and practices were developed to meet the social and economic needs of the time and created practices of exclusion that are still present in schools. In her book *Keeping Track: How Schools Structure Inequality*, Oakes (1985) provides an important historical perspective on the origins of tracking. This information and the challenging of assumptions about tracking serve as a wake-up call to many educators. Olsen (1996) argues,

> Knowing this history helps people to recognize that the long journey to inclusion, justice and equality in the schools has been fueled by responsible and courageous people who have been vigilant about monitoring exclusion. They raised their voices to protest inequities. Such stories help educators today to think about what kinds of dangers might exist in this historical era, and what kinds of roles they might play within a contemporary movement for equity and inclusion. (p. 55)

The school community needs to focus on what the data tell them about existing conditions, what needs to stay in place, what may need to change, and what additional information is needed. The data team should think carefully about how the discussions will be structured, because participants in this process will easily become overwhelmed if there is too much information or if ample time for discussion is not provided for sensitive and complex issues.

GUIDING THE DIALOGUE

Discussing issues of diversity and looking at issues of race and class, Jones (2000) states, "In doing this work, I've discovered that the toughest part of this challenge is not about looking at issues of racism. Our toughest challenge is in the fact that we simply do not know how to talk with each other" (p. 183). Jones's description of Senge's (1994; cited in Jones, 2000) four basic ways of conversing provides a tool to help professionals make conversations productive (see Table 5.1).

Dialogues become the most useful way of conversing when discussing issues of equity that arise from the inquiry. This is necessary to move the school community to deeper levels of reform. Delpit (1988) raises the issue of the role of power in dialogue. She argues that those in power often silence the dialogue when those who share the culture of poverty and children of color disagree with proposed solutions. She continues,

> I am also arguing that appropriate education for poor children and children of color can only be devised in consultation with adults who share their culture. Black parents, teachers of color, and members of poor communities must be allowed to participate fully in the discussion of what kind of instruction is in their children's best interest. Good liberal intentions are not enough. (p. 296)

For this dialogue to occur, there must be an opening up. Those in power must play a major role in creating conditions for full participation in discussion. In order

Table 5.1 Four Basic Ways of Conversing

1. **Raw debate** is complete advocacy on the part of each member engaged in conversation. Each member holds his/her position in conversations. Participants listen as a matter of strategy. There are winners and losers.
2. **Polite discussion**, the most dysfunctional form of conversation, is aligned with debate because participants hold their positions in the act of speaking. However, members mask their positions in politeness, never truly revealing their thinking. This form of conversation is extremely deceptive. It goes like this: "I understand your point, but . . ." or "That's a good point. However, have you read the latest research on . . . ?"
3. **Skillful discussion** includes a balance of inquiry and advocacy. This creates a very productive way of conversing. People go back and forth between these two forms of conversation as deemed necessary.
4. In **dialogue**, members suspend their positions and pursue avenues of inquiry for the purpose of developing a collective understanding. It is in dialogue that assumptions are probed and new discoveries are made.

to move the student agenda forward, it is important to know how others perceive issues in order to get clues about what must happen to improve conditions. Delpit (1988) acknowledges that we see things through our belief systems, but she argues that

> To put our beliefs on hold is to cease to exist as ourselves for the moment and that is not easy. It is painful as well, because it means turning yourself inside out, giving up your own sense of who you are, and being willing to see yourself in the unflattering light of another's angry gaze. It is not easy, but it is the only way to learn what it might feel like to be someone else and the only way to start the dialogue. (p. 297)

Delpit (1988) offers several guidelines, which are summarized here. Her full article provides rich detail that will be useful in guiding facilitated discussion around the data. The abbreviated guidelines are as follows:

1. Keep in mind that "people are experts on their own lives" (p. 297).

2. Don't be too quick to deny others' interpretations.

3. Believe that people are rational human beings even though we may not fully understand their rationalizations.

4. Risk vulnerability and your world being "turned upside down" in order to understand others' realities.

Saavedra (1996) has successfully used teacher study groups to affect the professional culture of teaching and to create changes in beliefs and practices. She points out that teacher transformation means that teachers study in a context

> in which teachers can confront their own cultural, social, and political identities, and the situations that have shaped and continually shape the expression of those identities. . . . In other words, through understanding their world and themselves with their world, teachers engage in the process of creating and shifting knowledge, meanings, ideologies and practices and thus transform themselves and conditions of their lives. (p. 272)

The context for the dialogues are study groups that meet on a regular basis to reflect, analyze, and critique their practices in relationship to how students benefit. Saavedra identifies eight conditions that will provide transformative learning. By participating in study groups, teachers were able to transform their practices and beliefs about diverse groups of students and their parents. They understood that their practices needed reform.

In schools where expectations are low; where content is weak; where practices are ineffective; and where students' race, ethnicity, and culture are not acknowledged or valued, study groups and professional development through dialogue can play a much-needed role. Creating cultures to transform beliefs and practices will bring richer analysis, interpretations, and implications for data. Becoming skilled in dialogue and using guiding questions such as those in the templates given here bring meaningful problem solving and solutions.

Figure 5.1 Data Dialogue Scenarios

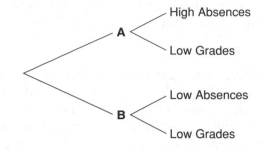

A	B	C	D
High Absences	Low Absences	Low Absences	High Absences
Low Grades	Low Grades	High Grades (Not Shown)	High Grades (Not Shown)

Figure 5.1 can be a useful template to analyze assumptions about existing data. For instance, as one school was inquiring about why some students had low grades, most teachers assumed it was because of attendance and pointed fingers at students. In structuring the conversation, the staff was guided to look at other possible assumptions. Four assumptions were proposed, and data were gathered to test the assumptions. What the faculty found was different patterns for different courses, and the initial assumption of low grades and high absences was more complex than had originally been assumed. There were many students who attended school every day and were getting Ds and Fs. What are the implications for instruction? Using a format to explore different assumptions and testing them can help ground the dialogue in the data.

Another strategy to create dialogue is to first ask staff members to give their perceptions of what the data will look like for certain indicators and then to compare these perceptions to the actual data collected. Questions should then be guided to compare assumptions to the data.

- Are there any patterns by racial/ethnic groups? By gender?
- What groups are doing well?
- What groups are behind? What groups are on target? Ahead?
- What access and equity issues are raised?
- Do the data surprise you, or do they confirm your perceptions?
- How might some school or classroom practices contribute to successes and failures? For which groups of students?
- How do we continue doing what's working and address what's not working for students?

Dialogue Templates

Using frameworks can help to structure dialogue; minimize or eliminate finger-pointing; and focus educators and others on issues, conditions, policies, and practices.

Figure 5.2   What Do the Data Tell You?

Group/Individual _____ Grade Level/Subject/School/District _____ Date _____ 1. How is student performance described?   *(By medians, quartiles, below, average, above, aggregate, etc.)* ....
2. How are different groups performing? Which groups are meeting the targeted goals? ....
3. What don't the data tell you? ....
4. What other data do you need? ....
5. What groups might we need to talk to? *(students, teachers)* ....

6. What are the implications for?
    • Developing or revising policies
    • Revising practices and strategies
    • Reading literature
    • Visiting other schools
    • Revising, eliminating, adding programs
    • Dialogues with experts
    • Professional Development goal setting, and monitoring progress?
 	
....
....

7. How do we share and present the data to various audiences? ....

Leaders and facilitators must be relentless in keeping the focus on improving all students' opportunity to learn in order to close the achievement gap. Figures 5.2 and 5.3 provide tools to help leadership teams, individuals, and groups focus on common issues that arise when reviewing the kinds of data that will be presented throughout the remainder of this book. Of course these are suggested formats intended to spark dialogue; they should be modified to meet the needs of a particular school setting.

When to Use

These or similar formats can be used to guide any discussions associated with reviewing data, particularly when decisions are being made about reform strategies.

Figure 5.3 Sample Questions From a School's Data Team

1.	Are there patterns of achievement based on SAT9 scores within subgroups: ethnicity, gender over the past three years?
2.	Are there patterns of placement for special programs by ethnicity, gender?
3.	What trends do we see with students who have entered our school early in their education vs. later? Is there a relationship between number of years at our school and SAT9 scores?
4.	Is there a relationship between attendance/tardiness and achievement?
5.	How do students who have been retained do later?
6.	How do our elementary students do in the middle school?
7.	What are the past SAT9 scores of 5th graders below grade level in reading?
8.	What are our next steps?

Administering the Forms

After overall explanations about the data and the process, dialogue groups of no more than 10 to 12 people should discuss the data. Groups can be by grade level, by content areas, or by other suitable configurations. Group norms should be established, and group meetings should be facilitated and recorded. Different groups can analyze different data sets. All group members should have access to relevant data in usable formats, such as tables and graphs, created by the data teams or others. Groups may choose to chart some of the data before they answer the questions. It may be a good idea to provide templates for charting.

How the dialogue occurs after discussing the data is critical. Facilitators need to be trained ahead of time and be prepared to facilitate the conversations. Some background reading might be appropriate depending on the data being analyzed. Figure 5.2 can help to structure the conversation around issues and conditions rather than placing blame. Sometimes when solutions are being proposed or when decisions are being made, it may be advisable to include professionals with expertise in certain areas. For instance, if you were discussing the success or lack of progress for different groups in mathematics or other higher-level courses, it would be important to have someone who is knowledgeable about these issues present.

Report outs (in which smaller groups report their discussion and deliberations to the whole group) and next steps are important (see Chapter 3). Also, these forms may be used in conjunction with some of the planning forms suggested in Chapter 11.

OUTCOMES FROM DIALOGUES

Rich solutions can emanate from dialogues, and I have participated in many. I will share a sample of some outcomes from data dialogues (Table 5.2). Keep in mind that these are only small samples of what schools and districts have discussed. The sample here illustrates outcomes for one district's school data teams. They developed inquiries, collected and analyzed the data, read about equity issues, shared their findings to assess the types of issues that emerged among the whole school, and then made action recommendations. Some of the school themes are not represented here because the issues were unique to a particular school. These are a few examples from their recommendations.

CONDUCTING THE INQUIRY: MEASUREMENT DIMENSIONS AND APPROACHES

The next four chapters (Chapters 6 through 9) demonstrate ways to gather information to conduct inquiries. Information from this chapter can help frame the dialogues for having conversations about the data as well as looking at outcomes, policies, processes, practices, and programs. Chapter 10 provides data-gathering templates and suggested indicators as a way of looking at combination and multiple data sources.

Many approaches to data gathering will be presented. Descriptive statistics are included. Qualitative approaches are also included. These approaches are particularly useful in all schools to uncover conditions that influence outcomes. A 1994 book by Anderson et al., *Studying Your Own School: An Educator's Guide to Qualitative Practitioner Research*, is especially useful in guiding qualitative inquiry in schools. I will briefly describe some of the qualitative approaches for schools and districts described by Anderson et al. (see Table 5.3 on page 82). Many will need to read more or receive training in these approaches. Data teams can lead the way. See the Bibliography for sources.

Table 5.2 Outcomes From Data Dialogues

District Theme	Action Recommended	Responsibility	Timeline
K-12 patterns of certain populations of students not succeeding: African American and Latino students; in some instances inequities are gender related	Major equity issue that must be addressed; assess district policies, practices, programs, and instructional approaches that contribute to these outcomes; make appropriate changes and provide appropriate professional development	Teachers, principals, district personnel	Immediate: March–May 1998
Need help in looking at student work expectations and instructional strategies	Design strategies with consultants and other staff development around issues of standards, expectations, and instruction	Teachers and district curriculum leaders	Summer 1998 and continuous
Some resistance to looking at data by racial and ethnic groups	Address these issues in summer institutes and continuous professional development; develop the teams' capacity to address these issues with the staff: identify appropriate literature, dialogue groups, and human resources	District must provide the support of facilitators and consultants to develop district capacity	Summer 1998 and continuous
Need more types of assessment; need systems to better assess growth as measured by SAT9	Schools teams will identify indicators and measures; district will acquire SAT9 tapes and will review test results and configurations of the data	Data teams and district	March 1998 and ongoing
Uniform standards and criteria in the evaluation of student work	Development of agreed-upon standards and performance assessments, SAT9, classroom work, report cards	District, schools	Summer 1998–2000
Need to assess instructional time and student achievement	Collect and analyze amount of instructional time in subjects at the elementary level and the quality of curriculum by program (gifted and talented vs. general population); math and language arts are possible focus areas	District, external facilitators, consultants	Summer 1998–1999
Finding a focus	Prioritize based on student outcome data, district focus, and so forth	District and school teams	Ongoing

Difficulty in presenting to staff: What do we do with our findings?	Presentation strategies will be developed during the summer institutes, as will strategies to create changes based on the information from the data analysis and interpretation	External facilitators and data teams	Ongoing
K-12 communication systems and articulation with community regarding expectations	Professional development for teachers in working with diverse parent backgrounds and in conversing with parents about expectations	Teachers, principals, district support	Fall 1998 and ongoing
Amount of time to do all the data team work is overwhelming; need more time and need to find ways to find that time	Implement data team organizational strategies to assess how resources (people, time, and money) are used, and make appropriate modification; needs to be addressed during summer institute with data teams; technology workshops	External facilitators, data teams, principals, central office, and superintendent	March 1998 and ongoing
Much of the existing data are inconsistent and incomplete	Diligence in checking the accuracy of data; new Eagle student database provides an opportunity to address this issue; design monitoring systems to check data accuracy and assign staff to monitor	District: data teams, principals, director of technology	March 1998 and ongoing
Need technology training	Spring workshops	Director of technology	Summer and Fall 1998 and as needed
Qualitative data should be included; we need help in designing questionnaire and interviews	Address in summer institute	Faculty consultant, external consultants	Summer 1998 and ongoing

Table 5.3   Qualitative Approaches

Method	Description
Interviews/Focus Groups • Conversations • Ethnographic • Structured • Surveys/Questionnaires • Checklists, rating scales, and inventories	A good tool to use when one wishes to know how a person feels about events that have happened or are happening. They are also important in gaining a perspective on how others understand and interpret their reality. Interviewing assumes a skill in listening and a nonthreatening manner in asking questions.
Observations • Participant Observation • Personal Action Logs, Checklists, and Rating Scales • Mapping • Material Culture Inventories • Visual Recordings and Photography	Observations focus on what is happening in a classroom, a playground, or a hallway, or on what a student or faculty member does in a specific situation over a delimited amount of time. They are best used when the researcher wants to see what is happpening in a classroom or playground; they can help demystify what is actually going on as opposed to what one might hope or assume is happening.
Archives and Documents	Archival refers primarily to historical research, and is the process of critical inquiry into past events to produce an accurate description and interpretation of those events and their meaning.
Journals and Diaries	Journals are personal documents that can also be used as a research tool to capture reflections and encounters. . . Journals can also promote educational objectives when used between teachers and students in the classroom . . . and encourage description, interpretation, and reflection on the part of the teachers as well as the student.

SOURCE: Anderson, G. L., Herr, K., & Sigrid Nihlen, A. (1994). *Studying your own school: An educator's guide to qualitative practitioner research.* Thousand Oaks, CA: Corwin.

6

Examining Outcomes

I t was 3:30 in the afternoon on a rainy April day. It was the first Monday of the month, faculty meeting day. Everyone knew that the test scores were in and that they would be looking at the results. The principal presented the scores, and everyone had copies of the information. There were a lot of numbers, and they were in small print. The teachers were trying to make sense of all these numbers. The information included grade-level summaries for two years. The school could tell if the scores had gone up or down. For instance, Grade 2 had scored at the 34th percentile in reading in 1999 and had scored at the 40th percentile in 2000; Grade 5 had scored at the 27th percentile in reading in 1999 and at the 25th percentile in 2000. Even though the second grade showed improvement, there were no particular standards that the school was aiming for. They just looked at whether the scores went up or down. The teachers had all worked last year to focus on reading, but they did not have any clues from this information as to why the second-grade scores improved and the fifth-grade scores declined. There was not the kind of information from test scores that could help guide instruction.

After attending some workshops given by the district on analyzing test score information, teachers on the data team found that there was more information available that could give them some clues about their results. They obtained disaggregated data by various student groups, by quartiles, by classroom, by individual student, and by content area strengths and weaknesses. They also established some consistent goals and standards for students. The expectations were for all students to achieve on or above grade levels.

The teachers met in teams and analyzed the information. They had a lot of "a-ha" moments. They found out that the second-grade curriculum and instruction were more focused on the standards, that students were moving out of the bottom quartiles, and that students who were English language learners were receiving appropriate support. The teachers attributed this to their professional development and team planning. The fifth-grade teachers were working just as hard, but they worked individually, did not emphasize the standards, and did not focus on language needs of students. Following these realizations, the principal and teachers designed a framework for looking at outcome measures, such as test scores and grades, and ways to use information to inform practice.

Overview

This chapter will provide suggestions on some types of data to collect and analyze related to student outcomes. These data include outcome accountability measures such as standardized tests and other outcomes such as grades and standards assessments and graduation and college-going rates.

Outcome data need to be looked at relative to what the expectations are for all students. If all students are expected to achieve on grade level or above or are expected to be eligible for college enrollment, the gaps or lack of gaps in achievement need to be noted for each group against that measure. The next step is to measure how far from the standard each group is. Simply measuring gap information from group to group can shortchange students. I have seen instances in which every group was below the standard. Although some groups were closer to the standard than others were, there was an achievement gap for every group relative to the achievement expectation. Schools most often measure achievement gaps from group to group and not against the standard they want all children to achieve. This can be shortsighted if the highest group is achieving at a below-level standard.

Because outcome data rarely provide schools and districts with enough information to decide on improvement strategies, there will be examples in this chapter of how to "peel the data." "Peeling the data" helps to focus strategies to affect outcomes.

LOOKING AT THE BIG PICTURE

In examining outcomes, schools and districts should set up systems to look at both short- and long-term outcomes. Looking at snapshot data at isolated points in time—by teacher, by student, by grade level, or by school—give some, but not sufficient, information about a school or district. Coherent decision making will depend on a systemic examination and analysis of patterns and reform efforts. Systems should be set up so the data can be gathered at the institutional, teacher, and student level over time. Inquiries should include the following: What happens to students as they move through the system? Who stays, who leaves, and for what reasons? What does the picture look like in kindergarten and at 12th-grade graduation for different students? Do students leave the system better off than when they entered? What do we expect our students to be able to do when they leave the system? For example, my expectation is that all students should be prepared to complete high school and to enter a baccalaureate degree-granting institution.

Beginning with kindergarten, Figure 6.1 illustrates some key outcomes over time for different groups of students. Data can be gathered over time to look at patterns related to graduation rates, test score patterns for cohorts of students, and other important outcomes. There are large leakages out of the system for African American

Figure 6.1   Who Goes to Four-Year Colleges?

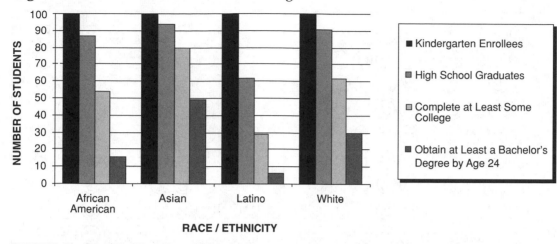

SOURCE: The Education Trust, Inc. *Achievement in America 2001.*

Secondary Source: U.S. Bureau of the Census. (2000). *Current population reports: Educational attainment in the United States.*

and Latino students. What is equally important to find out from data such as those in Figure 6.1 is what happened to the students who are not represented in these data after kindergarten.

Another more graphic way of looking at these data is shown in Figure 6.2. It displays one group. This can be done for each group. Looking at the disaggregated data for each group in a different display, we get a more poignant picture. Districts may want to use this type of chart to display systemic outcomes. Suggestions for looking at institutional processes that may be related to this outcome will be found in Chapters 7 and 8.

OUTCOME DATA FROM STANDARDIZED TEST SCORES: PEELING THE DATA

Standardized test scores still remain one of the principal measures used by the public to gauge school improvement. Many test companies are trying to become more responsive to current curriculum trends and are redesigning how and what they measure. Because students are still taking these tests on a regular basis, schools and districts need to analyze results and discuss the implications related to curriculum delivered. Have the students been taught what the test tests? Have they had practice with standardized test formats and been taught "test-wiseness" skills? Are the skills measured in the tests a part of the curriculum? If not, what is the school's obligation to prepare the students for these tests? And what alternative measures can the school or district present to the community to demonstrate that they are teaching students what they need to be successful in the 21st century? These are issues that must be considered if the focus is on students' best interests. It will also be important to document the percentage of students tested each year.

Figure 6.2   Sample Data: K-12 Outcomes for African American Students

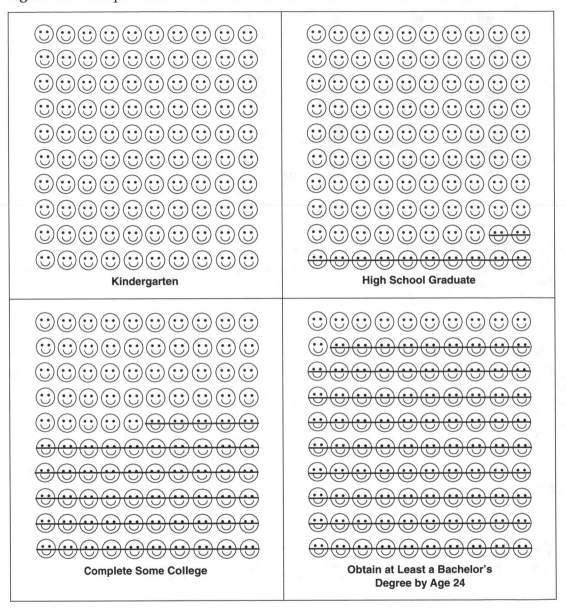

Most schools and districts receive considerable data on test results, but they rarely analyze or discuss these data in any systematic way. The following section will look at how to "peel the data" using different levels and ways of analyzing standardized test information—moving from aggregate data sets to information on curriculum and individual students. (See Boxes 6.1 and 6.2.)

The following examples give only some of the most common ways to look at test results. You can probably design some other ways to best suit your setting. This type of information should be shared with the school community. Before these meetings, the data team or others should prepare a framework for the dialogue, such as those suggested in Chapter 5.

Box 6.1 Peeling the Data: Levels of Looking at Data

1. District

2. K-12 feeder patterns

3. School levels

4. Grade level

5. Programs and tracks

6. Classroom-teacher

7. Student

Box 6.2 Peeling the Data: Ways of Looking at Test Information

1. Aggregate data (district, school, and classroom using means and medians)

2. Quartile data (looking at four different percentile bands: see figures in this chapter)

3. Cohorts over time (the same group of students as they move through the system)

4. Disaggregated data (looking at data by student groups, teachers, program)

5. Individual teacher

6. Individual student

7. Content cluster strengths and weaknesses (school, grade, class, student)

8. Content cluster alignment to the curriculum

9. Over time

Aggregate scores are the outer layers of information. Figures 6.3 through 6.5 (pages 88–89) show aggregate test scores over time. Figure 6.3 shows whole-school aggregate median percentiles, the point at which 50% of the students are below and 50% are above, in three subjects for a six-year period. The graph shows where the school is compared to the national norm median percentile (50%ile). With the exception of scores in writing (2001), the school is below the national median percentile. However, the graph shows progress between the base year and the most recent year in all three subjects. The school staff will need to dig deeper to find out what reforms might have caused these improvements and if this progress meets or falls short of their expectations. The progress in mathematics needs to be accelerated.

Figure 6.3   School Median Test Scores

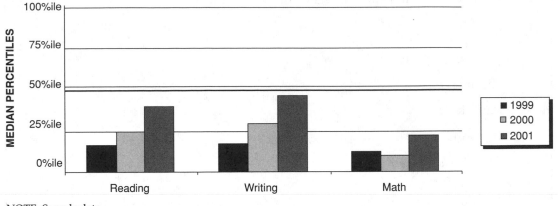

NOTE: Sample data.

Aggregate Grade-to-Grade Median Percentiles on SAT9 Performance

Figure 6.4 shows aggregate information on median percentile test scores by grade levels 1 through 9. These data still need to be disaggregated, but they show more information by using grade-to-grade rather than total-school medians as in Figure 6.3. These data show the difference in median percentiles from grade to grade

Figure 6.4   Performance on SAT9: Average Median Percentiles, 2000–2001

Expectation: Each grade should have ___% of students on grade level.

	Grade 1	Grade 2	Grade 3	Grade 4	Grade 5	Grade 6	Grade 7	Grade 8	Grade 9
Reading median	35%ile	35%ile	34%ile	31%ile	33%ile	33%ile	34%ile	32%ile	31%ile
Math median	51%ile	52%ile	44%ile	40%ile	45%ile	45%ile	42%ile	39%ile	42%ile

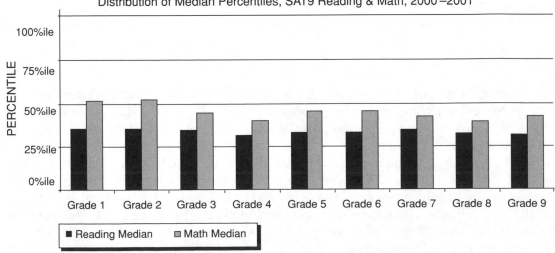

NOTE: Sample data.

for reading and mathematics. The median percentiles for reading are below those in mathematics at every grade level. Grades 4 and 9 have the lowest median percentiles. Other information will need to be gathered to find out why some grades appear to do better than others and what needs to be done to raise the scores, particularly in reading.

Peeling back further with data disaggregated by race and ethnicity, Figures 6.5a and 6.5b display how different groups are achieving in an urban high school. There are great disparities in achievement. There are wide gaps between African American and Latino students and the higher-achieving white students. A closer look reveals that the average scores for white students in many content areas are below the 50th percentile.

Figure 6.5a 2000 SAT9 by Ethnicity: Ninth-Grade Percentage at or Above Grade Level (50th Percentile)

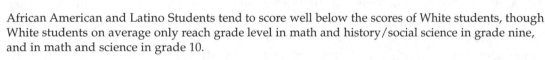

African American and Latino Students tend to score well below the scores of White students, though White students on average only reach grade level in math and history/social science in grade nine, and in math and science in grade 10.

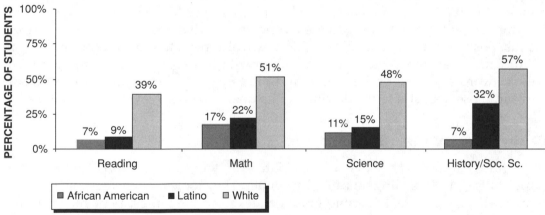

Figure 6.5b 2000 SAT9 by Ethnicity: Tenth-Grade Percentage at or Above Grade Level (50th Percentile)

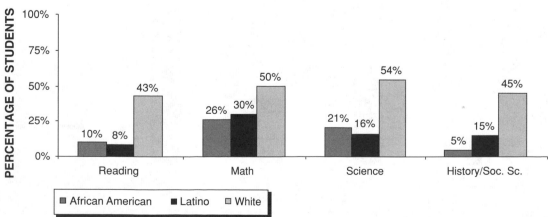

SOURCE: An urban high school, courtesy of Principals Exchange.

The Middle Rises but the Bottom Sticks

Test scores should also be examined by quartiles to determine whether students are shifting to higher or lower quartiles. These data are also important for parents who are concerned that as schools detrack, students in the upper quartiles will suffer academically. In using quartile information, the analysis focuses on shifts in quartiles, with the hope that the shifts will be from the lower quartiles to the upper quartiles. Table 6.1 (pages 92–93) includes the percentage of students in each quartile for three subject areas—reading, language, and mathematics—over three years. This represents one grade of students, but the analysis can be done by school; by grade group; by racial, ethnic, and gender groups; and by cohort groups.

Over time, a school community that is transforming its curriculum and instruction and raising its expectations for performance should see a decrease in students in the bottom quartiles and an increase in the higher quartiles. The reforms may take three to five or more years. Deeper-level reforms will take time. Schools should not have to resort to increasing scores by retaining certain students or by placing others in special education while the academic culture stays virtually the same.

Table 6.1 shows an increase in the percentage of students in the higher quartiles in total reading, language, and mathematics by year 3. There was a dramatic decrease in the percentage of students in the bottom quartiles in reading and language arts, but in mathematics the percentage of students in the bottom quartile remained virtually the same. Both trends will need to be looked at more closely, and information will need to be gathered concerning what may have affected these results, positively and negatively. The staff will also need to look at other indicators of student achievement and how these align with test scores. It appears that there were upward shifts out of the second and third quartiles. Was there a focus on students in those quartiles to the detriment of students who achieved at the bottom?

Quartiles by Gender Groups

Figures 6.6a and 6.6b show how one data team looked at Comprehensive Test of Basic Skills (CTBS) reading quartiles by gender. They looked at each grade, but only two are displayed here. In second grade, males form the largest percentages in the first, second, and top quartiles, but in third grade females have the largest per-

Figure 6.6a   Second-Grade CTBS Quartiles by Gender

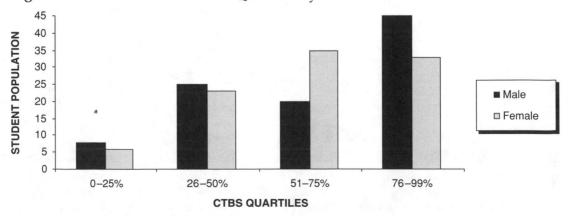

SOURCE: An urban elementary school.

Figure 6.6b   Third-Grade CTBS Quartiles by Gender

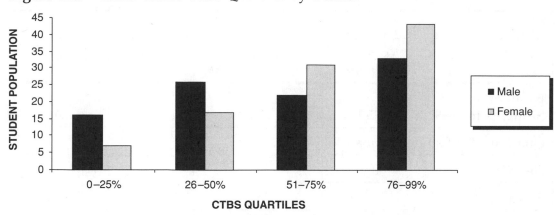

SOURCE: An urban elementary school.

centages in the top quartiles. Although these are two separate groups, it seems that further exploration of what is happening from grade to grade is warranted. It also appears that more students from both groups are scoring at the lower quartiles in third grade.

Peeling Back: Looking at Disaggregated Data by Language Proficiency Within Programs

This representation of the data shows year-to-year monitoring—how Grade 1 students score in Grade 2, Grade 2 in Grade 3, and so forth, by language groups. This is an example of information that can be gathered for any group.

Figure 6.7a compares the standardized test scores of different English reading proficiency cohorts to the district median percentile as they move through the

Figure 6.7a CTBS/U English Reading: Sample Interesting Elementary School

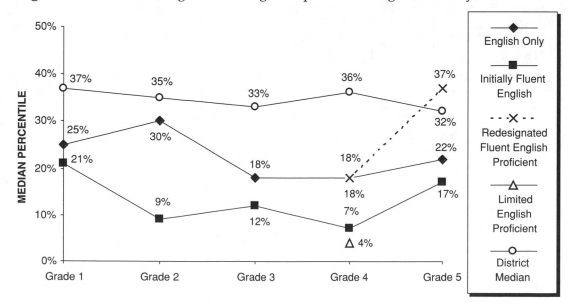

SOURCE: An urban elementary school.

Table 6.1   Test Scores by Quartiles Over Three Years

School:				
Grade 4	*Reading Vocabulary*	*Reading Comprehension*	*Reading Total*	*Language Mechanics*
Number of Students in 1999	75	76	75	76
Quartiles (% of students/quartile)				
76–99	0.0	2.6	1.3	3.5
51–75	17.3	18.5	17.3	13.2
26–50	26.7	28.9	30.7	25.0
1–25	56.0	52.6	50.7	57.9
Number of Students in 2000	84	85	84	84
Quartiles (% of students/quartile)				
76–99	7.1	5.9	4.8	17.9
51–75	21.4	23.5	22.6	21.4
26–50	27.4	30.6	31.0	27.4
1–25	44.0	40.0	41.7	33.3
Number of Students in 2001	78	78	78	78
Quartiles (% of students/quartile)				
76–99	17.9	10.3	15.4	23.1
51–75	15.4	21.8	17.9	23.1
26–50	14.1	30.8	26.9	21.8
1–25	52.6	37.2	39.7	32.1

SOURCE: An urban school district.

Language Expression	*Language Total*	*Math Comprehension*	*Math Concepts and Analysis*	*Math Total*
76	**76**	**76**	**76**	**76**
1.3	1.3	28.9	10.5	17.1
17.1	3.9	32.6	23.7	32.9
28.9	21.1	15.8	30.3	17.1
53.9	73.7	23.7	35.5	32.9 ◄
84	**84**	**84**	**83**	**83**
4.8	10.7	27.4	12.0	21.7
17.9	19.0	16.7	19.3	16.9
39.3	28.6	27.4	28.9	25.3
38.1	41.7	28.6	39.8	36.1
78	**78**	**78**	**76**	**78**
15.4	▲ 19.3	39.7	37.2	▼ 38.5
17.9	16.7	9.0	17.9	17.9
38.5	35.9	25.6	12.8	11.5
28.2	28.2	25.6	32.1	32.1 ▲

Good news: Reading, language, and mathematics scores indicate increases in the top quartile by year 3.

Bad news: By year 3, the bottom quartile percentage in math is similar to that of year 1.

Figure 6.7b   Aprenda Spanish Reading: Sample Interesting Elementary School

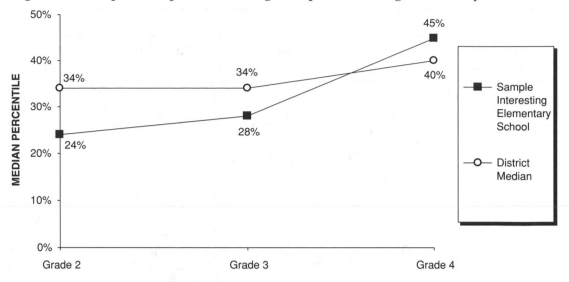

SOURCE: An urban elementary school.

grades. All groups are scoring below the district median at every grade level. The English Only (EO) students score above all groups, with the exception of the redesignated bilingual students, who score above the district median at Grade 4. At Grades 3 through 5, EO student scores appear to drop dramatically. What kinds of factors might be responsible for these dramatic shifts? These kinds of data raise questions about program quality. It appears that students who have been redesignated from the bilingual program have stronger skills, which enables them to score higher on the test. This appears to be supported by Figure 6.7b, which shows grade-by-grade median percentiles compared to the district median percentile for students who take the Spanish reading test (Aprenda). By Grade 4, the students are scoring above the district median.

However, as Figures 6.8a and 6.8b show, a somewhat different pattern emerges in mathematics. The EO students score above the district median at every grade except fourth, when they dip below the median. Redesignated students score below the district median at Grade 4, but they are way above the median and the EO students by Grade 5. The Initially Fluent English Proficient students consistently score below the district median. In the Spanish math test, the students score above the district median percentile at Grades 2 and 4.

This school community has important information to talk about. What kind of instruction is happening in the bilingual programs that appears to help students score at higher levels? Are these the skills that the school values? If so, what needs to be done to assist others in the school to achieve at higher levels? What resources are needed? Is the school completely satisfied with the bilingual program? Is there room for improvement?

Peeling Back Further: Looking at Student-Level Data

The next two tables demonstrate some ways to look at disaggregated data at the student level so there is a close-up view. Table 6.2 (page 96) shows SAT9 quartile data

Figure 6.8a CTBS/U Math: Sample Interesting Elementary School

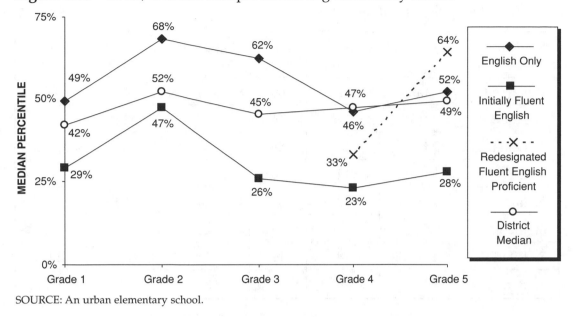

SOURCE: An urban elementary school.

Figure 6.8b Aprenda Spanish Math: Sample Interesting Elementary School

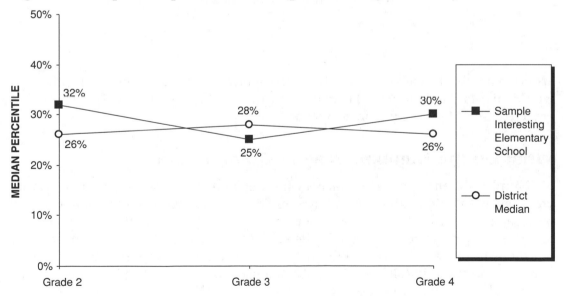

SOURCE: An urban elementary school.

in reading and mathematics for African American students. These data show who the teachers were for a two-year period. In examining these data, what patterns and information emerge? What are some implications for intervention? These data show that even though all of these students are scoring in the first quartile in reading, five of the eight are scoring in the second and third quartile in mathematics. Why is this so? What is happening in the instructional program? Do they have the same teacher in reading and mathematics? Are there language or cultural relevancy issues in the

Table 6.2   Second-Grade African American Students Who Scored in the First Quartile in Reading

Student's Name	Gender	Reading %ile	Math %ile	Language Score %ile	Teacher 1999	Teacher 2000
1. Larry C.	Male	17	60	4	M.P.	O.C.
2. Allen R.	Male	22	4	5	M.P.	A.F.
3. Donald E.	Male	21	69	56	H.L.	O.C.
4. Dave S.	Male	14	40	17	C.G.	O.C.
5. Jan K.	Female	22	69	24	M.P.	O.C.
6. Joe L.	Male	7	45	24	H.L.	O.C.
7. Rita D.	Female	18	12	15	C.G.	E.D.
8. Ben T.	Male	9	13	31	C.G.	E.D.

> All of these students are in the second and third quartiles in math, but in the first quartile in reading. Note: All of these students had the same teacher.

area of reading? Teacher O.C. has all of these students. What are the implications? It would be useful to look at all the other quartiles in both subjects to see what patterns emerge before deciding on the next steps.

What Do the Numbers Mean? Going Deeper

Numbers alone can't give teachers the detailed information they need about what needs to be taught. Figure 6.9 (pages 98–99) demonstrates how data can also be disaggregated by levels of accuracy in the reading and math skills that were tested. For example, teachers can isolate students' correct and incorrect answers for questions testing a vocabulary skill, such as using context to supply a missing word, or a math computation skill, such as subtracting decimals. This helps teachers decide what skills they need to stress more in their instruction. Test publishers and state departments of education will provide schools with the test objectives, the number of items and the relative emphases (number of items for each area). This assists in reviewing, aligning, and planning the curriculum. Of course, schools and districts must be careful not to limit their teaching to the content of a particular test, but if children will be taking that test, the content areas need to be part of what is taught. Why should children be tested on what they have not been taught? Another important factor is that test scores have many consequences for children related to placements and other educational outcomes.

Table 6.3 shows a sample of how the number of assessment items for different skills may be represented. In the column to the right of each set of numbers, teachers

Table 6.3   Content Standards

Content Standards	Number of Items	Number and Percentage of Students Demonstrating Accuracy*	Instructional Emphasis (percentage of instructional time spent on this content area) High—3, Medium—2, Low—1
Word Analysis			
Vocabulary Development			
Reading Comprehension			

*NOTE: Show these data for total and disaggregated groups.

can indicate the level of instructional emphasis (IE) they put on those skills and then use data like those in the following figures to compare the time spent and how well students tested in those areas. This will not answer the question of how well the skills were taught. Other measures will have to be used to find out about the quality of instruction.

Figure 6.9a shows the number of students tested over a three-year period and the percentage that demonstrated certain levels of accuracy. These are samples of some of the content areas tested in reading and mathematics. For example, in reading comprehension there has been a decline in the students demonstrating 70% or better accuracy in reading analysis. Teachers will need to assess classroom practices and content taught in light of this information. There are mixed patterns for reading and mathematics. These data need to be further analyzed by student groups.

Figure 6.9a   Vocabulary Skill

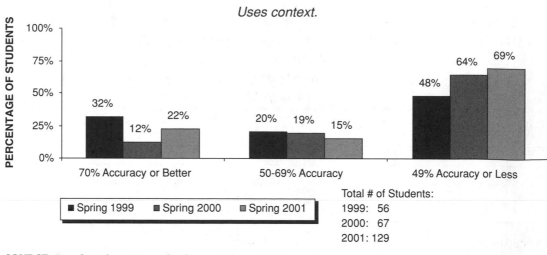

Uses context.

SOURCE: An urban elementary school.

Figure 6.9b   Reading Comprehension Skill

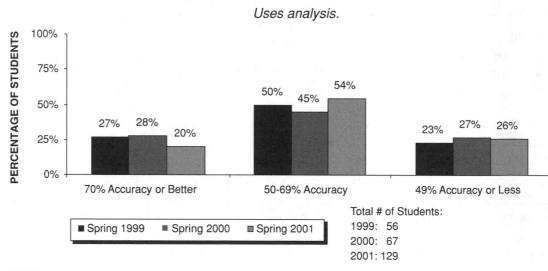

Uses analysis.

NOTE: Sample data.

STANDARDIZED TESTS FOR COLLEGE GOING

Percentage of Participation in PSAT

There are several college admissions tests administered nationally. Figure 6.10 (page 100) shows summary data collection formats and graphic representations for the percentage of 11th graders in a school taking the PSAT. Staff in small groups could chart these data. There has been an increase in the percentage of students taking the PSAT over the three years. If the school and district are aiming to get more students on the path to college, this is a positive trend. However, these increases may not yet be large enough—which groups demonstrated increases, by how much, and

Figure 6.9c Mathematics Computation Skill

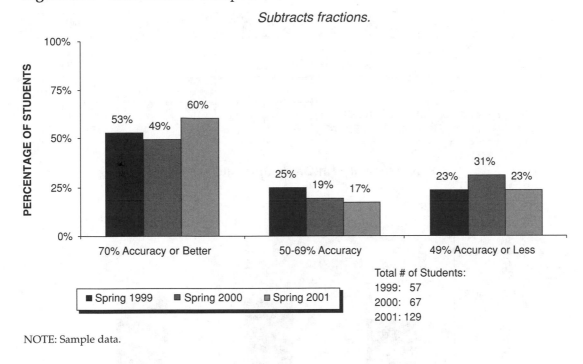

Subtracts fractions.

NOTE: Sample data.

Figure 6.9d Mathematics Concepts and Application Skill

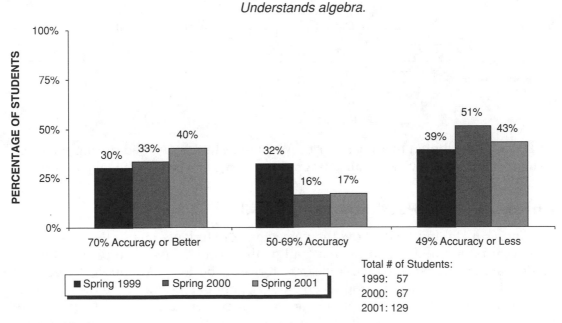

Understands algebra.

NOTE: Sample data.

Figure 6.10 Percentage of Participation in PSAT

	2002–03		2003–04		2004–05	
Total Number of 11th-Grade Students:	383		332		334	
	#	%	#	%	#	%
Number and Percentage of 11th-Grade Students Taking PSAT:	164	34	149	45	159	48

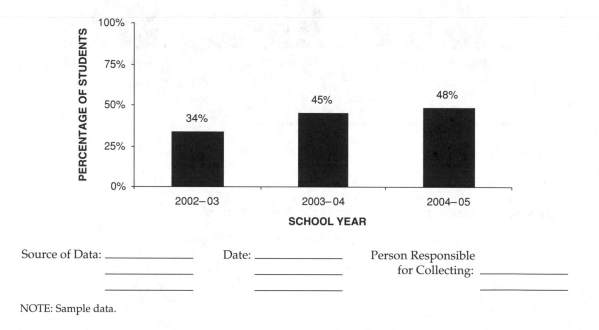

Source of Data: _____ Date: _____ Person Responsible for Collecting: _____

_____ _____ _____

_____ _____ _____

NOTE: Sample data.

what can be attributed to school efforts? Was the test administered during the week instead of on Saturday? Were all 11th-grade students encouraged to take the test?

Percentage of Participation in SAT

Figures 6.11a and 6.11b show the percentage of students taking the SAT over a three-year period and average verbal and math scores. If these two pieces of information are discussed together, a clearer story can be told. Although it might be assumed that scores would drop when a larger pool of students have the chance to take the test, in fact, when the percentage of 12th graders taking the SAT increased, the average scores were not affected by year 3. The average math score for year 1 (when only 26% of students took the test) was the same as for year 3 (when 42% took the test). The average verbal score (Figure 6.11b, page 102) slightly increased. On the other hand, if the scores had taken a dive, we would hope that the school would not deny students the opportunity to take the test but instead would make sure more students have the opportunity to learn the skills that are tested.

Figure 6.11a Percentage of Participation in SAT

School Year:	1996		1997		1998	
Total Number of Students:	362		305		320	
	#	%	#	%	#	%
Number and Percentage of Students Taking SAT:	94	26	119	39	133	42

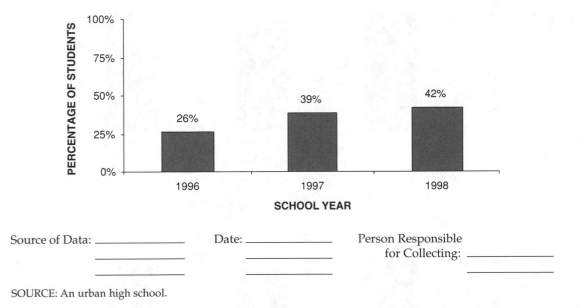

Source of Data: _____   Date: _____   Person Responsible for Collecting: _____

SOURCE: An urban high school.

On the Rise: Advanced Placement Test Scores

Figure 6.12 (page 103) monitors the percentage of students taking and scoring 3 or better for Advanced Placement tests. The numbers of students taking the test increased substantially from the initial year, but the last year showed a large decrease. The percentage receiving scores of 3 or better is fluctuating, but there are more than three times as many students passing as there were in 1991–1992. It would be important to find out if that has affected the substantial decrease and also to find out what the successful practices are that have contributed to the increases or decreases over time.

Outcome Measures for Standards Assessments

Table 6.4 (page 104) is an example of how one district monitored how students performed on standards assessments. There was a dramatic drop in the partially proficient range, from 67% in the first quarter to 22% in the fourth quarter. Most of the students were scoring in the proficient and advanced ranges by June. This seems to be good news for the fourth grade. However, almost a quarter of the students are still classified as partially proficient. A closer look at these students and the instruction they received is warranted. The next step would be to disaggregate the data.

Figure 6.11b Average SAT Verbal and Mathematics Scores

School Year:	1996	1997	1998
Average SAT Verbal Score:	385	363	387
Average SAT Math Score:	414	396	414

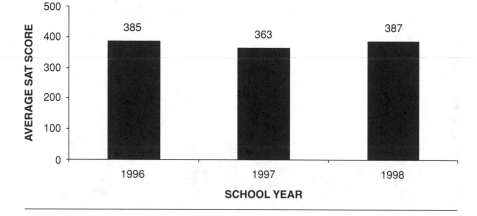

Verbal

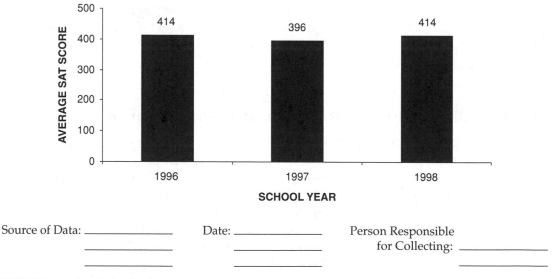

Math

Source of Data: _____   Date: _____   Person Responsible
_____   _____   for Collecting: _____
_____   _____   _____

SOURCE: An urban high school.

Multiple Student Outcomes

Table 6.5 (page 105) displays information on multiple outcomes by gender, race, and ethnicity. The classwork, grade, and standardized test scores are each given a proficiency level, and then a total is calculated for a summary score. Teachers can look at patterns across measures. For instance, David, an African American male, has a high score on the test but is receiving only a 1 on classwork and in his grades. Are

Figure 6.12 Advanced Placement Test Scores: Five-Year Summary

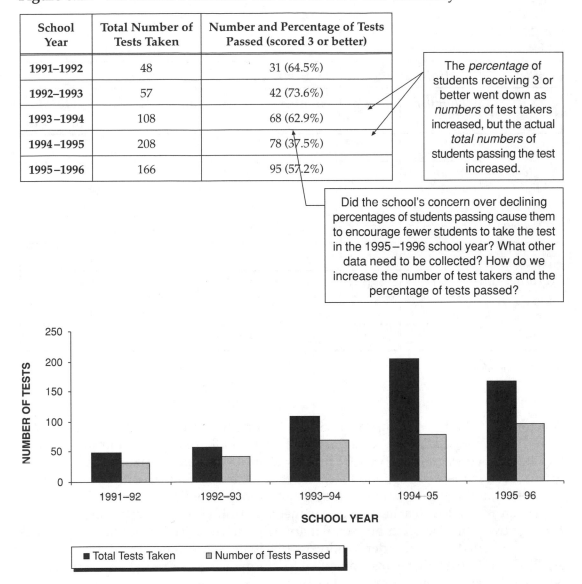

School Year	Total Number of Tests Taken	Number and Percentage of Tests Passed (scored 3 or better)
1991–1992	48	31 (64.5%)
1992–1993	57	42 (73.6%)
1993–1994	108	68 (62.9%)
1994–1995	208	78 (37.5%)
1995–1996	166	95 (57.2%)

The *percentage* of students receiving 3 or better went down as *numbers* of test takers increased, but the actual *total numbers* of students passing the test increased.

Did the school's concern over declining percentages of students passing cause them to encourage fewer students to take the test in the 1995–1996 school year? What other data need to be collected? How do we increase the number of test takers and the percentage of tests passed?

■ Total Tests Taken   ▨ Number of Tests Passed

SOURCE: Urban school.

there some instructional issues that need to be addressed? David's summary score is partially proficient. How accurate is this score? Nancy, a white female, is doing better in classwork and grades than on the test. Does she need some help in this area? Her summary score is advanced. Also, standards will need to be established relative to what determines successful performance. Should some areas receive more weight than others? How is quality content defined?

MONITORING STUDENT GRADES

Grades are the most frequent feedback given to students and parents about how young people are doing in subjects in school. Students can get numerical grades or letter ratings as early as the primary grades, such as "O" for outstanding, "S" for sat-

Table 6.4   Achievement on Standards Assessments, 2000–2001

Grade: 4th
Date:

Quarter	Partially Proficient		Proficient		Advanced		
	Number	%	Number	%	Number	%	Total Students
One (October)	40	67	15	25	5	8	60
Two (December)	35	56	20	32	7	11	62
Three (February)	20	30	36	55	10	15	66
Four (June)	14	22	40	63	10	16	64

SOURCE: An urban school.

isfactory, or "I" for needs improvement. At the upper elementary level, letter grades of A–F may be used. At the secondary level, we usually find student grades of A–F. Grades can be summarized as frequency distributions and looked at by subject, grade level, student group, and teacher. Schools can set goals to decrease the number of fails, to increase students' grade point averages, and so on.

When we look at teachers or departments with high failure rates and set goals for improvement, we often hear explanations such as, "I (we) have high standards and the others don't." In order to address this issue, schools need to define what an A, B, C, and so forth means and what performance is expected of a student to achieve the corresponding grade. If standards are set for content and performance, more consistency will be possible in measuring and interpreting what grades mean. Even though such consistency in standards does not exist in most places, schools should still do grade analyses. Discussions that are generated from these analyses can help to create conditions where teachers see the need for standards. Many schools or districts have uniform units or end-of-grade assessments. These measures are based on agreed-upon content and standards that are expected to be taught. This helps to counter some of the arguments related to individual standards, and the conversations can be directed toward content and instructional practices.

Why Did Our Students' Grades Go Down After Fourth Grade?

Table 6.6 (page 106) represents a way to show summary data on student grades for Grades 4 through 6. These types of data can be further disaggregated by individual

Table 6.5   Multiple Student Outcomes in Reading

Student	Gender	Race-Ethnicity	English Language Learner	Classwork Level	Grade	Norm-Referenced Test	Total/3	Partially Proficient (3–4)	Proficient (5–7)	Advanced (8–9)
1. Shawn	F	AA	N	3	3	3	9	X		
2. David	M	AA	N	1	1	3	4	X		
3. Juan	M	L	Y	1	2	1	4	X		
4. Martin	M	W	N	2	2	2	6		X	
5. Christie	F	W	N	2	3	2	7		X	
6. Nancy	F	W	N	3	3	2	8			X
7. Ana	F	L	N	1	1	2	4	X		
8. Robert	M	AA	N	2	1	2	4	X		
9. John	M	W	N	1	2	2	5		X	

NOTE: Sample data. Scores of 3–4 are classified as partially proficient, scores of 5–7 as proficient, and scores of 8–9 as advanced.
AA: African American; L: Latino; W: white.

Table 6.6 Analysis by Grade Level, Spring 2001

Grade expectation (e.g., "All students receive grades of C and above"): Total number of students in 2001: Fourth grade: 88 Fifth grade: 89 Sixth grade: 88					
Subject	*Grade Level*	*As*	*Bs*	*Cs*	*Ds*
Communication	4	25%	31%	34%	9%
	5	14%	26%	43%	14%
	6	13%	33%	35%	19%
Reading	4	23%	33%	33%	11%
	5	15%	25%	42%	15%
	6	14%	32%	37%	17%
Writing	4	24%	32%	35%	9%
	5	16%	24%	45%	12%
	6	15%	30%	36%	20%
Mathematics	4	20%	35%	35%	10%
	5	16%	36%	36%	12%
	6	12%	40%	36%	10%
Science	4	13%	31%	42%	14%
	5	24%	25%	36%	15%
	6	23%	27%	38%	12%

With the exception of science, there is a decrease in the percentage of As students receive as they move up the grades and an increase in Ds received.

NOTE: Sample data.

teachers, by student groups, and by program types. In this particular table, we see that students generally receive higher grades in Grade 4 than in Grades 5 or 6. Is the school satisfied with this distribution? What other information is needed? What might be contributing factors to the difference between Grades 4, 5, and 6? The differences do not seem to be as wide in mathematics. Why? What kinds of improvements should be aimed for in spring 2001? An important unanswered question is whether standards for grades have been set across the school? This is a key determiner regarding whether the students' skills really dropped dramatically after Grade 4, or if inconsistency in grade standards is playing a role.

How Do Students' Grades Compare Across Departments?

The secondary grade analysis shown in Table 6.7 represents two semesters of grade distribution by departments. The information is grouped by discipline or program. Overall, 20% or more of the students are receiving Ds and Fs in every area. For the most part, there is a slight improvement in the second semester. In the academic subjects, in fall 2001, 49% of students received Ds and Fs in science. This was the highest percentage of Ds and Fs for all academic subjects, and there was only slight improvement in the spring. In mathematics, in the fall, 44% of students received Ds and Fs—this decreased by 1% in the spring. Departments should do further analysis. Why are some departments failing fewer students? What accounts for the high percentage of low grades in English as a second language (ESL) and special education? In driver education?

Peeling Back: What Accounts for Differences in Students' Grades Within the Mathematics Department?

Courses within departments can be further analyzed, as shown in Table 6.8 (page 109), which shows that there is a high dropoff in the number of students taking higher-level mathematics beyond geometry. What types of advising are students receiving? Why are they not taking higher-level courses? Additionally, three courses show very high percentages of low grades: Math 9A, Basic Math A, and Algebra 1A. What supports are provided to students who are failing? Do teachers make mid-course corrections? What types of professional development are occurring? Why did low grades increase so much from Math 9A to Basic Math A? It appears that students do better in high-level courses, but is this related to attrition? Are there patterns by racial and ethnic groups?

Peeling Back Further: Which Teachers Give What Grades—and Why?

Table 6.9 (page 110) shows grade distribution for Basic Mathematics broken down by teacher. Teacher B fails high numbers of students. This teacher and teacher D appear to account for the assignment of most of the low grades in this course. All of the teachers have about the same number of students. Why are some teachers failing students at much higher rates than others are? Is this related to different instructional strategies? What types of assistance do students receive? What types of assistance might teachers need? Is this "remedial" course necessary? Should students be in higher-level mathematics? Administrators will need to become involved with these issues.

Disaggregation of Grade Point Averages for Males by Race/Ethnicity

Figure 6.13 (page 111) shows student grade point averages (GPA) disaggregated by race and ethnicity for males at a high school. Grades were first summarized for

Table 6.7 Grade Analysis by Department

Grade Expectations:

Department	2001–2002 School Year	Total Number of Students	As	Bs	Cs	Ds	Fs
English	Fall	2,375	12%	22%	30%	19%	17%
	Spring	2,367	16%	23%	28%	17%	16%
Advanced English	Fall	29	11%	32%	32%	22%	3%
	Spring	29	5%	33%	31%	21%	0%
Foreign language	Fall	1,195	20%	21%	28%	19%	12%
	Spring	1,105	23%	25%	25%	14%	13%
Mathematics	Fall	1,973	10%	16%	30%	18%	26%
	Spring	1,970	13%	18%	26%	19%	24%
Science	Fall	1,332	9%	15%	28%	24%	25%
	Spring	1,330	11%	16%	24%	22%	25%
Social studies/history	Fall	1,703	14%	30%	42%	10%	4%
	Spring	1,705	13%	25%	31%	17%	14%
Art	Fall	535	22%	24%	29%	14%	11%
	Spring	536	23%	23%	27%	13%	14%
Business	Fall	324	25%	26%	24%	12%	13%
	Spring	327	23%	22%	25%	13%	17%
Driver education	Fall	285	19%	24%	26%	10%	21%
	Spring	282	18%	22%	24%	16%	20%
Health	Fall	348	22%	12%	36%	19%	11%
	Spring	346	28%	16%	19%	18%	19%
Music	Fall	243	34%	22%	20%	12%	12%
	Spring	245	35%	24%	18%	9%	14%
Physical education	Fall	1,701	42%	20%	15%	8%	15%
	Spring	1,705	46%	15%	16%	9%	14%
Computers	Fall	364	25%	25%	30%	11%	9%
	Spring	370	26%	20%	33%	9%	12%
Related arts/ vocational education	Fall	504	26%	27%	32%	5%	10%
	Spring	506	20%	27%	29%	15%	9%
ESL	Fall	309	12%	22%	30%	16%	20%
	Spring	307	14%	26%	28%	15%	17%
Reading	Fall	27	35%	23%	23%	10%	9%
	Spring	22	33%	22%	22%	14%	9%
Special education	Fall	457	20%	21%	18%	20%	21%
	Spring	459	32%	20%	16%	15%	17%

NOTE: Sample data.

Table 6.8 Grade Analysis: Mathematics Department

Course	2001–2002 School Year	Total Number of Students	As	Bs	Cs	Ds	Fs
Math 9A	Fall	366	10%	15%	36%	22%	17%
	Spring	352	12%	19%	28%	17%	22%
Basic Math A	Fall	184	14%	6%	29%	26%	25%
	Spring	187	11%	8%	20%	16%	42%
Topics Math	Fall	29	13%	26%	33%	16%	12%
	Spring	27	10%	24%	41%	13%	10%
Algebra 1A	Fall	559	4%	10%	20%	32%	34%
	Spring	540	8%	15%	23%	24%	28%
Algebra 2A	Fall	252	15%	24%	33%	18%	10%
	Spring	247	16%	22%	26%	20%	13%
Geometry	Fall	391	15%	22%	36%	20%	27%
	Spring	389	13%	18%	28%	18%	20%
Math Analysis	Fall	146	23%	28%	34%	12%	3%
	Spring	142	22%	25%	31%	14%	6%
Calculus	Fall	45	30%	34%	20%	10%	6%
	Spring	40	31%	33%	20%	11%	4%

SOURCE: An urban high school.

Highest drop of students taking higher-level math courses.

Courses with highest percentage of Fs.

each student by averaging all grades received, and these were then averaged together with the averages of peers. We can see trends for a period of three years. By 2001 it appears that all groups' GPAs have improved. The achievement gaps between Asian, white, African American, and Latino students have narrowed, but a gap still remains. What needs to be done to improve achievement for all groups and to eliminate gaps among groups? How do you get all groups to achieve at high levels?

Disaggregation of Grades

Table 6.10 (page 112) displays grades for African American and white students over several years for three schools. The district has not established a standard of

Table 6.9 Grade Analysis by Math Teachers for Basic Mathematics

Teacher	Total Number of Students	As	Bs	Cs	Ds	Fs
		#	#	#	#	#
		%	%	%	%	%
A	30	4	6	10	4	6
		13	20	33	13	20
B	35	0	0	4	4	27
		0	0	11	11	77
C	33	5	7	5	12	4
		15	21	15	36	12
D	30	1	3	2	8	16
		3	10	7	27	53

SOURCE: An urban high school.

Teachers with highest
percentage of Fs

expectation for what percentage of Ds for any group is acceptable. There is a wide disparity between African American students and white students receiving D grades. African American students' percentages of Ds are very high compared to those of their white counterparts. In schools A and B the percentages are rising. In school C there is a decline in the percentage of Ds over time. For white students, there is a slight decrease in the percentage of Ds at school A and an increase in school B, and school C seems to remain about the same over time.

There needs to be some deeper data work and dialogue in all three schools. It seems that such a large percentage of African American students receiving Ds would be unacceptable. Chapter 7 will suggest some ways to peel the data back further to get at some possible answers to the problem.

The Importance of Disaggregating Within Broad Racial/Ethnic Groups

Figure 6.14 (page 113) was shown previously in the book (see Figure 3.1), but it is being used again to emphasize the need to disaggregate even in schools that have what are considered to be homogeneous racial and ethnic groups. Figure 6.14 further disaggregates the GPAs of Asian students into subgroups. Here we see that some groups of students—Lao, Hmongs, and Cambodians in this case—are achieving lower GPAs than are other Asian groups, such as Chinese and Japanese students. This demonstrates how important it is to recognize the variances that will be found in all broadly drawn racial and ethnic categories—African Americans, whites, Native

Figure 6.13 High School GPA (Males)

Race/Ethnicity	June 1999	June 2000	June 2001
African American	1.96	2.27	2.30
Native American	2.68	2.50	2.75
Asian	2.99	2.75	3.10
Latino	2.00	2.31	2.30
White	3.20	2.99	3.43
Total	2.57	2.56	2.78

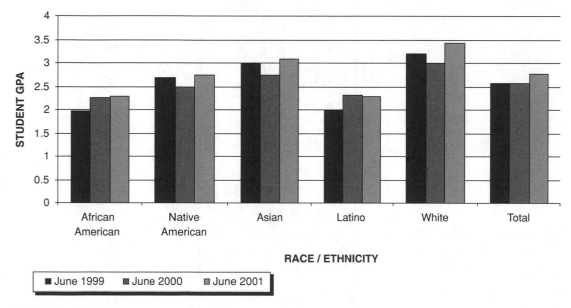

NOTE: Sample data.

Americans, Latinos, and Asians. The more aware educators can become of the unique experiences and backgrounds of different subgroups—as well as of individual students—the more informed and useful the data analysis will be.

DISPLAYING MIDDLE AND HIGH SCHOOL COURSE ENROLLMENT AND STUDENT OVERALL PROGRESS IN COLLEGE PREPARATORY COURSES

Monitoring course enrollment is especially critical. Ensuring that all students are engaged in higher levels of learning and that teachers are developing instructional practices to help students be successful are goals for schools committed to access and equity. Schools must continually keep track of whether students are enrolling

Table 6.10 Percentage of African American and White Sixth- Through Eighth-Grade Students Receiving GPAs of D and Below District Expectation

School	African American				White				Total School			
	1995–1996	1996–1997	1997–1998	1998–1999	1995–1996	1996–1997	1997–1998	1998–1999	1995–1996	1996–1997	1997–1998	1998–1999
A	45.2%	47.5%	40.7%	45.6%	21.8%	17.3%	16.6%	19.2%	27.3%	24.0%	21.6%	25.3%
B	40.7%	40.3%	41.2%	53.6%	14.7%	14.6%	15.9%	18.1%	18.5%	18.3%	19.4%	23.0%
C	42.2%	41.3%	38.7%	37.5%	16.4%	16.6%	16.8%	17.8%	27.4%	27.5%	27.1%	27.4%

SOURCE: A school district.

Figure 6.14 High School GPA (Males): Disaggregation for Asian Groups

Race/Ethnicity	June 2000	June 2001	June 2002
Cambodian	1.67	1.79	1.80
Chinese	3.52	3.90	3.82
Hmong	1.80	2.15	2.00
Japanese	3.70	3.95	3.75
Korean	3.31	3.50	3.73
Lao	1.9	2.00	2.50
Vietnamese	3.40	3.60	3.83
All Asian males	2.76	2.98	3.06

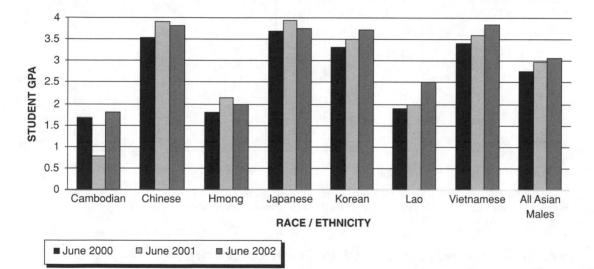

NOTE: Sample data.

in and passing higher-level courses and whether there is a reduction of lower-level courses.

A Look at Who Is in Algebra

Eighth-grade data over two years might be displayed as illustrated in Figures 6.15a and 6.15b. Figure 6.15a is blank and can be used as a template for many data activities. Teachers, administrators, students, and parents can all be involved in filling in the bars from summarized data provided to them. The completed Figure 6.15b, which can be hand drawn, shows progress for most groups over the two years. It shows that there are large gaps that remain among groups. This should generate a focused discussion about what needs to be done to close the gaps.

Figure 6.15a   Course Enrollment

School:					Goal:				
AA - African American A - Asian									
NA - Native American L - Latino W - White									

	AA	NA	A	L	W	AA	NA	A	L	W
100%										
75%										
50%										
25%										
0%										
			2002–2003					2003–2004		

What Are We Doing Right? Rising Enrollments in College Preparatory and Honors Courses

Three-year trend data for one high school's college preparatory and honors enrollment are presented in Figure 6.16 (page 116). This three-year monitoring reveals that there is a much higher percentage of students taking college preparatory courses by year 3, from 57% to 80%. If the school is aiming for 100% enrollment, it appears that they have made significant progress. What is working? What still needs to be done? Are beliefs changing? What practices have changed?

What Happens to Our Math Students After Geometry?

Figure 6.17 (page 117) shows combined data on course enrollment and course passage. These data cover a three-year time span and are disaggregated by race and ethnicity. For all groups, more students are enrolled in and passing algebra and geometry. However, data show that substantially fewer students take the more advanced college preparatory mathematics courses across all racial and ethnic groups, and there are more substantial dropoffs for African American and Latino

Figure 6.15b   Eighth-Grade Course Enrollment in Algebra: Sample Presentation of a School's Summarized Data

School:					
AA - African American		A - Asian			
NA - Native American		L - Latino		W - White	

Goal:

	AA	NA	A	L	W
2002–2003	37%	20%	80%	31%	67%
2003–2004	54%	36%	92%	58%	74%

NOTE: Sample data.

students than there are for Asian and white students. What contributes to this? What types of academic counseling are students receiving? Lower pass rates are also evident for African American and Latino students for all three years. What types of opportunities are being provided to support academic success? What kinds of study skills do students have? What instructional strategies work well?

Table 6.11 (page 118) illustrates information about a cohort of students who started in algebra. As they moved through the grades, there were substantial decreases in the numbers of students taking higher-level math courses, that is, those courses that Chapter 2 cited as good indicators for successful college enrollment and completion. A cohort that began with 489 students in algebra had only 40 in an advanced math course by their senior year. Schools have to ask, is this acceptable? The data need to be further disaggregated by student groups. Do some groups drop out at higher rates than others? Given these data, what are the next steps?

Figure 6.16 High School Students Enrolled in College Preparatory and Honors Classes

School year	1999–2000		2000–2001		2001–2002	
Total number of students enrolled	1,971		1,882		1,954	
	Number	%	Number	%	Number	%
Number and percentage of students enrolled in college preparatory and honors classes	1,117	57	1,450	77	1,560	80

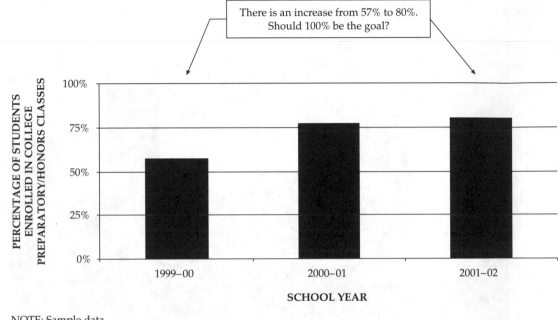

There is an increase from 57% to 80%. Should 100% be the goal?

NOTE: Sample data.

OUTCOMES: STUDENT GRADUATION RATES

Middle School Graduation Rates by Race/Ethnicity and Gender

Figure 6.18 (page 118) shows a data collection format used to monitor middle school eighth-grade enrollment at the beginning of the year and the percentage of students who graduate at the end of the academic year. The data are disaggregated by race, ethnicity, and gender. These data are more informative if the same group of students is counted at each point. Eighteen percent of the students enrolled at the beginning of the year did not graduate. African American students graduated at higher rates than Latino or other students did. Why are some students not graduating? Why are Latino and other students graduating at much lower rates than African American students? The school community needs to gather more data and to continue to monitor these rates.

Figure 6.17 Percentage of Active Students Passing College Preparatory Math by Race/Ethnicity

2002 Courses	African American		Asian		Latino		White	
	Number of Students	% Pass	Number of Students	% Pass	Number of Students	% Pass	Number of Students	% Pass
Algebra I	175	38	102	88	156	37	85	76
Geometry	173	64	94	92	104	65	78	88
Algebra II	40	63	78	95	53	67	52	91
Elementary Functions	22	82	44	96	20	80	47	96

2003 Courses	African American		Asian		Latino		White	
	Number of Students	% Pass	Number of Students	% Pass	Number of Students	% Pass	Number of Students	% Pass
Algebra I	191	49	116	90	179	50	92	87
Geometry	164	75	96	93	106	75	83	91
Algebra II	64	75	82	96	66	80	60	94
Elementary Functions	25	89	56	94	32	85	33	92

2004 Courses	African American		Asian		Latino		White	
	Number of Students	% Pass	Number of Students	% Pass	Number of Students	% Pass	Number of Students	% Pass
Algebra I	240	62	124	92	192	61	102	90
Geometry	192	68	102	90	122	76	75	90
Algebra II	84	72	94	96	83	71	62	92
Elementary Functions	15	100	64	95	45	98	34	93

Table 6.11 High School Mathematics Cohorts

	Algebra	*Geometry*	*Algebra 2*	*Math Analysis/Calculus*	*Statistics*	*Math B*	*Math C*
9th graders	479	87 (honors)					
10th graders	250	203	60				
11th graders		130	148	44	1	103	29
12th graders			47	40	18	20	58

SOURCE: An urban high school, courtesy of The Principals Exchange, Whittier, CA.

Figure 6.18 Eighth-Grade Enrollment and Graduation Rate by Race/Ethnicity and Gender

	All Students		African American		Latino		Other	
	Number	Percentage	Number	Percentage	Number	Percentage	Number	Percentage
Eighth-Grade Enrollment, Beginning of 1999-2000 School Year								
Total	1,616	100	852	100	666	100	58	100
Male	768	100	405	100	342	100	22	100
Female	848	100	447	100	364	100	37	100
Graduating From Eighth Grade, End of 1999-2000 School Year								
Total	1,317	81	739	87	541	81	37	64
Male	624	81	343	85	268	78	13	59
Female	693	82	396	89	273	75	24	65

Percentage of Eighth-Grade Students Graduating

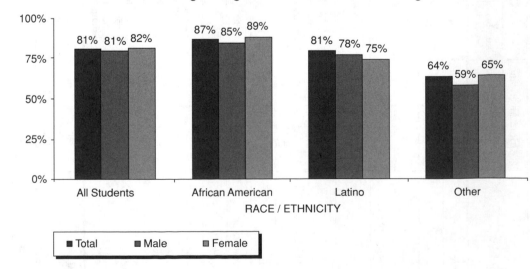

SOURCE: Urban middle school.

Figure 6.19 High School Graduation Rate by Race/Ethnicity

Race/Ethnicity	June 1994	June 1995	June 1996
African American	90%	85%	92%
Asian	97%	98%	96%
Latino	81%	91%	95%
Native American	87%	86%	89%
White	95%	96%	97%
Total	94%	95%	96%

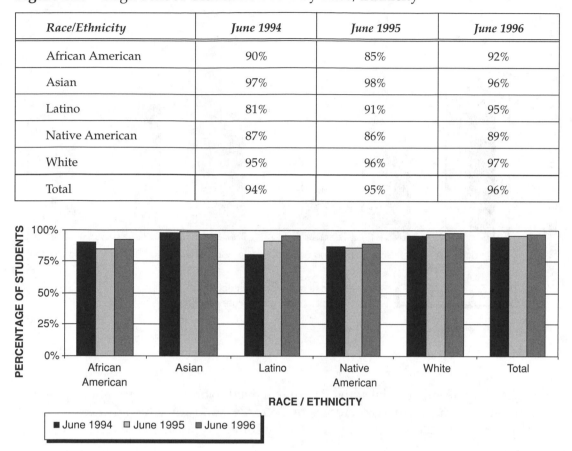

SOURCE: Urban high school.

High School Graduation Rates by Race/Ethnicity

A data collection form for high school (or other level) graduation rates over time is shown in Figure 6.19. The data are disaggregated by race and ethnicity. The graduation rates for all groups appear to have improved, with the exception of Asian students, who show a decrease. Native American students have the lowest rates. Although rates have improved, they are still low. What needs to happen in order to maintain increases in the graduation rates?

COLLEGE-GOING RATES

A Districtwide Look at College-Going Rates by High School

Figure 6.20 shows a seven-year comparison of a district's college-going rate for six high schools. High school E, which had the highest percentage of students going to college in 1996, was the only high school with a decrease in 2001. High schools C

Figure 6.20 District High Schools College-Going Rates

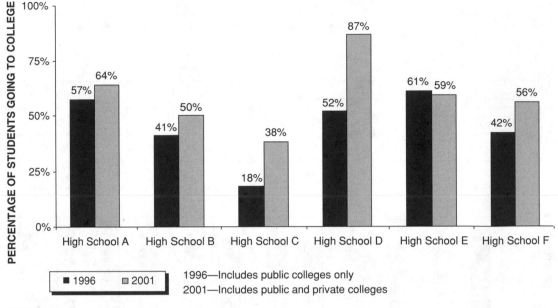

SOURCE: Urban school.

and D have made substantial gains. There will need to be discussions about practices and strategies that produced increases or decreases, and for which groups.

The data also need to be disaggregated by college type, as in the following tables and figures.

A Four-Year Look at the District's College-Going Success

The summary collection form and the graphics that follow reflect ways to look at actual college-going rates over time by level of postsecondary institution. Figure 6.21 compares the district to the state college-going rate. For the four years for which state information is available, it appears that the district averages remain at or below the state averages. Goals and other issues related to college attendance will need to be reviewed.

Monitoring for Two- and Four-Year College Enrollment by Race and Ethnicity

Blank forms for this purpose can be used for community or baccalaureate-granting institutions (see Figure 6.22a, page 122). A look at the data from an actual school district that used the forms (Figure 6.22b, page 123) reveals different patterns for different groups. In year 2, African American students decreased in community college enrollment and increased enrollment in four-year colleges or universities; Asian students increased in community college enrollment and decreased in four-year college or university enrollment; and Latino students increased in both community college enrollment and in four-year college or university enrollment. White students showed a slight gain in both two-year and four-year college enrollments.

Figure 6.21 Percentage of Graduates Entering Public Colleges and Universities

School Year	Two-Year Community Colleges		Four-Year State University		Any College or University	
	District	State Average	District	State Average	District	State Average
1999–2000	41%	40%	11%	11%	53%	53%
2000–2001	30%	31%	10%	12%	45%	55%
2001–2002	38%	36%	9%	12%	53%	53%
2002–2003	41%	40%	12%	13%	56%	54%

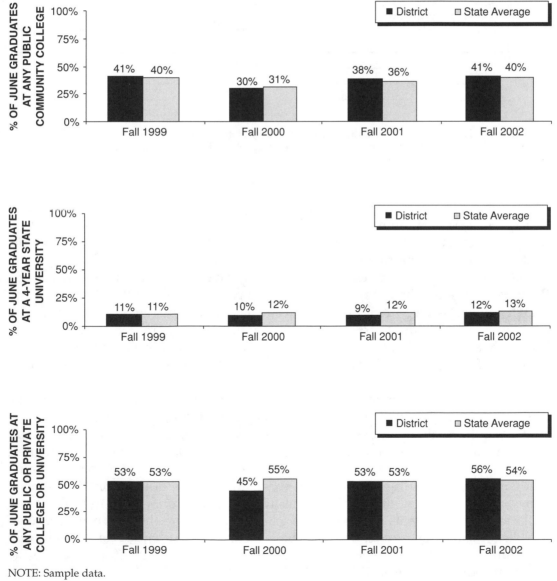

NOTE: Sample data.

Figure 6.22a   Enrollment Figures for All Freshmen Entering Institutions by Race/Ethnicity

Use a separate form for each higher education level.
Name of institution: _____

School Year	All Students		African American		Native American		Asian		Latino		White	
	#	%	#	%	#	%	#	%	#	%	#	%
2002–03												
2003–04												
2004–05												
2005–06												

Source: _____   Date: _____   Person
_____   _____   Responsible: _____
_____   _____   _____

Notes: _____
_____
_____
_____
_____

This gives the school community and district a base of information to analyze. Next, they can present the data disaggregated by school. Faculty, parents, and students could participate in charting the data from summary statistics.

Actual college-going rates must be verified by student enrollment in college. Planned college-enrollment rates might be compared to actual rates. However, any college-going rates reported should be the actual and not planned rates. Otherwise, the school may well present a false picture, because planned rates are usually much higher than actual rates. A comparison of the two will help schools to look at the level of difference and to raise questions about what is occurring so strategies can be reviewed.

In states like California, where the majority of students attend in-state public institutions, schools and districts can obtain enrollment information for most of their students quite easily. In other states, where the majority of students go to private colleges, this may involve contacting more sources for the data. Some schools request that students send postcards from college after enrollment. Some schools do annual graduate follow-up surveys to find out what students are doing after high school. Some actually verify enrollment by requesting the data directly from the colleges. In order to do this, students need to let the school know where they have elected to go to college before they leave. This can be a labor-intensive endeavor. Schools and communities must first consider this tracking to be important information so the proper resources are invested in developing a system.

Figure 6.22b Comparison of Students' and Parents' Expectations for College Enrollment to Percentage of June 1999 and June 2000 Graduates Enrolled in College

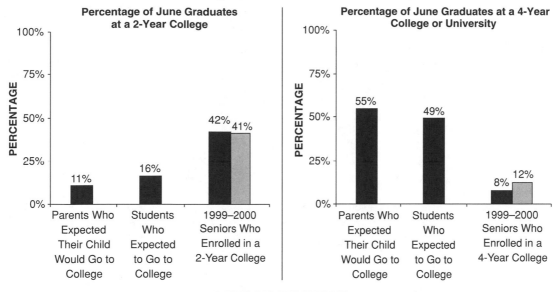

AFRICAN AMERICAN

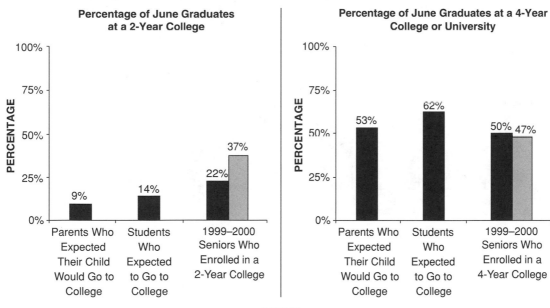

ASIAN

(continued)

Figure 6.22b Continued

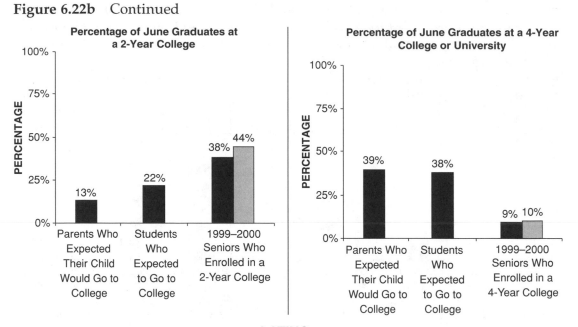

LATINO

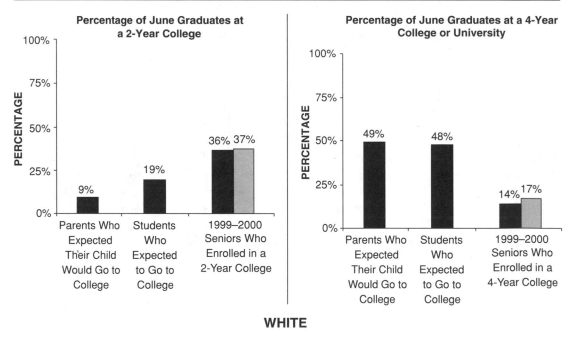

WHITE

SOURCE: An urban school district.

NONACADEMIC MEASURES RELATED TO OUTCOMES

Educational opportunities can be affected by the amount of lost learning time. Student opportunity-to-learn time lost because of suspensions, attendance, and other reasons needs to be assessed. Gender disaggregation is also important. It is generally found that males are referred for and receive more disciplinary penalties than females and that African American males are suspended and expelled disproportionately to their percentage in the population. Teacher time also needs to be assessed. Teacher attendance and out-of-classroom time may also be factors related to student achievement. These data need to be disaggregated and combined with achievement measures by student groups, by teacher, and at the student level.

Poor attendance is usually cited as one of the reasons for low achievement by students. But before such generalizations are drawn, there are many aspects of attendance that need to be monitored, including students' daily attendance at school and class-by-class attendance. Some students may be absent more frequently from some classes than from others. Many schools find that there are certain days or class periods that have higher or lower absenteeism. To what is this related? Students may be a source of good information.

The next chapter discusses equity measures related to processes and practices that can have a major impact on the types of outcomes discussed in this chapter.

7

Assessing Policies and Practices

Working with a leadership team of teachers and coordinators, the principal of an inner-city elementary school focused a great deal of time on improving the academic culture of the school. Together, they participated in retreats, visited other school sites, read literature about school reform, and set a major goal: "Every child will achieve at or above grade level."

In the second year of the process, the principal was asked how she planned to measure the success of all this hard work. She looked perplexed and said, "I don't know, maybe by the students' standardized tests?" She had not thought about, nor did she have any notion of, what else might be used to measure progress toward higher student achievement in classrooms or schoolwide. The school had no systematic ways to look at the policies, practices, or process changes in the school. Perhaps most important, they had not instituted processes for continually assessing the school's current conditions as a base for reform plans. And this was a principal who truly wanted to focus on equity, student achievement, and teaching and learning issues.

When the teachers at the same school were asked a similar question, they too had not thought much about how to look at reform, other than by test scores. They had some ideas about how school reforms might affect their work as teachers, but they were not always able to link this to better outcomes for students. They also possessed virtually no strategies for finding out what they needed to know about measuring reform, including establishing a variety of baseline data. This had never been a priority. Starting new activities took priority over assessing their impact.

Unfortunately, when the students' standardized test scores came back that year, the public verdict was that the school had made no progress in raising achievement. In spite of the staff's attempts to work collegially, implement new curricula, invest time in ongoing professional development, and hold grade-level meetings to discuss teaching strategies, student performance on the standardized tests did not rise. The teachers and administrators were greatly demoralized by the announcement of the scores because they had no other measures to gauge the impact of their work or whether their work was effective.

Thereafter, the reform effort was severely diminished—until the principal and teachers examined other indicators of progress and found encouraging signs of growth. The staff examined their efforts to reform the academic culture of the school, to raise expectations, and to teach students at higher academic levels. Two years later, the school's standardized test results rose dramatically, as did other measures of the academic health of the school. From then on, the school always used multiple indicators to identify and report progress, and they built continual internal reflection and measurements of practices into the day-to-day culture of the school.

Overview

This chapter examines in great depth a critical stage of the reform process that requires multiple layers of reflection and investigation by the school community. Processes and practices affect student outcomes, but little time is spent in systematically looking at the everyday workings of the institution. Most of the answers to why outcomes appear as they do are embedded in norms and practices. Research gives clues as to what are effective and ineffective institutional practices. We also have lots of information on how certain institutional practices affect equitable outcomes.

Discussing what impact reform may bring to the work lives of key participants can help to crystallize the real need for reform and the potential for lasting effects for students. This deeper level of reflection must continue as the school or district evolves its visions, sets goals, and develops strategies.

Assessing where your school or district is involves probing perceptions about why things are as they are. It means asking the hard questions: What are we doing? What is working? What is not working? Educators need to evaluate the services they offer students and how they are performed.

Questions should lead not to finger-pointing but to identifying institutional policies and practices that affect student achievement. Determining where the school is requires individual and collective reflection. A climate of trust, risk taking, and openness must be fostered. Although an external facilitator is often employed to begin the process, the school community must ultimately adopt a commitment to asking and answering the questions. This becomes at once a continual schoolwide assessment effort and an ongoing individual effort, because reform is ultimately personal and requires behavioral modification. Reflective questions that provoke professionals to assess their underlying assumptions in preparation for deep-level reforms are essential.

This chapter will demonstrate ways to look at school and classroom practices. Suggestions will be offered on ways to

- Gather information to analyze institutional policies, practices, and cultures
- Examine existing school documents to reveal problems and practices
- Assess equitable classroom practices

PART I: INSTRUMENTS

This section will provide instruments and other tools to find out about the school culture and practices. The suggested indicators are based on research related to effective school cultures and practices. The first part of the section will present questionnaires and surveys. The second part will present ways to look at school documents to assess effective and ineffective practices.

ASSESSING PERCEPTIONS OF ATTITUDES, READINESS, AND COMMITMENT TO REFORM AT THE SCHOOL

Many times, reforms are initiated in a school or district without any clues as to where people are relative to the reform. For example, a school that moves to detrack or to group students heterogeneously will have far more success if the majority of educators are dissatisfied with current levels of student achievement and believe that all students should at least be prepared for college. If this is not the current view at the school, then reform agents need to be aware that the first order of business will be to work on transforming the attitudes of their colleagues. Otherwise their efforts will be blocked.

A structured survey can tell you where your school community is on the continuum of reform—and the possibilities for reform. It may reveal satisfaction with the status quo. On the other hand, it may reveal that many more educators than expected are already trying to learn and use strategies proven to meet the needs of diverse student populations. A survey of these efforts can catalyze collaboration among the educators.

Too often, broad sweeping judgments are made about members of the school community based on limited information. Asking people to reflect on their perceptions prior to beginning the reform process involves them early on, gives them the message that what they think is important, and provides rich data and information for the future. The instrument Perceptions of Attitudes, Readiness, and Commitment to Reform (Figures 7.1a and 7.1b, pages 129–136) was designed for this purpose. It can be modified for use in a variety of settings.

When to Use

This survey is best used when the discussions about the need for the school to improve student achievement are initiated. It can be used to create baseline data relative to where the school is at the beginning of the process and possibly one, two, or three years later to assess the degree of change in perceptions.

Administering the Instrument

The survey should take approximately 30 minutes for participants to fill out. The purpose, as described earlier, should be explained to those participating. The survey

(text continues on page 136)

Figure 7.1a Perceptions of Attitudes, Readiness, and Commitment to Reform

Name: _____ School: _____ Date: _____ Role: ___Teacher ___Administrator ___Support Staff ___Paraprofessional ___Parent ___Student
<div align="center">**Part I: Perceptions of Beliefs and Practices**</div>
Please take a few minutes to think about *your own* perceptions of where your school is relative to student achievement.

1. Student Achievement
 	
  a) What percentage of your school's staff is dissatisfied with current levels of student achievement?
 	
         0%   25%   50%   75%   100%

2. Expectations
 	
  a) What percentage of the students does the staff believe are capable of achieving at or above grade level in all subject areas?
 	
         0%   25%   50%   75%   100%
 	
  b) What percentage of K-12 students does the staff believe should be prepared to pursue a college or university education?
 	
         0%   25%   50%   75%   100%
 	
  c) What percentage of students does your staff believe are capable of succeeding in the college-preparatory pattern of courses required for university eligibility?
 	
         0%   25%   50%   75%   100%

3. Aspirations for and Information About Higher Education
 	
  a) What percentage of your student population do you believe is interested in going to a college or university after high school?
 	
         0%   25%   50%   75%   100%
 	
  b) What percentage of your student population and their parents are prepared to make well-informed decisions about college?
 	
         0%   25%   50%   75%   100%

4. Curriculum and Instruction
 	
  a) What percentage of your student population is learning a rigorous, challenging curriculum built around higher-order thinking skills and problem solving?
 	
         0%   25%   50%   75%   100%
 	
  b) What percentage of the teachers in your school are investigating and trying to learn and use strategies that are proven to meet the needs of diverse student populations, e.g., cooperative learning, untracking, sheltered English, culturally relevant strategies?
 	
         0%   25%   50%   75%   100%

(continued)

Figure 7.1a   Continued

---

5. School Practices

   a) What percentage of the staff is interested in eliminating tracking and other grouping practices that can inhibit student academic achievement?

0%	25%	50%	75%	100%

   b) What percentage of the staff engages in formal discussions about current educational practices that work for *all* students?

0%	25%	50%	75%	100%

   c) What percentage of the staff shares their ideas for school improvement?

0%	25%	50%	75%	100%

Part II: Perceptions of Support for Collegiality

Please check "Yes" or "No":

1. Is there a climate in your school that promotes joint problem solving around the issue of raising student achievement?

   Yes ____   No ____

2. Is time set aside on a regular basis for staff to develop and share strategies for improving student achievement?

   Yes ____   No ____

Part III: Perceptions of Current School Status

On the whole, my school is: (Check the one that *most closely* describes your school.)

   ____ *Not Ready*
   - No consensus about the school's vision.
   - No desire to reform.
   - Unaware of low-level curriculum and its implications for college going.
   - Satisfied with current levels of achievement.

   ____ *Ready for Reform*
   - Building consensus about the school vision.
   - Substantial desire among the staff for reform.
   - Efforts to create a team to lead reform.
   - Widespread evidence of dissatisfaction with levels of student achievement.
   - Baseline data on achievement analyzed, shared, and discussed.

   ____ *Implementing Reform*
   - Shared school vision has been developed.
   - Staff development and budget reflect the vision.
   - Joint problem solving on school structure, curriculum and instruction, and increasing student achievement and 4-year college-going rates.
   - Reforms in instructional/counseling practices beginning.
   - Using data in decision making.
   - Team leadership.

Figure 7.1a   Continued

____ *Beginning Evidence of Reform*
- Strategies and practices are more aligned to vision.
- Higher level of staff commitment.
- Increased interest in teaching students a rigorous, balanced curriculum and courses.
- Beginning to dismantle schoolwide practices that inhibit student achievement (i.e., tracking).
- Indicators of improved student achievement exist.
- Indicators of reforms in the academic culture exist.
- Monitoring plan, continuous use of data.
- Reallocation of resources.

____ *On the Move*
- Movement aligned with vision.
- Evidence of schoolwide belief in higher expectations for students.
- Staff initiating practices which accelerate student achievement.
- Sustained gains in student achievement.
- All students are aware of and are being prepared for 4-year college opportunities.
- Consistent and ongoing monitoring using data.
- Reallocation of resources.

Part IV: Concerns

Please consider your own beliefs about the barriers or enhancements to student learning in your school in answering the following questions.

1. What concerns do you have about *curriculum and instruction* that may be affecting the achievement of students on your campus?

2. What concerns do you have about *school and district practices* that may be affecting the achievement of students on your campus?

3. What concerns do you have about *support for collaboration and growth* that may be affecting the achievement of students on your campus?

4. What concerns do you have about *school leadership* that may be affecting the achievement of students on your campus?

SOURCE: Part IV: Concerns—Permission of STAR Center, University of Texas.

Figure 7.1b   Perceptions of Attitudes, Readiness, and Commitment to Reform: Sample of a School's Summarized Data

Name: _____

School: _____

Date: _____

Role: ___Teacher ___Administrator ___Support Staff ___Paraprofessional ___Parent ___Student

Part I: Perceptions of Beliefs and Practices

Please take a few minutes to think about *your own* perceptions of where your school is relative to student achievement.

1. Student Achievement

a) What percentage of your school's staff is dissatisfied with current levels of student achievement?

		0%	25%	50%	75%	100%
School	#		5	13	18	4
Responses	%		13%	32%	45%	10%

2. Expectations

a) What percentage of the students does the staff believe are capable of achieving at or above grade level in all subject areas?

		0%	25%	50%	75%	100%
School	#		3	7	25	5
Responses	%		7%	18%	62%	13%

b) What percentage of K-12 students does the staff believe should be prepared to pursue a college or university education?

		0%	25%	50%	75%	100%
School	#		6	21	10	3
Responses	%		15%	53%	25%	7%

c) What percentage of students does your staff believe are capable of succeeding in the college-preparatory pattern of courses required for university eligibility?

		0%	25%	50%	75%	100%
School	#		3	15	19	3
Responses	%		7%	38%	48%	7%

Figure 7.1b   Continued

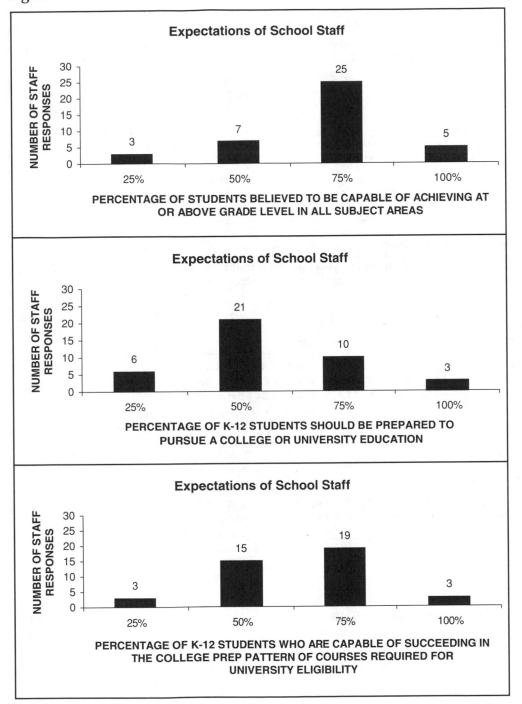

(continued)

Figure 7.1b   Continued

---

3. Aspirations for and Information About Higher Education

a) What percentage of your student population do you believe is interested in going to a college or university after high school?

		0%	25%	50%	75%	100%
School	#		6	19	11	4
Responses	%		15%	48%	27%	10%

b) What percentage of your student population and their parents are prepared to make well-informed decisions about college?

		0%	25%	50%	75%	100%
School	#	10	14	12	4	
Responses	%	25%	35%	20%	10%	

4. Curriculum and Instruction

a) What percentage of your student population is learning a rigorous, challenging curriculum built around higher-order thinking skills and problem solving?

		0%	25%	50%	75%	100%
School	#		7	27	4	2
Responses	%		18%	67%	10%	5%

b) What percentage of the teachers in your school are investigating and trying to learn and use strategies that are proven to meet the needs of diverse student populations, e.g., cooperative learning, untracking, sheltered English, culturally relevant strategies?

		0%	25%	50%	75%	100%
School	#			18	7	15
Responses	%			45%	18%	37%

5. School Practices

a) What percentage of the staff is interested in eliminating tracking and other grouping practices that can inhibit student academic achievement?

		0%	25%	50%	75%	100%
School	#		8	15	10	7
Responses	%		20%	37%	25%	18%

b) What percentage of the staff engages in formal discussions about current educational practices that work for *all* students?

		0%	25%	50%	75%	100%
School	#		14	15	6	5
Responses	%		35%	37%	15%	13%

Figure 7.1b Continued

c) What percentage of the staff shares their ideas for school improvement?		0%	25%	50%	75%	100%
School	#		12	14	8	6
Responses	%		30%	35%	20%	15%

Part II: Perceptions of Support for Collegiality

Please check "Yes" or "No":

1. Is there a climate in your school that promotes joint problem solving around the issue of raising student achievement?

Yes ___ [14]   No ___ [26]

2. Is time set aside on a regular basis for staff to develop and share strategies for improving student achievement?

Yes ___ [10]   No ___ [30]

Part III: Perceptions of Current School Status

Perceptions of Current School Status
Sample Presentation of a School's Summarized Data

Not Ready 38%, Ready for Reform 35%, Implementing Reform 15%, Beginning Evidence of Reform 12%, On the Move 0%

can be administered in several ways. The questions can be modified so that individuals may give their personal perceptions or their perceptions of others in the organization relative to reform. If the school community is interested in finding out how different constituencies view a situation, this should be indicated on the form. Care should be taken to administer the survey at a meeting where participants have not reviewed it ahead of time. This avoids preconsultation among various interests so that the views indicated can be as individual in nature as possible. Names should be optional. This survey should also be given to parents and other major stakeholders in the school community.

Data Analysis and Presentations

After the survey has been administered, the data team should summarize the data. Then, in small group discussions with guided questions, the school community should discuss what they believe the data tell and the possible implications for reform. For example, the sample data in Figure 7.1b (Question 2a) show that 62% of staff believes that students can learn at high levels, but Question 5a indicates that only 37% are interested in eliminating tracking. Ask how these two findings can be reconciled in light of the research on tracking that shows how it depresses student achievement. Ask each group to discuss their responses and then to report out to the whole group.

The session should close with "next steps" planned to move the reform process forward. There may very well be some gaps in beliefs and expectations identified. These will be important to address. Participants should be encouraged to give evidence to support their responses. There also may be different perceptions relative to groups—teachers, administrators, parents, and so forth—regarding what the current status of reform is at the school. Frequently administrator and teacher perceptions are quite different on Part II, "Perceptions of Support for Collegiality." It will be important to discuss why those differ.

Discussion and Cautionary Notes

Often elementary staff and parents do not see the link between college going and student preparation at the elementary level. Presentations and discussions about sorting, labeling, expectations, and curriculum practices at the elementary level—and how these affect future opportunities—are important. It is important for constituents to understand the purpose of this survey and to fill it out thoughtfully. Sharing the data is critical and can be pivotal to guiding the reform process. Each group should be skillfully facilitated. The facilitators may need briefings prior to the meeting. An external facilitator may be needed, so that (a) the entire staff can be focused on the issues, and (b) no one on the staff is viewed as controlling this process. This is best done when participants are in a setting that is conducive to dialogue—not in a hurried faculty meeting.

PROCESS INDICATORS

School and district change efforts usually have no process to develop and look at indicators of progress and results. They need tools to really think about what it will look like when they accomplish their objectives, as well as timelines for change and clear understandings of what the improvements are designed to accomplish. The Process Indicators in this section (Tables 7.1a and 7.1b, pages 138–141) were designed as working documents to be used by schools and districts developing their own indicators for improvement efforts. These Process Indicators do not by any means represent the only way to establish indicators. For example, the major emphasis here is on processes used to transform a school's academic culture rather than on individual student outcome indicators. However, the form could be modified for use in that way. Other indicator systems are presented later in this chapter.

When to Use

The Process Indicators form (Tables 7.1a and 7.1b) is a tool to help the school or district community to focus on how they will measure intended outcomes. Therefore, whenever possible it should be developed before the initiation of improvement efforts. We have found that initiators of change are often vague about their goals and objectives. The discussion sparked by developing the Process Indicators helps clarify goals and implementation strategies. The instrument can also be used to examine current efforts, helping to set the stage to gather baseline data for the subsequent monitoring systems, which will be discussed in Chapter 11.

Using the Form

The school or district must first prioritize improvement processes and efforts. Then one of two approaches might be taken:

1. The data team, the leadership team, or both do the initial work with the Process Indicators form, developing a draft plan with timelines and key participants noted. At least three to four uninterrupted hours are needed for this work. The teams may also need the assistance of an evaluator experienced in using both qualitative and quantitative measures of school change. This person should act as a guide in building the school community's capacity to do the work with minimal assistance in the future. Next, small groups representative of the school community should review and comment on the team's draft, with the data or leadership team acting as facilitators. The feedback should be reviewed, the form revised, and the final copy distributed and discussed with the school community. These steps will help to build ownership for the change effort at the beginning of the process.

2. The second approach option is to engage the entire school community from the outset. Descriptions of intended or existing improvement efforts as well as goals and objectives should be available to all staff and parents. All should fill in the first two columns of the instrument. The school community should then be grouped by interest or familiarity with the improvement efforts to complete the second half of

(text continues on page 142)

Table 7.1a   Process Indicators: Schoolwide Organizational Change in the
Academic Culture

School: _____

Date: _____

Decide your indicators of change ("Structures and Desired Change") and then
complete other columns. (Refer to the *Sample Process Indicators* in Table 7.1b.)

Structures and Desired Change	Processes for Change	Indicators	How Measured
I. Planning/ Decision Making			
II. Staff-Parent Emphasis			
III. Professionalism/ Responsibility *Internal*			
III. Professionalism/ Responsibility (continued) *External*			
IV. General Conditions of Change			
V. Curriculum Change			
VI. Instruction			
VII. Other			

Form designed by Linda F. Winfield. Revised by Ruth S. Johnson, 1996.

Table 7.1b Sample Process Indicators: Schoolwide Organizational Change in the Academic Culture

School: _____ Date: _____			
These are some ways that your school can begin to look at indicators of change. This list is not exhaustive. You should also look at indicators identified in the school profile, such as attendance, test scores, etc.			
Structures and Desired Change	*Processes for Change*	*Indicators*	*How Measured*
I. Planning/Decision Making • Create leadership teams for schoolwide change. • Create data teams. • Create department teams.	• Selection processes are developed. • Professional development. • Team building. • Meetings, formal/informal. • Monitoring teams' effectiveness.	• Increased planning and dialogue around academic issues and changing structure and practices focused on student achievement. • Decision making/ integration. • Structure/focus of meetings changed. • Buy-in. • Shared vision. • Increased participation of all team members, school staff. • Contents of meeting discussions and emphasis. • Attendance—how much and by whom.	• Observations of level of discussion about academic achievement. • Analysis of agendas. • Logs and notes on observations of teams in action. • Meeting notes. • Surveys.
II. Parent Involvement • Involve parents in student achievement.	• Communication. • Use a variety of strategies. • Communicate in parents' dominant language. • Collaboration. • Incentives/ remove barriers. • Student folders sent home weekly. • Evening and Saturday morning meetings.	• Increased parental involvement: e.g., attendance at community events and school events. • Parents requesting information increases. • Attendance in parenting classes. • Increase in homework completed. • Weekly folders sent home and signed by parents. • Parents initiating, suggesting, implementing, and evaluating.	• Surveys and focus groups of parents and teachers. • Analysis of student grades. • Amount of and types of books read, etc. • Folders signed. • Attendance roster. • Conference rosters. • Meeting agendas and notes.

(continued)

Table 7.1b Continued

Structures and Desired Change	Processes for Change	Indicators	How Measured
III. Professionalism/ Responsibility			
• Develop and implement a professional development plan. • Create inquiry groups.	• Provision of opportunity and structures for professionals to meet in clusters such as grade level, staff development; release time for joint planning and discussion. • Change format of staff development faculty meetings to allow for more interactive discussion around improving student achievement. • Provide opportunities for teachers and administrators to visit each other and teachers in other schools. • Provide opportunities for all in school community to attend conferences and workshops.	• Increased and continuous collegial and joint problem-solving meetings to reflect on and monitor strategies to raise student achievement. • Increase in sustained in-depth staff development (decrease in one-shot in-service). • Less isolation of teachers. • Staff increasingly views improved student achievement and school functioning as its responsibility. • Focus on student achievement in all meetings. • Increased teacher participation in curriculum, instruction decisions, policies and practices affecting achievement. • Senior teachers along with less experienced teachers volunteer to become involved in school and classroom improvement. • Staff experiments, keeps up-to-date, teacher is a researcher, risk-taker. • Increase in peer coaching, teacher receiving feedback about curriculum and instruction. • Peer coaching.	• Surveys over time. • Logs kept by teachers and principals. • Interviews—individual/group observation. • Videotapes. • Evaluation of staff development. • Observation data by administration and specialists. • Student outcome data. • Effective class referrals, suspensions. • Teacher plans. • Parent feedback.

Table 7.1b Continued

Structures and Desired Change	Processes for Change	Indicators	How Measured
		• Increase in number of teachers actually implementing high-level curriculum and improved teaching. • Number of visits to classrooms by teachers, administrators, and outside specialists.	
IV. General Conditions of Change			
(Expectations, Changes in Practices/Structures, Norms of Schools) • Revise curriculum. • Address and confront low expectations. • Change grouping practices that negatively sort and label students. • Teach all students at and above grade level. • Implement schoolwide discipline program. • Implement weekly assemblies emphasizing student achievement. • Implement a schoolwide homework policy. • Implement schoolwide support services. • Allocate and reallocate resources to use in raising student achievement. • Monitor all of the above changes.	• Professional development. • Increase time for teachers to meet. • Sessions that focus on the general conditions of low expectations and group practices. • Inquiry groups.	• 100% of classes implementing new curricula. • Increased number of students learning at higher levels. • College awareness. • Percent increase in improved grades. • Decreased discipline referrals. • Decreased suspensions. • Focus by staff on problem solving.	• Course enrollment. • Reading and math scores. • Level of work completed. • Numbers over time. • Percent increase in attendance for teachers and students. • Decreased suspensions, referrals over time.

Form designed by Linda F. Winfield. Revised by Ruth S. Johnson, 1996.

the instrument. At least two hours should be allotted for this work, with release time used. The leadership or data teams then review the information and revise and present the final draft to the school community.

The leaders of this process will have to know the culture of their school to determine the best approach to constructing the Process Indicators. Whatever the approach, the school community should be involved meaningfully in these beginning stages.

Once the decisions are made about expected outcomes and how they will be measured, data collection, timelines, persons responsible, and other work need to be determined. Some person(s) need to be in the leadership at this point, preferably the data team.

Data Analysis and Presentation

A mock data presentation may be created to show the power of the information. However, this form is intended to plan how to measure changes.

Discussion and Cautionary Notes

Much rich discussion can evolve about expectations of change, the scope and scale of the changes. Within a school community there are different expectations of what can be accomplished as well as varying levels of clarity regarding what changes are intended. This process can help the staff to focus on why they are moving in a certain direction and how they will know when they get there. When the school community sees the outcomes of their efforts, they can make informed decisions about what they need to continue to do and what adjustments they need to make. They can also celebrate their accomplishments.

This process can be tedious for some and engaging for others. Those that will do the follow-up work should understand the important contribution their efforts will make. They need adequate time. Local colleges and universities or school offices of evaluation might assist with designing surveys and instruments and the manipulation of data. A skilled facilitator may be needed.

If the school community has no involvement in this process, it is difficult to get any kind of enthusiasm from them later. They will very likely view it as an external force being imposed on them and will have little feeling for the importance of the process or of data. They may argue about the validity of the indicators.

Meanwhile, involving the school community from the beginning pays big dividends. Information becomes available early on regarding the school community's

- Level of knowledge about improvement efforts
- Assumptions about how to measure outcomes or success
- "Spin" on whether the proposed strategies succeed, and why or why not

A final benefit of this process for members of the school community worth mentioning is the opportunity for what should become rich and ongoing dialogue in all arenas of the school's or district's work. Participants receive feedback about their own ideas during the process. They are able to be part of discussions that lead to decisions, rather than being left to wonder why their suggestions have been taken or not.

ASSESSING INSTITUTIONAL REFORM IN THE ACADEMIC CULTURE OF SCHOOLS

What are some ways to assess whether a school is moving toward a culture of high achievement? Unfortunately, there are few meaningful, systematic ways to examine reforms related to equity in academic culture. Little help has been available to educators, especially at the elementary level. How can educators know which reforms in the school culture will likely lead to substantive achievement differences for students? How can they determine whether reforms are only superficial, or if practices, norms, and policies are changing for the lasting benefit of students?

The restructuring literature provides some clues about the types of fundamental systemic reforms that we need to look for, those that appear to have the highest potential to build the capacity of the institution to improve student outcomes. Such areas of reform include professionalism, organizational practices (collegiality and reflection), curriculum and instruction, and expectations for learning. Some key conditions to assess in the overall academic climate include the following:

- Expectations (Brophy & Good, 1974; Edmonds, 1979; Grant & Sleeter, 1988; Haycock, 2001; Hilliard, 1991; Johnson, 1995; Oakes, 1985; Persell, 1977; Winfield, 1986)
- Professionalism, work conditions (Barth, 1990; Fullan, 1993; Darling-Hammond, Berry, & Thoreson, 2001; Little & McLaughlin, 1993; Maeroff, 1993; Olsen et al., 1994; Rosenholtz, 1991)
- Curriculum, instructional practices, learning opportunities (Banks, 1988; Cicourel & Kitsuse, 1963; Cohen, 1991; Goodlad & Keating, 1990; Haberman, 1991; Hart & Jacobi, 1992; Haycock & Navarro, 1988; Howard, 1991; Irvine, 1990; Jones, 1994; Ladson-Billings, 1994; Oakes, 1985; Olsen et al., 1994; Pelavin & Kane, 1990; Sleeter, 1991; Wheelock, 1992)
- Leadership, planning, decision making (Barth, 1990; Estler & Boyan, 1988; Fullan, 1993; Maeroff, 1993; Olsen et al., 1994; Sergiovanni, 2001; Stout, 1993)
- Parent and community involvement (California Tomorrow, 1995; Chavkin, 1989; Clark, 1983; Epstein, 1984; Fine, 1993; Henderson, Marburger, & Ooms, 1989; Leitman et al., 1995; New York ACORN Schools Office, 1996; Nicholau & Ramos, 1990; Olsen et al., 1994)

The central focus of systemic reform must be the creation of academic environments that produce high-level achievement outcomes for all students, regardless of background. Fundamental reforms are required in organizations, governance, policies, programs, practices, and the inclusion of parents and community. Such reforms involve shifts in power, resources, values, and roles.

The instrument Assessing Institutional Reforms in the Academic Culture of Schools (Figure 7.2a) should be used in schools where the focus is on student achievement and where there is a commitment to look at institutional practice. However, it can also be used as a wake-up call for schools to better understand how their institutional practices contribute to high or low achievement. Many educators who have taken these surveys have worked in low-achieving schools for so long that they had no idea what conditions existed in high-achieving schools. Using instruments like this one can move staff away from simply placing blame on parents and

(text continues on page 148)

Figure 7.2a Assessing Institutional Reforms in the Academic Culture of Schools

Name (optional): _____   School: _____
Position: _____   Date: _____

(Fill in for postassessment *only*.)
Filled out instrument in 200 ___ ? *Yes* ____ *No* ____

Directions: Please fill in the circle under the number that you believe best represents your school. One (1) is the lowest rating and five (5) is the highest.

Area	*Underachievement*	*Rating*					*Higher Achievement*
Leadership/Planning/ Decision Making	* Little or no collaboration between administrators and teachers about strategies to raise student achievement.	1 -O-	2 -O-	3 -O-	4 -O-	5 -O-	* Frequent and regular collaboration and joint problem solving to design and evaluate strategies to raise student achievement with a focus on access and equity.
	* Mostly top-down style of leadership; leadership teams function in isolation from colleagues; roles and commitment unclear;	1 -O-	2 -O-	3 -O-	4 -O-	5 -O-	* Frequent collaboration with administrative leaders; teams skillfully engage with each other and planning and decision-making involves all major stakeholders.
	* No use of data.	1 -O-	2 -O-	3 -O-	4 -O-	5 -O-	* Regular planning and use of data for inquiry; disaggregation of data.
	* No vision or strategic planning; add-on fragmented programs; no inclusion of stakeholders.	1 -O-	2 -O-	3 -O-	4 -O-	5 -O-	* Consensus on shared vision for school; focus on systemic issues that reform institutional policies and practices.
	* Meetings focus solely on operations, adult agenda.	1 -O-	2 -O-	3 -O-	4 -O-	5 -O-	* Meetings and activities have a clear focus on instruction.

What evidence supports your assessment? _____

Area	*Underachievement*	*Rating*					*Higher Achievement*
Professionalism/ Responsibility	* Low achievement and poor school functioning blamed on others.	1 -O-	2 -O-	3 -O-	4 -O-	5 -O-	* Staff views improved achievement and school functioning as its responsibility; analyzes institutional practices; highly committed staff; includes the entire school community.
	* 20% or more teachers lack credential.	1 -O-	2 -O-	3 -O-	4 -O-	5 -O-	* 90–100% of the teachers are fully credentialed.
	* Few teachers, counselors, and administrators are engaged in continuous meaningful professional development that will result in improved academic achievement.	1 -O-	2 -O-	3 -O-	4 -O-	5 -O-	* All professionals are continuously developing their professional skills.
	* Most professionals are not up-to-date in fields.	1 -O-	2 -O-	3 -O-	4 -O-	5 -O-	* Staff experiments; keeps up-to-date in fields; experiments with new strategies; evaluates progress and regularly uses data; teacher is a researcher; visitations to other sites with successful practices.
	* Nonrelevant, isolated, sporadic, or nonexistent staff development; in-service is the only form of staff development.	1 -O-	2 -O-	3 -O-	4 -O-	5 -O-	* Systematic, comprehensive, and tied to staff needs—up-to-date strategies, peer teaching, coaching, collegiality.

What evidence supports your assessment? _____

Figure 7.2a   Continued

Area	Underachievement	Rating					Higher Achievement
Standards Curriculum	* Curriculum and courses are not aligned with state/ national standards.	1 -O-	2 -O-	3 -O-	4 -O-	5 -O-	* Curriculum and courses are aligned with state/national standards.
	* Few students are engaged in standards-based tasks.	1 -O-	2 -O-	3 -O-	4 -O-	5 -O-	* All students are engaged in rigorous standards-based tasks; 90–100% of students score at levels demonstrating mastery.
	* Little or no agreement on consistent process to measure and report student performance.	1 -O-	2 -O-	3 -O-	4 -O-	5 -O-	* Consensus and commitment to ensuring standards-based rigor in curriculum and course work for all students; consistent framework for measuring student progress and providing feedback.
	* Curriculum actually taught is thin, fragmented.	1 -O-	2 -O-	3 -O-	4 -O-	5 -O-	* Students are taught a rigorous, balanced curriculum, rich in concepts, ideas, and problem solving.
	* Remedial instruction is isolated to low-level skills based on discrete facts.	1 -O-	2 -O-	3 -O-	4 -O-	5 -O-	* All students are taught a curriculum that is at or above grade level; students pushed toward higher-order thinking.
	* No technology included in the curriculum.	1 -O-	2 -O-	3 -O-	4 -O-	5 -O-	* Students have technology integrated into curriculum.

What evidence supports your assessment? _____

Area	Underachievement	Rating					Higher Achievement
Instruction	* Mostly lecture format; students passive, emphasis on low-level skills.	1 -O-	2 -O-	3 -O-	4 -O-	5 -O-	* A variety of successful, challenging, and interactive instructional strategies are used, such as cooperative learning, directed lessons, extended engagement time for learners; use of high-quality technology and software programs.
	* Multicultural issues and concepts are not integrated into standards-based instruction. No use of students' authentic learning outside of school to connect what is being taught in school.	1 -O-	2 -O-	3 -O-	4 -O-	5 -O-	* Multicultural issues and concepts are integrated into standards-based instruction. Use of students' authentic learning outside of school to connect what is being taught in school.
	* Repetitive low-level drills, heavy use of workbooks.	1 -O-	2 -O-	3 -O-	4 -O-	5 -O-	* Higher-level skills taught; progress assessed frequently; production rather than reproduction of knowledge is encouraged.
	* Lots of pullout programs isolated from regular classroom instruction; emphasis on remedial instruction.	1 -O-	2 -O-	3 -O-	4 -O-	5 -O-	* Students taught all subjects that lead to college entrance; addresses needs of diverse student populations.
	* Student abilities and achievement assessed solely on standardized skill-based tests.	1 -O-	2 -O-	3 -O-	4 -O-	5 -O-	* A variety of indicators are used to measure student performance.
	* No use of standards-based assessments.	1 -O-	2 -O-	3 -O-	4 -O-	5 -O-	* Appropriate and frequent use of standards-based assessments.

What evidence supports your assessment? _____

(continued)

Figure 7.2a Continued

Area	Underachievement	Rating					Higher Achievement
Expectations	* Academic goals are unfocused; no attention to access and equity.	1 -O-	2 -O-	3 -O-	4 -O-	5 -O-	* Goals are clearly focused on student achievement, access, and equity.
	* Students from low-income and certain ethnic backgrounds are viewed as not having the potential to gain high-level knowledge and skills.	1 -O-	2 -O-	3 -O-	4 -O-	5 -O-	* All students viewed as potential high achievers—staff believes all students are capable of mastering the high-level knowledge and skills.
	* Students considered not capable of taking required courses for 4-year postsecondary institutions.	1 -O-	2 -O-	3 -O-	4 -O-	5 -O-	* Students have access, are supported and prepared for 4-year postsecondary institutions.
	* Staff conversation reflects much negativity about children; staff assumes no responsibility for low levels of achievement.	1 -O-	2 -O-	3 -O-	4 -O-	5 -O-	* Staff constructively focuses on institutional and instructional practices that need changing and engages in discussions about ways to help students learn at high levels.
	* Students are informally and formally labeled in negative ways, e.g., slow, remedial, dropouts.	1 -O-	2 -O-	3 -O-	4 -O-	5 -O-	* Students are not negatively labeled.

What evidence supports your assessment? _____

Area	Underachievement	Rating					Higher Achievement
Learning Opportunities Grouping/Tracking/ Labeling	* Students separated by perceived ability into rigid homogeneous groups.	1 -O-	2 -O-	3 -O-	4 -O-	5 -O-	* Flexible grouping for short periods of time; most/all instruction in heterogeneous groups.
	* Lower-level and remedial groups get least-prepared teachers, watered-down curriculum.	1 -O-	2 -O-	3 -O-	4 -O-	5 -O-	* All students have opportunities to be taught by best-prepared teachers.
	* Only high-achieving students taught advanced-level information/ skills/technology.	1 -O-	2 -O-	3 -O-	4 -O-	5 -O-	* All students get same rigorous core curriculum—variety of strategies including technology are used.
	* Few options for low-achieving students.	1 -O-	2 -O-	3 -O-	4 -O-	5 -O-	* Students form study groups; extended days are provided, other student supports are introduced and implemented; practices are altered when necessary to better serve students.
	* Levels that students' function at is seen as unalterable.	1 -O-	2 -O-	3 -O-	4 -O-	5 -O-	* All students viewed as having the capacity to achieve at higher levels.

What evidence supports your assessment? _____

Figure 7.2a Continued

Area	Underachievement	Rating					Higher Achievement
Parent Involvement	* Parents are considered indifferent toward child's achievement.	1 -O-	2 -O-	3 -O-	4 -O-	5 -O-	* Staff, parents, and leaders use a variety of strategies to motivate and accommodate parents as partners in their children's education. Families learn to become effective advocates for their students.
	* Education viewed as a domain of professionals; little or no collaboration between staff and parents.	1 -O-	2 -O-	3 -O-	4 -O-	5 -O-	* Collaborative process where staff and parents assume joint responsibility for student performance, homework, communication.
	* Parent involvement limited to a few persons; insensitivity to cultural differences hinders participation.	1 -O-	2 -O-	3 -O-	4 -O-	5 -O-	* Parents, leaders, and staff use effective strategies to achieve broad participation and representation of all ethnic groups in activities.
	* Parents, students, and other community members are not aware of and rarely provided information about preparing students for higher education.	1 -O-	2 -O-	3 -O-	4 -O-	5 -O-	* Parents, students, and community partners actively participate in planning and implementing of programs.
	* Information rarely translated into the parents' dominant languages; communications seldom relate to achievement.	1 -O-	2 -O-	3 -O-	4 -O-	5 -O-	* Translation to parents' dominant languages consistently provides for effective school communication (oral and written) focused on student achievement.

What evidence supports your assessment? _____

Area	Underachievement	Rating					Higher Achievement
Support Services for Students	* Few or no tutoring services, tutoring usually in the form of a homework club; limited numbers of students utilize services.	1 -O-	2 -O-	3 -O-	4 -O-	5 -O-	* Ample support services closely integrated with instructional program; variety of tutoring programs offered with a flexible schedule; coordinated with core curriculum; regular participation of students who need assistance.
	* Little coordination among special programs; no mechanism to catch students "falling through the cracks."	1 -O-	2 -O-	3 -O-	4 -O-	5 -O-	* Special programs integrated into regular instruction; counseling programs aligned.
	* No agreed-upon plan for handling attendance, discipline, vandalism problems, uncaring environment; no review of implications on academic achievement.	1 -O-	2 -O-	3 -O-	4 -O-	5 -O-	* Agreed-on procedures for handling attendance and discipline problems, reduced referrals, suspensions, caring environment; monitoring impact on academic achievement.

What evidence supports your assessment? _____

communities to an awareness that the academic culture of the school contributes to the achievement patterns of children.

When to Use

This instrument is best used in a retreat or in sessions of a day or more. It is also best used in a context where the professionals have had the opportunity to read, discuss, and hear about issues such as tracking, expectations, and professional development. This will help ensure that the individuals filling out the instrument have a reasonable knowledge base for indicating where they believe their school to be along the continuum. Ideally this should be done at the beginning of the reform process and at intervals, such as annually or every other year, depending on the area being assessed.

Administering the Instrument

Before administering this instrument to any group of educators, parents, or community members, its purpose must be explained well. It may be useful for more than one person to talk about the importance of the instrument to demonstrate a range of perspectives. Participants should understand that they are taking a critical look at their school and that it will be used positively, not for "finger-pointing." This instrument can also be modified for teachers to look at their individual classrooms.

The whole school community can participate in the administration of the instrument Assessing Institutional Reforms in the Academic Culture of Schools (Figure 7.2a, pages 144–147). Participants should individually fill out the instrument. Names are optional, but everyone should fill in "position." However, there may only be one administrator (very likely for an elementary school principal), so that person may have to take the risk of being identified. The form includes a line for postassessment: "Filled out in 200_ Yes_ No_." This will be filled out when the instrument is readministered at a later date to assess progress. This is important information to fill in each time to compare perceptions of people who have been in the reform process over time to new participants.

Participants should be encouraged to complete the question, "What evidence supports your assessment?" After rating an area, this evidence provides valuable information for assessment. If desired, each person may also write on a separate page how he or she justifies his or her ratings. It should take approximately 20 to 30 minutes for individuals to fill out the instrument, first reflecting on their own personal practices and then on the school as a whole.

After completing the form, in small groups with a designated facilitator and recorder, participants should share their responses with each other. Answers can be plotted on a larger instrument. Because this part of the exercise may be overwhelming, it may be helpful to designate three or four areas to focus on for the first examination. This approach was used effectively in one district; following the discussion, the team identified five areas to focus on for improving student achievement.

A school group may wish to have an initial discussion and then give participants time later to discuss the conditions further or to gather more documentation before beginning to move toward strategies. If this approach is used, the next intensive session should be held within two weeks. This will also give time to prepare a more graphic presentation of the outcomes of the survey. Ask questions about the results, such as, "Were you surprised by the results? What appear to be positive findings? What findings are causes for concern? What are the implications for action?"

The initial discussion time immediately following administration should be approximately 45 minutes to an hour. The results should continue to be reviewed on an ongoing basis and referred to in planning and decision making.

Data Analysis and Presentations

Individual responses can be tallied for each item in a group setting, as described earlier. As suggested, a few conditions at a time can be selected so the process does not overwhelm the group. An optional approach for tallying the data may be found in Figure 7.2b. Here, the 1 and 2 ratings are collapsed together and the 4 and 5 ratings are collapsed together in order to analyze highs and lows. These are represented on the graphs. The 3 ratings were considered average and not represented on the graph, but they could be included if desired. The percentage of participants who rated the school at the lower ends and those who rated it at the upper ends were then calculated.

Such data presentations can be used to engage the staff in discussions about school conditions and what must be reformed to move toward a high-achieving

Figure 7.2b   Assessing Institutional Reforms in the Academic Culture of Schools: Sample Baseline Presentation of a School's Summarized Data

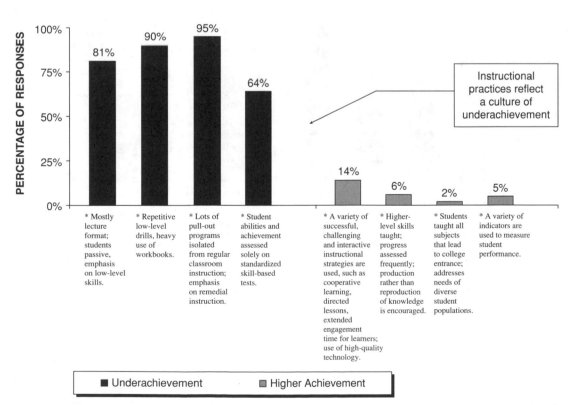

(continued)

Figure 7.2b Continued

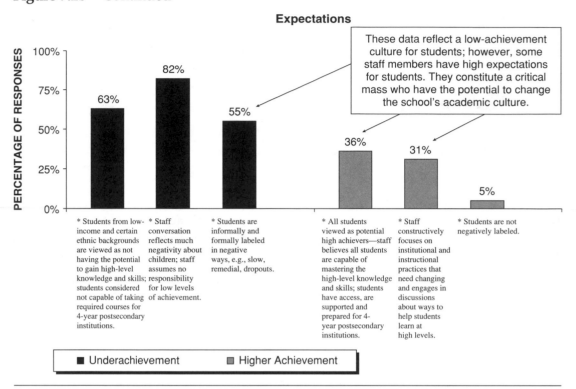

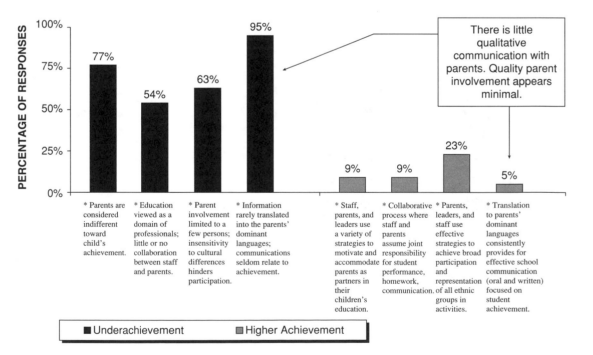

Figure 7.2b   Continued

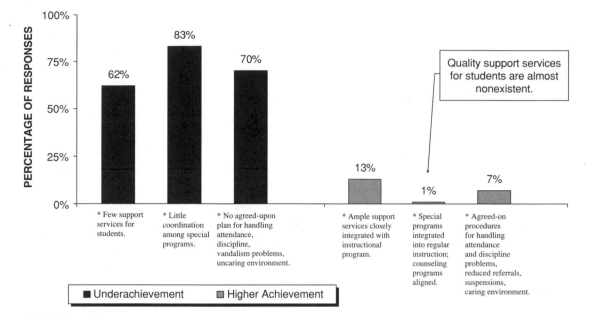

Support Services for Students

NOTE: Sample data.

culture. The data should also be disaggregated by respondents' roles or positions in the school community. Are there differences in perceptions along these lines? If so, these need to be discussed. The facilitators of the discussion must urge participants to give documentation for their responses so that decisions are not weighted toward who is the best speaker or who has the most powerful role.

The results of the initial survey should be kept to compare with results at a future date. A list of who participated in the survey, including their roles or positions, should also be kept.

Discussion and Cautionary Notes

In using this instrument, it is important to go over the categories and terms so there are clear operational definitions. For example, the staff may need to use the literature defining "rigorous, balanced curriculum" in the curriculum area. A school could modify this instrument based on new research. Descriptors of reform may be used instead of numerical ratings, if thought through carefully. After the staff has done its own internal analysis, the school may want an outside evaluator to assess the school using the same instrument. This will offer additional grounding about where the school stands. The information can then be analyzed and decisions made for school development. This instrument can also be used for baseline data about the reform in school culture and, if carefully done, can serve as a progress indicator of reforms that can lead to advances in student achievement.

The following information gives examples of how to show where a school community was at two different points in the reform process—before the reform began and three years later. Although the sample presented here documents a three-year period, schools would do well to administer this on an annual basis and then bring in an outsider to document progress at the three-year point. Every area does not necessarily need to be gauged annually. The areas that the school is most strongly focusing on at a given time should be assessed. Again, the school community should decide what would work best in their culture.

Data Analysis and Presentation

These data can be presented as in Figure 7.2c, where dramatic reforms were revealed in the academic culture of the school. For example, in the area of Planning and Decision Making, 65% indicated top-down management in year 1. In year 3, only 4% thought the school was managed this way.

Two samples of findings are shown in the area of Expectations. For example, in year 1, 83% of the staff indicated that student failure was linked to their parents and background, but in year 3, only 16% believed this. In year 1, only 8% of the staff perceived that the school constructively focused on strategies to help students learn. By year 3, 55% perceived that this was occurring.

OTHER INSTRUMENTS TO ASSESS EQUITY

There are several instruments available to assess equity. The Kentucky Department of Education has an Equity Analysis and Data Gathering Instrument, and the College Board developed instruments for Equity 2000 (now with school-based services). Contact information can be found in the Resource section of this book. There is also information on the World Wide Web.

SCHOOLS' AND DISTRICTS' ASSESSMENTS OF DELIVERY OF PRECOLLEGE GUIDANCE

The norms and practices related to guidance for college are rarely assessed in schools. For decades, college counseling was usually reserved for a selected group of students, and other students, mostly low-income students of color, received little information and were expected to terminate their formal education at high school, go directly to work or the military, or at best take vocational training. As schools and districts move toward closing the achievement gap around college going, it will be important to assess the area of college guidance.

The following anecdote is from a young Latino woman's urban school experience with her guidance counselor. This university student had read an article on tracking, and it awakened her consciousness about her own high school experience. In a reflection session, she wrote the following:

> I had to fight to enroll in the college preparatory classes, and I was told that the classes would be too difficult for me, even though I had a 4.9 (on a 5-point scale) GPA in junior high school.
>
> The counselor was trying to track me into a non–college preparatory track, even though I had proven myself academically capable. I imagine that

Figure 7.2c   Assessing Institutional Reforms in the Academic Culture of Schools: Sample Baseline Presentation of a School's Summarized Data

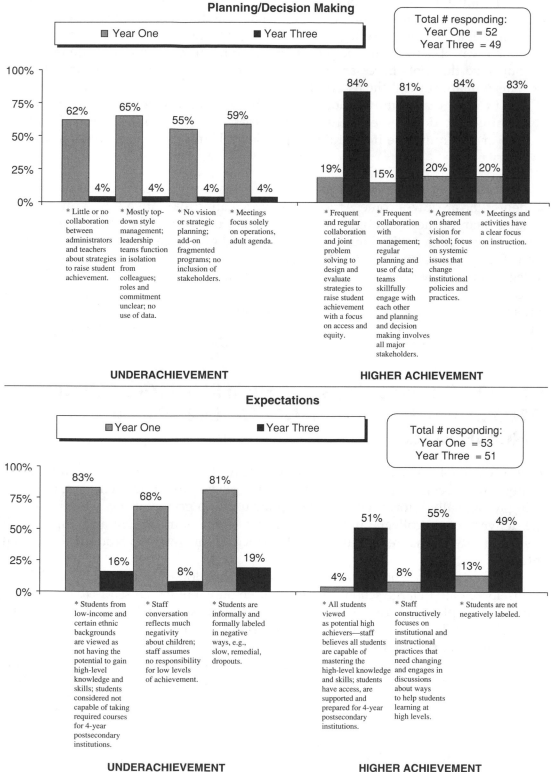

SOURCE: Urban school.

his opinion that I would not succeed in difficult courses must have been based on my ethnicity.

I realize that I was strong enough to fight for my future and that not all students are as strong as I, nor do they have the knowledge of what classes will prepare them for college. I had the knowledge and the ability to fight, thus I was able to overcome this obstacle. Unfortunately, many students do not have the tools necessary to overcome these obstacles and are tracked. This will affect them the rest of their lives.

I realize that in most schools across the country, it is in the hands of the counselor to determine the future of so many students. They have a lot of power and must use it carefully to provide all students equal access to the curriculum.

Unfortunately, this is not an isolated case. This story is heard all too often from students who are low-income, African American, Latino, or Native American students making their journeys through school. Students from all racial and economic backgrounds have high aspirations—dreams that need guidance to connect to an action plan. That plan includes taking algebra, geometry, algebra 2, and other higher-level college preparatory classes in middle and senior high school and understanding the process for applying to college—including taking college entrance exams and filling out applications for admission and financial aid. Demystifying who goes to college and helping students and families to navigate the complex system of getting to college are critical functions.

CHARACTERISTICS OF HIGH-PERFORMING AND LOW-PERFORMING COUNSELING PROGRAMS

Typically, schools provide college counseling only at the senior high level, after most students have been included or excluded from college preparatory courses. If we are going to radically reform who has the opportunity to go to college, we must begin the delivery of precollege guidance as early as elementary school and approach it systematically to ensure that all students—not just the very top students—are well informed.

This function does not have to rest on counselors alone. Many schools don't have counselors at all; in large schools there are often only a few counselors to go around. Broad-based planning that includes students, parents, teachers, administrators, counselors, and community-based organizations is necessary to create a delivery system that will reach all students and families.

Characteristics of High-Performing and Low-Performing Counseling Programs (Table 7.2) was developed specifically to help schools and districts assess counseling practices. The content is based on the report by the College Board *Keeping the Options Open* (1987).

When to Use the Instrument

This instrument can be used in two ways: one, as a vehicle for discussion of beliefs about who should go to college and therefore who should have access to

Table 7.2 Characteristics of High-Performing and Low-Performing Counseling Programs

Directions: Circle the number that you think best reflects the performance of your school's/district's counseling programs and explain why.

Low-Performing Programs	How Is My School Doing? (1 = low, 5 = high)	High-Performing Programs	Why?
A set of loosely related services performed almost exclusively by counselors.	1 2 3 4 5	A well-defined planning process that leads to well-coordinated services for all students.	
Students "fall through the cracks."	1 2 3 4 5	An ongoing monitoring system is set up to constantly assess student performance and provide services where needed.	
Counselor operates in isolation from the school, community, and district.	1 2 3 4 5	Counselor serves constructively on teams in planning for improvement of student achievement.	
No coordinated planning process to provide for the needs of students; plans are viewed as a bureaucratic requirement.	1 2 3 4 5	Planning process involves everyone in the school community: students, parents, teachers, administrators, and counselors.	
District gives little support.	1 2 3 4 5	District provides services and support to schools by • Providing technical assistance in their assessment of needs and evaluation. • Providing special allocations of resources to schools serving large numbers of low-income and underrepresented students. • Periodically reviewing school plans. • Identifying elements that should be coordinated across and among schools.	
Make no use of data to analyze and improve the learning of students on a regular basis.	1 2 3 4 5	Use data on a regular basis to analyze and improve the learning of students.	
Individual progress of underrepresented students is not monitored and/or data is not available or easily accessible.	1 2 3 4 5	Counselors actively monitor the progress of underrepresented students in college preparatory classes by analyzing access and success data and provide assistance and intervention when needed.	
No attention is paid to research.	1 2 3 4 5	Counselors analyze and share research information on tracking, retention, and heterogeneous grouping.	
Counselors are not viewed as "reform agents" in schools.	1 2 3 4 5	Counselors demonstrate leadership skills as "reform agents" in schools.	

Form designed by Phyllis J. Hart, The Achievement Council, Los Angeles, CA.

information. It can help frame the discussion and keep it focused on issues rather than on blaming others for why students aren't being served: "The counselors don't do their job"; "The teachers expect less"; "The parents don't want their kids to go to college." The second use would be after a school or district is convinced that real reform needs to occur and wants to assess the guidance delivery system and plan for meaningful reform. Ideally, the instrument should be used during a retreat focused on improving college opportunity structures for all students. It can, however, be used during the school day at meetings scheduled for the purpose of improving guidance.

Administering the Instrument

This instrument should be used to gather a variety of perspectives, including those of a broad range of parents, students, teachers, counselors, and administrators. Each person should rate (1–5) where he or she thinks the school is in relation to the issue, with a descriptor as to why. A conversation among the group comparing perceptions and rationales can provide valuable information and discussion, whether or not consensus is reached. It will provide a snapshot of where this group thinks the school is and an opportunity to prioritize one or two focus areas for improvement. It should be revisited annually to monitor progress and make necessary revisions. Successes should be shared with staff and the broader community.

Data Analysis and Presentations

It is important to use this instrument in conjunction with disaggregated data to see what improvements have taken place, particularly for historically underrepresented students. Are students leaving elementary schools with the knowledge of what courses to take in middle and high school to prepare for college? Have they been exposed to college and university campuses? Are more students from the underrepresented race, language, and gender groups being placed in college preparatory courses? Are they successful in these classes? Are the safety nets there and working? Have college-going rates improved? Are scholarships and financial aid dollars increasing?

Together with periodic snapshots from the guidance document, these data can powerfully motivate improvement of the K-12 precollege guidance delivery system. They can be used to demonstrate that guidance is more than the affective domain: It is educational, academic, and proactive in improving college opportunities for all students.

Discussion and Cautionary Notes

This instrument should be used as a tool to evaluate precollege guidance and to involve others in the reform process. It should also help identify where the gaps are and inform what kind of help others need to do a more effective job. If educators see it primarily as a tool to evaluate counselors, it will not achieve its intended purpose. Proceed with caution. Those engaging in the process should do some preliminary reading and discussion. Part of the discussion should revolve around the entire school's roles in K-12 precollege guidance and counseling.

COUNSELOR COLLEGE PREPARATORY RECORD KEEPING FOR INDIVIDUAL STUDENTS

Preparation for college needs to begin in kindergarten—and earlier if possible. At the elementary level this requires monitoring of teaching and learning to make sure it is focused on high expectations, high-level content, a diversity of instructional approaches, and parent involvement. All of the instruments and forms provided in this book are related to analyzing issues of access and equity so students and their parents can choose their own opportunities and options, rather than having them chosen by "the system." This section will discuss ways to more sharply focus on college preparation.

College preparation, enrollment, and retention involve creating a culture in which students expect that college will be a reality in their future. Parents will need to participate in this endeavor with the school. Many parents who are not college graduates will require information about what is needed to assist their children in making college enrollment a reality. Instructional quality and content can be monitored by using instruments in this book. Other monitoring information usually comes out of state reviews, such as the Program Quality Review in California and similar evaluations in other states that address curriculum quality issues. But additionally, schools need to monitor what is happening in classrooms. Administrators should observe teachers' expectations of students, content quality, strategies, and assessment.

Table 7.3a is an example of how a high school monitored individual student attendance, coursework, grade point averages, test participation, submission of applications for college acceptance, and financial aid. These help to monitor individual students as well as counselor support. All of these forms can be adapted for computer use. Counselors, teachers, and administrators need to consistently monitor the preparation process. Too many students have missed out by the time they get to their senior year and have not taken the necessary courses for college entrance. In Table 7.3b one student, Jones, needs to take geometry. He has not filled out college applications, and a parent conference is needed. Someone will need to check back later to see if these gaps have been filled. This information can be readily available if computerized. Some schools are requiring all students to take a college preparatory sequence, because those courses most often impart the types of knowledge that workers will need for the 21st century. If these courses are required, passing rates and other indicators still must be checked.

WHICH COUNSELORS ARE PROVIDING COLLEGE ACCESS TO STUDENTS?

Table 7.4 (page 160) shows five years of monitoring individual counselors on the percentage of their counselees enrolled in college preparatory and honors classes. It appears that the number of counselees preparing for college increased most in year 4. What happened that year and in the years leading up to it? In year 1, only 43.3% of students were enrolled in college preparatory courses. By year 5, 82% were enrolled. All counselors show similar percentages of students enrolled. Counselor F has the

Table 7.3a Counselor College Preparatory Record Keeping for Individual Students in Grades 9–12

School _____
Counselor _____
Grade Level _____
Year _____

Note: This form is designed to assist counselors in keeping track of counseling sessions regarding college plans and processes, as well as for reporting purposes. This can be used in conjunction with a four-year plan. (Could be put on an NCR form, having parent and student sign)

		A	B	C	D	E	F	G	H	I	J	K	L	M
Student	Race/Ethnicity	Student ID #	Attendance	GPA	Coursework on Schedule for 4-year College? Yes/No	Coursework Needed if No in C	Career Goal	PSAT, PACT	ACT, SAT	ACH Test	SAAC	College	College	Major	Conference With Parent

Table 7.3b Counselor College Preparatory Record Keeping for Individual Students in Grades 9–12: Sample

School _____
Counselor _____
Grade Level _____
Year _____

Note: This form is designed to assist counselors in keeping track of counseling sessions regarding college plans and processes, as well as for reporting purposes. This can be used in conjunction with a four-year plan. (Could be put on an NCR form, having parent and student sign)

Student	Race/Ethnicity	Student ID #	A Attendance	B GPA	C Coursework on Schedule for 4-year College? Yes/No	D Coursework Needed if No in C	E Career Goal	F PSAT, PACT	G ACT, SAT	H ACH Test	I SAAC	J College	K College	L Major	M Conference With Parent
Johnson	African American	12,345		3.5	Yes		Chemist		1,200		✓		✓	Chemistry	✓
Jones	African American	98,765		2.5	No	Geometry	Actor		950					Drama	
Martinez	Latino	11,543		2.7	Yes		Doctor		1,050		✓		✓	Pre-Med	
Smith	White	13,678		2.9	Yes		Lawyer		1,000				✓	Pol. Science	✓

Table 7.4   Students Enrolled in College Preparatory and Honors (CP/H) Classes by Counselor

Counselor	Year	# of Counselees	# Enrolled in CP/H	% in CP/H	Annual Difference
A	1	303	129	42.5	
	2	280	135	49.0	+6.5%
	3	276	158	57.0	+8.0%
	4	284	212	75.0	+18.0%
	5	263	210	80.0	+5.0%
B	1	345	160	46.3	
	2	318	161	50.6	+4.3%
	3	352	220	63.0	+12.4%
	4	263	207	79.0	+16.0%
	5	361	292	81.0	+2.0%
C	1	351	157	44.7	
	2	315	176	55.8	+11.1%
	3	345	195	57.0	+1.2%
	4	298	232	78.0	+21.0%
	5	319	269	84.0	+6.0%
D	1	349	153	44.7	
	2	326	164	50.3	+6.5%
	3	332	187	56.0	+5.7%
	4	304	251	78.0	+22.0%
	5	325	266	82.0	+4.0%
E	1	19	142	41.8	
	2	21	142	44.2	+2.4%
	3	323	177	55.0	+10.8%
	4	289	229	79.0	+14.0%
	5	309	269	87.0	+8.0%
F	1	362	149	41.1	
	2	338	159	47.0	+5.9%
	3	343	186	52.0	+5.0%
	4	320	231	72.0	+20.0%
	5	321	254	78.0	+6.0%
TOTALS	1	2,344	1,016	43.3	
	2	2,105	1,035	49.1	+5.8%
	3	1,971	1,117	57.0	+7.9%
	4	1,882	1,450	77.0	+20.0%
	5	1,954	1,560	82.0	+5.0%

SOURCE: Urban school district.

lowest, with 78% enrolled, and counselor E has the highest, with 87% enrolled. What needs to be done to maintain this progress? What other data might need to be collected?

COUNSELOR'S PLANS FOR COUNSELEES

Table 7.5 was developed in collaboration with counselors. The form monitors each counselor's students' plans for college going. Collaboratively, counselors and administrators can use this to monitor progress and focus academic counseling. This can help to prevent students from "falling through the cracks."

Table 7.5   Individual Counselor Annual College-Going Report

This report form should be used in consultation with the VP of Counseling and give a sense of progress, to make midcourse adjustments, reward successes, support counselors and students, and help define the focus and direction of the counseling program.

College-Going Report for Seniors

This data should be gathered by each counselor annually and submitted to the VP of Counseling. The VP should give a summary status report to the principal. Each principal could then report this summary to appropriate district administrators. The report should include the following suggested categories:

School: _____   Year: _____

Counselor: _____   Total # of Seniors in Fall: _____

Total # of Seniors in Spring: _____

Number and Percentage of Seniors to:	#	%
4-year public colleges/universities		
4-year private colleges/universities		
2-year public colleges		
2-year private colleges		
Military		
Work		
Graduated from high school		
Dropped out		
Transferred		

By ethnicity for higher education:	4-year public		4-year private		2-year public		2-year private	
	#	%	#	%	#	%	#	%
African American								
Asian								
Latino								
White								

Number of SACC forms mailed: _____

Number of Cal Grants received: _____

Race/Ethnicity	Cal Grant A		Cal Grant B		Cal Grant C		Pell Grant		College Scholarships		Local Scholarships	
	#	%	#	%	#	%	#	%	#	%	#	%
African American												
Asian												
Latino												
White												

Number of seniors who took the SAT: _____

SOURCE: An urban high school.

PART II: EXISTING SCHOOL DOCUMENTS

Rich sources of data exist in schools that can tell compelling stories about equitable and inequitable policies and practices. These documents are sometimes referred to as "artifacts" (Crawford & Dougherty, 2000). Looking at existing documents in a school can help to assess how the school distributes its most valuable resources: time, people, and money. These documents include the master schedule, student and teacher schedules, time allocations and use of time, teacher assignments by experience, credentials, and student outcomes, and counselor practices.

Agendas are also useful in assessing what items are discussed at meetings over time. These documents can reflect what values and norms are operating at the school. The documents can give rich clues to what policies and practices need to be eliminated, revised, or added. Some of those documents are listed in Table 7.6, but there are many more that schools can analyze.

HOW DOES THE MASTER SCHEDULE REFLECT PRACTICES AND GOALS?

Every school has some kind of schedule. These can be ideal tools for looking at equity issues. The secondary schools have master schedules. These schedules can include not only periods and subjects offered, but also what teachers are assigned to courses and the numbers of students in each course. The schedule can be analyzed for the following:

- Analyze the types and numbers of courses being offered. Are courses being offered that will prepare students to be competitive and provide eligibility for college? Are higher-level courses increasing over time and remedial courses decreasing? What is the ratio of vocational to academic courses?
- Other inquiries that can be done include monitoring the number of students in each section of a course at different points in time. For instance, what is the enrollment in geometry in September, November, February, and June? Are the numbers stable or dwindling? What do the numbers look like at the higher levels? Which teachers are teaching at different levels from year to year?
- Master schedules can be compared from year to year and within years to give a picture of the direction the school is moving in. This is important in schools that are increasing academic rigor and addressing equity issues.

Schools with year-round schedules need careful analysis related to issues of access and equity. More experienced teachers prefer the track in which they have the summer off, leaving other tracks to more inexperienced teachers. Year-round schools with large numbers of ESL students often place them all on one track. This scheduling frequently denies ESL students opportunities to takes higher-level courses. If only one or two sections of a higher-level course are taught, they are usually not offered on the ESL track. This is a major equity issue. Schools need to examine these practices and explore ways to open access. Some suggested examination should include the following:

- Distribution of courses: Are higher-level courses only offered on certain year-round tracks?

Table 7.6   Analyzing School Documents

Documents	Types of Possible Equity Information	Comments
Master Schedule	Increases and decreases in the number and type of courses offered; course enrollments at different points in time; teacher assignments	The schedule needs to be updated at key points in time and analyzed for plus or minus changes.
Teacher Schedules	Distribution of teacher quality; which students get the most effective teachers? How is time used? Measure academic and nonacademic time for all and different groups. Which subjects/courses get more or less time?	Needs to be combined with student achievement outcomes. Many ninth graders have school adjustment problems. Are they receiving the most effective teachers?
Student Schedules	Which students get what courses and which teachers and when? How much time is nonacademic?	Need to also look at student athlete schedules-many skip the last period for away games; what classes are scheduled? What about ESL students?
School Calendar	What is the instructional flow? Are there lots of breaks in instruction? How is allotted time being used?	Many schools have empty times when little or no quality instruction is occurring.
Subject Time and Homework Time Allocations	Find inconsistencies at the elementary level in the amount of subject matter time from teacher to teacher. What is the amount of homework that is done at home or in school?	Inconsistencies and time allocations need to be examined. What relationship does this have to academic achievement?
Teacher Plan Books	Planned content to be taught. Are teachers planning instruction to meet standards and at what level? What is the amount of time spent on different subjects? What types of materials and approaches are being used?	Analysis should be compared to student outcomes.
Counselor Record Keeping	How do counselors keep records on students? What kinds of counseling are different groups of students receiving?	Analyze access to information, the types of information, and when students receive information.
Budgets	How are resources used? Has it had an effect on student achievement or has there been more fragmentation of programs?	New programs and resources need constant evaluation. Which programs get the most resources? Are they linked to student needs?
Agendas of Meetings	What does the school focus on? Do agendas reflect a culture that focuses on student achievement or routines? Do they reflect the written goals or the informal goals?	Analyze agendas over a period of time to find out the amount of type spent on routine items vs. discussions that are focused on teaching and learning.

Table 7.7a   School A Remedial Science Courses

	Period 1	Period 2	Period 3	Period 4	Period 5	Period 6
Room 254	A4161 Life Science A	A4244 Life Science A	A4173 Physical Sci A	A4112 Life Science A	A4891 Life Science A	
Room 307	A4050 Biology A	A4160 Biology A	A4083 Biology A		A4896 Biology A	A4876 Life Science A
Room 251	A4075 Physiology A	A4608 Biology A		A4892 Biology A	A2390 Adv Biology A	
Room 302	A4392 Adv Phys Sci A		A4875 Adv Phys Sci A	A4234 Physical Sci A	A4436 Physical Sci A	A4715 Physical Sci A
Room 250	A4421 Biology A		A4254 Biology A	A4513 Biology A		A4886 Biology A
Room 255	A4068 Chemistry A	A4585 Adv Phys Sci A		A4057 Chemistry A	A4834 Chemistry A	A4890 Adv Phys Sci A
Room 307	B3889 Physical Sci A		B3773 Physical Sci A	B3564 Physical Sci A	B3893 Life Science A	B3094 Life Science A
Room 254	B3561 Biology A	B3583 Life Science A	B3890 Physical Sci A	B3525 Physical Sci A	B3887 Physical Sci A	
		B3542 Biology A	A3563 Biology A	A3457 Biology A	B3457 Biology A	B3520 Biology A
Room 251	B3872 Physical Sci A	B3772 Physical Sci A	B3515 Physiology A		B3060 Biology A	B3864 Biology A
Room 255	B2449 Chemistry A	B3572 Chemistry A	B3551 Adv Phys Sci A	B3594 Adv Phys Sci A		B3888 Physical Sci A
		C3545 Physical Sci A	C3624 Physical Sci A	C3577 Biology A	C3896 Physical Sci A	C3578 Biology A
Room 252	C3581 Life Science A	C3544 Biology A	C3593 Biology A	C3886 Life Science A	C3129 Biology A	
		C3592 Adv Phys Sci A	C3892 Physical Sci A	C3634 Physical Sci A	C3391 Physics A	C3535 Adv Phys Sci A
Room 253	C3601 Biology A	C3582 Biology A	C3623 Physiology A		C3787 Biology A	C3906 Physiology A
Room 257	C3591 Adv Phys Sci A	C3602 Chemistry A	C3633 Chemistry A		C3603 Adv Phys Sci A	C3603 Adv Phys Sci A

SOURCE: An urban high school.

- Distribution of teacher quality
- Distribution of resources
- Distribution of electives
- Distribution of extracurricular activities
- Distribution of knowledge about opportunities for higher education

The master schedules provided in Tables 7.7a and 7.7b are actual schedules from two urban high school science departments; these show course offerings at schools

Table 7.7b School B Remedial Science Courses

	Period 1	Period 2	Period 3	Period 4	Period 5	Period 6
Room 704	1321 AP Chemistry	1322 Chemistry B	1322 Adv Bio B	1324 AP Biology	1325 Hon Chem B	
Room 755	1357 Biology B	1333 Biology B	1352 Biology B			
Room 801	1342 Phys Sci B		1344 Adv Phys Sci B	1245 Adv Phys Sci B	1346 Adv Phys Sci B	
Room 754	1331 Biology B	1332 Biology B	1353 Biology B	1354 Biology B		1356 Biology B
Room 753	1361 Adv Phys Sci B	1362 Adv Phys Sci B	1363 Adv Phys Sci B	1364 Adv Phys Sci B	1365 Adv Phys Sci B	
Room 802	1371 Adv Phys Sci B	1372 Chemistry B	1373 Phys Sci B	1374 Phys Sci B	1375 Adv Phys Sci B	1376 Adv Phys Sci B
Room 108				1124 AP Physics		
Room 801	1431 Biology B	1432 Biology B	1433 Biology B		1435 Biology B	1436 Biology B
Room 701	1381 Biology B	1382 Biology B	1383 Biology B	1384 Biology B		
Room 755				1404 Biology B	1405 Biology B	1406 Biology B
Room 702	1404 Biology B	1402 Biology B		1394 Biology B	1395 Biology B	1396 Biology B
Room 703	1411 Chemistry B		1413 Physics B	1414 Physics B	1415 Chemistry B	1416 Physics B
Room 804	1421 Physics B	1422 Adv Phys Sci B	1423 Chemistry B	1424 Chemistry B		

SOURCE: An urban high school.

with similar demographics—75 percent Latino. By examining these schedules one can assess school expectations and goals. School A (Table 7.7a) shows that 28 of the total science offerings (bold boxes) are remedial courses that do not count for college. The students in these courses are given the message that they are not college material. School B (Table 7.7b) shows a very different picture. Only three courses are remedial. School B, which serves more children from very low-income families than School A, is doing extremely well.

Table 7.8 is a simple analysis done by a vice principal in an urban school. The goals were to increase the levels and rigor of math classes. The school seems to be accomplishing its goals, with the exception of pre-calculus and calculus. They need to continue and carefully monitor their efforts. The count from the master schedule is shown in Table 7.8. The table also indicates that more students appear to be ready to take higher-level courses.

Table 7.8 Comparison of Mathematics Courses Offered in 1999–2000 and 2000–2001

	Number of Sections	
Course	*1999–2000*	*2000–2001*
Algebra 1	40	36
Geometry	11	21
Algebra II	6	19
Pre-Calculus	5	3
Calculus	1	1

ASSESSING DOCUMENTS, POLICIES, AND PRACTICES ON HOW TIME IS USED

When analyzing documents and looking at policies and practices, an analysis of how time is used is critical. Allington and Cunningham (1996), Crawford and Dougherty (2000), Oakes (1985), The Principals Exchange (2001a, 2001b), and others have found that there are disparities in the use of academic and nonacademic time related to student achievement. Their analyses in schools show that students who are in lower-achieving, low-income schools and those who are placed in lower tracks and remedial classes experience less academic time. Although many believe that we need longer days and longer school years, if we extend time and use it unwisely, it will probably not yield much better results in terms of academic achievement. What schools and districts should analyze is the use of the existing time. There will be some examples in this chapter, but schools should think about more ways to look at how they use time and the link to student achievement.

Allington and Cunningham (1996) state,

> Across virtually every study of classroom effectiveness in elementary schools one finding stands out. That is, teachers who allocate more time to reading and language arts instruction are the teachers whose children show the greatest gains in literacy development. Another finding is that the amount of time allocated to teaching reading and writing varies substantially between schools. (p. 106)

In work with a low-achieving urban elementary school Allington and Cunningham found that teachers spent on average 45 minutes a day in reading instruction, in contrast to a suburban school that spent two hours a day on reading.

Oakes (1985) found that low-track classes spent much more time on control issues and low-level content in contrast to higher-track classes, where the focus was on academic learning and little time was wasted. The Principals Exchange (Whittier, CA), in their school evaluations, has found lots of wasted time at the beginning and end of the year in low-achieving schools. The disorganization related to scheduling, lack of books, and other issues results in a climate where teachers do not begin the prescribed curriculum until three weeks into the school year, and some stop formal instruction in May or after testing.

Some students may need more time for learning. Rather than using retention, schools need to analyze how to extend the day, tightly align tutoring with regular coursework, and possibly extend the year; they must also analyze the use of existing time and the value of nonacademic activities.

EXAMINING SCHOOL CALENDARS

An analysis of school calendars (Table 7.9) can reveal information about the distribution of instructional time and wasted use of instructional time. In some schools teachers do not start teaching grade-level materials until two to three weeks into the school year, citing the fact that students' schedules are not firmed up and that students are in and out and don't have books. Therefore teachers use this time to go over last year's work or have the kids watch videos and so forth. After the tests in April or May, some schools collect the books and have students do inconsequential types of assignments. School leaders need to pay as close attention to the amount of instructional time as to the level of content and pedagogy.

Using the school calendar, an analysis can be done on the number of instructional days devoted to teaching the prescribed curriculum such as reading, Algebra I, English 9, biology, and so forth. From the 180-day calendar shown in Table 7.9, the following pattern emerged.

The total shows that out of 180 days of in-school time, students are missing out on 53 days of instructional time. This represents over two months of school time in which students are not being appropriately instructed. The beginning and end of school are particularly problematic in terms of lost time, and these may be the first areas that need to be addressed. This sample is not atypical of what happens in many urban and low-achieving schools. The "academic press" is missing.

TEACHER PLAN BOOKS

Teachers' plan books can be rich sources of data for school leaders. The analysis, however, can only be useful if the information in a plan book adequately reflects what the teacher plans and then actually does.

An example of an analysis of an elementary school is shown in Table 7.10 (page 169). The analysis of the plan books was based on looking at the percentage of planned work meeting grade-level standards. It shows that according to teachers' plan books there is diminished work at grade-level standards for students in higher grades. What might be some implications for dialogue? What other information might be necessary? These data should be further disaggregated by teacher.

PART III: ASSESSING EQUITABLE CLASSROOM PRACTICES

Chapter 1 provided information on the impact of teacher quality on student achievement. It is important for schools to assess teaching practices related to equity and student achievement. Some professional development in this area will probably be

Table 7.9   Sample School Use of 180-Day Calendar

Allotted 180-Day School Year Time Schedule	How Time Is Spent	Holidays, etc.	Total Days Prescribed Instruction
September 5, 2001–October 1 *15 Days*	Review of last year's work 15 days		0 out of 15 allotted
October 1–November 24 *35 Days*	Prescribed instruction 33 days Unit testing 2 days	4 holidays	33 out of 35 allotted
November 25–December 23 *18 Days*	Prescribed instruction 16 days 2 days assembly, holiday parties	2 holidays	14 out of 18 allotted
December 23–January 31 *18 Days*	Prescribed instruction 15 days 3 days end-of-semester testing	10 holidays	16 out of 18 allotted
February 1–March 31 *40 Days*	Prescribed instruction 37 days 1 day Presidents' assembly 2 days review and end of unit testing	5 holidays	37 out of 40 allotted
April 1–May 31 *37 Days*	Prescribed instruction 17 days 10 days of test preparation 5 days state testing	7 holidays	22 out of 37 allotted
End of May 31–June *16 Days*	Prescribed instruction 5 days Testing, handing in books, trips, other end-of-year activities, etc.		5 out of 15 allotted
Total *180 Days*			Total 127 out of 180 allotted days spent on prescribed curriculum.

71% of total days allotted to prescribed instruction.

NOTE: Sample data.

Table 7.10 Percentage of Teachers' Planned Work Meeting Grade-Level Standards

Grade	Percent Grade Level Language Arts Standards	Percent Grade Level Mathematics Standards	Total Percent Grade Level Standards
1	100	100	100
2	100	40	70
3	50	100	75
4	50	80	65
5	30	80	55
6	10	30	20

SOURCE: An urban school.

necessary. There are many strategies to look at classroom practices. Many principals and classroom teachers are being trained to observe in classrooms. Programs such as GESA (Generating Expectations for Student Achievement) focus on issues of equity by addressing the impact of perceptions and beliefs on teacher practice. This section will provide some instruments and suggested data strategies that can be effective if they are focused and are done by skilled data gatherers. These are but a few ways, but they are focused on equity issues. Some suggested strategies are the following:

- Surveys
- Teacher observations
- Videos
- Student observations and shadowing
- Interviews, focus and study groups
- Parent and student information

A research framework for looking at opportunity to learn in classrooms is provided by Stevens (1993). Table 7.11 illustrates the framework.

SURVEY—THE EQUITABLE SCHOOL CLASSROOM

Previous instruments proposed ways for schools to measure whether they were moving toward a culture of high achievement and equity. Often teachers are isolated and teachers' knowledge about what other settings might look like is limited. Although equity is a desirable outcome, many do not have a notion of what this looks like in the real world of schools and classrooms. Systematic ways to assess this important issue are lacking. The Profile of an Equitable Classroom (Table 7.12, pages 171–174) was developed by The NETWORK, Inc. to assess equity in classrooms. The instrument describes what an equitable classroom looks like on a number of dimensions and can be used in any classroom. Schools and districts can develop their own instruments. The NETWORK, Inc. also offers a partner instrument, The Equitable School

Table 7.11 Opportunity to Learn: A Conceptual Framework Developed from International and National Research Studies to Investigate Students' Access to the Core Curriculum

Variable/Source	Definition
1. Content Coverage (Leinhart, 1983; Leinhart & Seewald, 1981; Walker & Schaffarzick, 1974; Wiley, 1990; Winfield, 1987; Yoon et al., 1990)	1. Teacher arranges for all students to have access to the core curriculum. Teacher arranges for all students to have access to critical subject matter topics. Teacher ensures that there is curriculum content and test content overlap.
2. Content Exposure (Brophy & Good, 1986; Wiley, 1990; Winfield, 1987)	2. Teacher organizes class so that there is time-on-task for students. Teacher provides enough time for students to learn the content of the curriculum and to cover adequately a specific topic or subject.
3. Content Emphasis (Floden et al., 1981; Goldenberg & Gallimore, 1991; LeMahieu & Leinhardt, 1985; McDonnell et al., 1990; Oakes, 1990; Shavelson & Stern, 1981; Stern, 1981)	3. Teacher selects topics from the curriculum to teach. Teacher selects the dominant level to teach the curriculum (recall, higher order skills). Teacher selects which skills to teach and which skills to emphasize to which groups of students (ability grouping and tracking or regrouping).
4. Quality of Instructional Delivery (Brophy & Good, 1986; Stevenson & Stigler, 1992)	4. Teacher uses teaching practices (coherent lessons) to produce students' academic achievement. Teacher uses varied teaching strategies to meet the educational needs of all students. Teacher has cognitive command of the subject matter.

SOURCE: Stevens, F. (1993). *Opportunity to learn: Issues of equity for poor and minority students.* Washington, DC: National Center for Educational Statistics.

Continuum. To obtain these instruments, plus other information and complete directions for administration, see the Resource section of this book.

Administering the Instrument

Specific details on administering the Profile of an Equitable Classroom should be obtained from the publishers. The instrument could be used at the initiation of reform to gather baseline information and at various stages of implementation. The

(text continues on page 175)

Table 7.12 Profile of an Equitable Classroom

By: Raymond M. Rose, Frances A. Kolb, and Nancy Barra-Zuman

This instrument begins to answer the question *"What does an equitable classroom look like?"* The components of an equitable classroom are those elements that we can see or hear; that is, they are measurable and observable.

Components:
Physical Environment
Curriculum
Language
Teaching Methodology
Behavior Management
Academic Evaluation
Classroom Integration

Profile of an Equitable Classroom was developed to be used in any classroom. The companion instrument, *The Equitable School Continuum*, also developed by The NETWORK, Inc., describes an equitable school. Curriculum materials and training have been developed in all subject areas to provide more specific assistance.

Version 3.1
The NETWORK, Inc.
136 Fenno Drive
Rowley, MA 01969-1004
© 1991

Reprinted with permission from: The NETWORK, Inc. 2001

Ideal	*Acceptable*	*Unacceptable*
I. Physical Environment		
Definition: The physical environment of the classroom includes displays on all bulletin boards, posters, and presentations used to decorate the room. It also includes the greetings and messages that are posted on walls. The location of desks, and general physical organization of the room are included as well.		
• The teacher visually portrays male and female representatives of various races, cultures, and physical disabilities in both traditional and non-traditional roles, and in pictorial displays. • The teacher structures the environment (e.g., seating arrangements and physical placement of furniture) to facilitate integration of all members of the class. • The teacher insures that adaptations are made in equipment and room organization so that the effect is a barrier-free environment.	• The teacher provides gender and race neutral visual images in pictorial displays. • The teacher structures the physical environment to be barrier-free when it is necessary.	• The teacher visually portrays people only in roles traditional for their race, gender, or culture. • The teacher portrays only one gender, race, or culture in visual displays. • The teacher's visual displays portray gender, race, ethnic, or physical disability stereotypes.

(continued)

Table 7.12   Continued

Ideal	Acceptable	Unacceptable
II. Curriculum		
Definition: The formal and informal content, which is taught in the classroom through lessons, activities, and modeling. Curriculum includes all aspects of a teacher's programs and activities that make up the complete program of education for the purpose of educating students.		
• The teacher's classroom activities are multi-cultural and gender-fair. The teacher includes classroom lessons to increase awareness, and counter the past effects of race, gender, ethnic, or physical disability bias and discrimination. • The teacher actively encourages students to accept and value diversity in themselves and others. • The teacher presents instruction and content that reflects a multi-cultural perspective. • The teacher encourages and enables students to examine their world from a variety of cultural perspectives.	• The teacher's classroom activities are multi-cultural and gender-fair. • The teacher sometimes will include activities that will result in students cooperating with other students.	• The teacher does not include the contributions of women or racial and ethnic minorities. Or the teacher fails to inform students that the people studied are not members of the dominant culture. • The teacher presents stereotyped views of groups of people. • The teacher presents materials that present only a single ethnocentric view of history, education, and culture.
III. Language		
Definition: The language and language style used in the classroom by the teacher, and what the teacher allows students to use.		
• The teacher uses inclusionary terms for people in all written and oral communication. • The teacher works with students to help them develop inclusionary language forms and styles and encourages all students to use those terms in their own communications. • The teacher discusses the negative impact of the use of derogatory terms in reference to race, gender, ethnic groups, or physical disabilities.	• The teacher uses inclusionary terms for people in all written and oral communication.	• The teacher uses derogatory terms in reference to any race, gender, or ethnic group. • The teacher repeatedly uses gender-limited language. • The teacher repeatedly mispronounces students' names. • The teacher is indifferent to the fact that students use derogatory terms in reference to any race, gender, ethnic, or physically disabled group.

Table 7.12 Continued

Ideal	Acceptable	Unacceptable
IV. Teaching Methodology		
Definition: The style, time, and method of attention directed at students by the teacher in the process of instruction.		
• The teacher provides the same amount of teaching attention to all students, but varies the type of attention to meet the student's need and style. • The teacher directs the classroom discussion to enable all students to participate. • The teacher provides a variety of different types and styles of attention to students to provide for the individual needs of students. • The teacher analyzes their interactions with students for differential patterns and takes action to counteract and balance differences.	• The teacher provides teaching attention to all students, but varies the type of attention to meet the student's need and style. • The teacher directs the classroom discussion to enable the majority of students to participate.	• The teacher provides students with different amounts of attention based on students' race, gender, ethnicity, or physical disability. • The teacher allows a student or group of students to dominate the class. • The teacher does not provide for the individual needs of students. • The teacher expresses no concern, nor takes any action to address imbalances in student interaction patterns.
V. Behavior Management		
Definition: The style, time, and methods used by the teacher to control student behavior in the class.		
• The teacher explicitly informs students in advance of acceptable and unacceptable behavior, and the consequences of their behavior. • The teacher reprimands all students equally for infractions of classroom or school rules. • The teacher regularly praises all students for good behavior. • The teacher does not allow or condone students to harass each other.	• The teacher usually informs students of their behavioral expectations. • The teacher reprimands all students equally for infractions of classroom or school rules. • The teacher praises all students for good behavior. • The teacher does not allow or condone students to harass each other.	• The teacher does not make rules clear to students. • The teacher reprimands students differently for behavioral infractions based on the students' race, gender, or national origin. • The teacher attributes stereotyped characteristics to a race, gender, physical disability, and/or national origin group in their efforts to control student behavior. • The teacher does not take action to prevent students to harass other students based on race, gender, ethnicity, and/or physical disabilities.

(continued)

Table 7.12 Continued

Ideal	Acceptable	Unacceptable
VI. Academic Evaluation		
Definition: The style and systems used by the teacher to evaluate and report student academic performance.		
• The teacher has a set of high academic expectations for all students without respect for the students' race, gender, ethnicity, or physical disabilities. The teacher communicates those expectations to all students. • The teacher praises students for the intellectual quality of their work, irrespective of the students' race, gender, national origin, or physical disabilities from a set of criteria which has been announced to the students. • The teacher uses a variety of methods to evaluate student academic performance.	• The teacher has a single set of academic expectations for all students without respect for the students' race, gender, ethnicity, or physical disabilities. • The teacher acknowledges the intellectual quality of students' work, irrespective of the student's race, gender, national origin, or physical disabilities from a set of criteria which has been announced to the students. • The teacher has a limited number of methods of evaluating student performance.	• The teacher uses a different set of criteria for evaluating the academic work of students, based on the student's race, gender, national origin, or physical disability. • The teacher evaluates students differently for the same performance, basing the evaluation on the student's gender, race, physical disability, and/or ethnicity. • The teacher uses only a single method to evaluate student performance.
VII. Classroom Integration		
Definition: The structure and activities, which the teacher formally and informally uses to facilitate student social and academic cooperation.		
• The teacher promotes cooperation and integration of students through activities, which help students of different skill levels, genders, physical disabilities, races, and ethnic groups to work together more effectively. • The teacher structures classroom activities in order to promote the development and exercise of leadership skills among a variety of students.	• The teacher assigns classroom seating patterns, project groups, and other structured activities to integrate students by race, gender, physical disability, and/or ethnic group.	• The teacher groups students for any activity by race, gender, ethnicity, or physical disability. • The teacher allows segregated patterns to exist by allowing students to group themselves. • The teacher assigns classroom tasks on the basis of a student's race, gender, ethnicity, and/or physical disability. • The teacher does not encourage a multi-racial/multi-cultural type of student leadership. • The teacher structures classroom tasks so as to have competition between different genders, races, ethnic groups, and/or physical disabilities. • The teacher places students in same-skill instructional groups for all academic instruction.

instrument shows three categories—"Ideal," "Acceptable," and "Unacceptable"—to describe where a classroom falls on the continuum. Because some of the components will take time to reform, different parts might be administered at relevant times. Categories could be tallied under each component and displayed on bar graphs to show ranges of equity within classrooms. If possible, it would be useful to disaggregate the data by respondents' race/ethnicity and number of years teaching to see if patterns emerge. This could present implications for staff development.

If a self-reporting process is used in which members of the school community individually fill out the instrument, a cross-check of these perceptions may be sought from outsiders, who may rate the environment differently. This can inspire a richer discussion that leads to a more accurate picture. Whatever actions are implicated through the instrument should be planned so they can be well implemented and successfully accomplished. Some schools may have lots of "Unacceptable," leading staff to feel overwhelmed; others may not. Participants should have sufficient opportunity to implement reforms before the instrument is readministered.

TEACHER OBSERVATIONS

Teacher observations should be frequent and focused. Table 7.13 offers one way to gather data and quantify by teacher, by grade, and by school. Table 7.14 offers information using narrative data. This information can target specific support for teacher development and assess teacher strengths related to student achievement. All the terms used need operational definitions so there are common meanings in conversations. Schools and districts should use information from the literature to help frame the definitions.

Table 7.13 can gives clues related to different teachers' strengths. Schools need to clearly describe each area and to develop agreed-upon criteria. Teacher D appears to have strength in several areas. How do those talents get shared? No teacher

Table 7.13   Observation Summaries, Fall 2001: Grade 4

Teacher	Equitable Learning Environment			Engaging and Supporting All Students			Teaching the Standards: Subject Matter Depth			Quality of Instructional Delivery		
	–	X	+	–	X	+	–	X	+	–	X	+
Teacher A	1			1				1		1		
Teacher B		1		1			1				1	
Teacher C		1			1			1			1	
Teacher D			1			1		1				1
Total for Grade	1	2	1	2	1	1	1	3		1	2	1
Key: Weak – Adequate X Superior +												

SOURCE: Instrument revised with permission from the Principals Exchange, Whittier, CA.

Table 7.14 Observer's Conclusions

Observer: Focus of Observation:	Teacher: Date:
Conclusion	*Examples*
All African American students were in lower-level groups and were being taught below standards.	The content they were being taught was weak and the teacher assistant taught them for the total class time allotted for reading.
Little evidence of relevant teaching	The teacher did not attempt to relate the content to the students' lives, and there were many times when this could have happened. Students were not actively engaged in their learning.
Recommendations based on above observations	1. At a minimum, grade level content standards should be appropriately taught to all students. Consider professional development in the areas of content and instruction, as well as participation in TESA (Teacher Expectations Student Achievement). Make sure that students have access to high-quality instruction at all times. Consider restructuring the use of teaching assistants. 2. Provide extensive support and professional development in culturally relevant teaching and the ways that it is related to student achievement. The teacher needs immediate strategies in ways to check for comprehension.
Meeting date to discuss observation:	

Instrument revised with permission from the Principals Exchange, Whittier, CA.

is superior in "Subject Matter Depth." What are the implications for professional development?

Narrative observations are also important. Many forms and formats are available. The one in Table 7.14 is formatted so the observer states his or her conclusions and then gives specific examples of what was observed. Evidence to support the observation is critical, particularly when addressing equity issues. Therefore, the observers should be knowledgeable about what is being observed.

Another excellent source for data is through the use of videotaping. Teachers can use this for their own self-evaluations, or teachers can dialogue in groups. Guidelines should be used to help guide the conversations.

Table 7.15   Comparison of Levels of Instruction Taught and Levels of Student Work Received

Grade	Percent of Instructional Time on Grade Level Standards	Percent of Student Work Meeting Grade Level Standards
1	100	92
2	95	85
3	80	60
4	70	55
5	60	50
6	100	40

SOURCE: An urban school.

Teacher interviews, focus groups, and study groups are also useful in looking at classroom practices. Consider questions such as the following:

- Curriculum: How do you decide what to teach? What documents influence what you teach?
- Assessment/intervention: How do you determine if students are learning? What do you do when students don't meet your goals? What do you do with assessment results?
- General information: What at your school is promoting student achievement? What is not promoting student achievement? What are your recommendations for promoting student achievement? (Questions courtesy of the Principals Exchange, 2001a, 2001b.)

Teachers can analyze the amount of instructional time they spend on grade-level content versus the level of work they receive from students. This has implications for understanding how effective the instructional delivery was for different groups of students. An example gathered from some urban teachers is found in Table 7.15. It reveals uneven patterns from grade to grade. In spite of the fact that the teachers in Grade 6 stated that they spent 100% of the time on grade-level standards instruction, only 40% of the work received was at grade level. The next steps might involve an examination of how the instruction was delivered.

Study groups were described in Chapter 5. Refer to that chapter for processes to conduct these types of inquiry groups.

OBSERVING STUDENTS IN CLASS AND SCHOOL

This strategy is one that is particularly useful in finding out what students are experiencing in classes and in other aspects of the school culture. Students can be identified by academic achievement using indicators such as test scores, course

Table 7.16   Student Observation

Observer: Date:	Student: Academic Level, etc.:	
Time/Setting	*Observation*	*Comments*

enrollments, grades, and so forth. They are rated as low, average, or high achievers. A day or some part of the day is selected when students will be observed and their experiences recorded. Pay attention to what is happening to the student as a result of the school experience. This can provide rich data about what is working for students and what is not. Observations can also be done to assess the academic experiences of diverse racial/ethnic and gender groups. The observation format can be open-ended or structured. As many observations should be done as possible in order to observe patterns. Of course, having other adults in the class may affect the dynamics, but I have found this strategy to still be useful. The students are not told that they are being observed, and sometimes teachers are not told which students are being observed in an attempt to keep the setting as natural as possible. (See Table 7.16.)

PARENT AND STUDENT INFORMATION

Parents and students are valuable sources of information. They need to be integral in assessing practices and progress. Chapter 8 will provide some suggestions related to parents and students.

8

Listening to Student and Parent Voices

At a staff meeting where teachers, counselors, and administrators are deliberating the low achievement of students in their school, the subject of parent involvement surfaced. There are comments such as, "If the parents showed more interest and came to school more often the kids would do better. They don't care about their child's academic achievement. The students have no ambitions. They don't want to do the work. They don't turn in the homework, so why bother to assign it?"

At a meeting with parents, the following comments are heard: "The homework is never checked by teachers. We need homework directions in Spanish. Kids should have homework every night. Teachers need to explain homework. More homework—20 to 30 minutes for K through 2 and one hour for Grades 3 through 5. My child has too many substitutes, and they don't follow the plans the teachers leave. My child enjoys reading. We want evening classes for parents. The school needs to jump-start the program and be consistent from teacher to teacher. Tutoring needs to be done by a qualified person with a focus on the area for remediation—not old homework. Videos should not be shown during the week. How much time goes to special events and draws away from regular instruction? There are inconsistent standards at a grade level—and inconsistent expectations for students. Office personnel need to be more approachable. Perfect attendance breakfast was great! I want my child to go to college. Will he be prepared?"

In a meeting with students, the following comments are heard: "We don't do homework because no one checks it. I don't understand the homework. I do my homework in class. I want harder work. I ask for help, but the teacher has no time to help me. She leaves right after school. We can't bring our books home because we have to share them with another class. The work is too easy. I'm bored. I am tired of watching videos all day long. We always do projects in a group. I am tired of that."

Overview

The scenarios above clearly show that parents, students, and educators can have very different perceptions about why things are the way they are. The voices of students and parents are often left out when we assess school cultures and expectations. This is particularly true in schools where there are large numbers of low-income children. The educators make assumptions about the aspirations of both parents and students based on limited data. Students' and parents' opinions are frequently not valued. Because they may not respond to the school's approaches of communication, it is assumed that parents are uninterested or don't care. I have found in the data that I have collected and analyzed and from others that this is simply not true. The expectations and aspirations for educational attainment are high. There is often cultural dissonance between the school, the parents, and the students in the manner that information, knowledge, and access get communicated. It is important to get these missing voices on record and to use the data for shaping reform strategies.

Assumptions that teachers, counselors, and administrators hold about parents and children who are of color and low income need to be tested for accuracy. This chapter will suggest some approaches for inclusion of parent and student voices that will help test those assumptions. These suggestions should not be viewed as comprehensive but as examples of approaches.

California Tomorrow, a nonprofit organization whose mission promotes opportunity and participation, has developed a useful document that describes some strategies for using student voice as well as the benefits and drawbacks of each strategy (see Figure 8.1). This can serve as a useful tool in designing inquiries that include students.

STUDENT AND PARENT-GUARDIAN QUESTIONNAIRES

Many low-income parents and parents of color as well as their children have had limited access to information about what is needed to prepare for postsecondary education. At the high school level, data show that counselors spend 80% of their time with seniors who are going to college. The questionnaires presented in this section were developed for middle and senior high schools, but modifications can be made for elementary schools. The surveys can generate valuable information about aspirations, students' access and opportunities in the schools, and parents' and students' expectation for higher education.

When to Use or Develop Surveys

The following questionnaires should be used at the beginning of the reform process:

- High School Student Questionnaire (Figure 8.2, pages 183–185)
- High School Parent-Guardian Questionnaire (Figure 8.3, page 186)

Figure 8.1 Tools of the Trade

USING STUDENT VOICE STRATEGIES:
When should you elicit student voice? While all approaches to eliciting student voice are useful, each has distinct drawbacks and benefits. You'll need to think about how to protect students and ensure confidentiality, particularly if they'll be addressing subjects that arouse adults' anxiety or hostility. The following chart may help you to select the best approach in terms of student safety, intimacy, and adult receptivity.

STUDENT VOICE APPROACH	BENEFITS/DRAWBACKS/CONSIDERATIONS
Focus groups (to brainstorm issues and get a sense of priorities; to explore a limited number of issues and get greater depth of understanding)	**Benefits**: Students feed on each other's comments, and you can get more depth than in written forms of response; can get responses from many students in the time it would take to interview just one; students like to talk. **Drawbacks**: Time and labor intensive to set up; lose individual stories and detail; sometimes unusual experiences don't get expressed because of peer pressure to discuss shared concerns. **Overall**: Great way to get overall themes and patterns, to get sense of priorities, to get reactions to ideas, to hear student words.
Surveys and questionnaires	**Benefits**: Relatively easy to administer; can get interview responses from many more students than through focus groups; anonymous responses can provide more protection for students and sometimes more honest responses. **Drawbacks**: Any written form of response is harder for students and often yields less depth and "meat" than formats where they talk; surveys often not taken seriously by students; restricted to forced choice or relatively simple responses. **Overall**: Good for finding out the extent of a problem, for getting responses across large numbers of students. Can be difficult to design a good questionnaire.
Quick-writes (quickly and informally written response to a given prompt)	**Benefits**: Easy to administer; takes little time; can get lots of students' responses; encourages writing; can be done across multiple classrooms without any particular teacher skill; responses are in students' words (compared to surveys in which they choose prewritten responses). **Drawbacks**: Sometimes what students have to say is filtered and limited by their writing ability and comfort; restricted to a single prompt. **Overall**: Good for response to specific prompt.
Panels	**Benefits**: Real students talking to real teachers—the face-to-face contact can be powerful; somewhat protected format for students; responses are in the voices of students. **Drawbacks**: Students can become shy or intimidated by the face-to-face "in front of the room" format; teachers need to be prepared to listen respectfully.
Shadowing and observing	**Benefits**: Allows teachers to really see and feel what a student's day and life are like in a school; offers more holistic cues into student experience than a report from a student about their experience. **Drawbacks**: This is a one-on-one activity, very labor-intensive; hard for many teachers to participate or for any teacher to shadow observe numerous students.
Fishbowls (a few people have a discussion, often in response to a prompt, while others listen in)	**Benefits**: Less structured and less scary than a panel, but allows teachers to see students and hear them talk; the discussion nature of a fishbowl allows students to feed off each other and for the facilitator to probe for deeper responses; requires less preparation than a panel. **Drawbacks**: Allows less depth of individual stories than interviews or panels.

(continued)

Figure 8.1   Continued

Interviews	**Benefits**: Good for getting individual stories and perspectives in depth; for reconstructing someone's experiences and history, for eliciting perspectives about an issue, etc.; can be more comfortable and often powerful for students because they are talking to a real person (compared to surveys); more revealing than surveys or questionnaires because of depth of response and opportunities for probes; more chance for individual voices than focus groups or panels; can be powerful connections between the teacher and student. **Drawbacks**: Very labor-intensive; interviews take a lot of time to prepare, conduct, and analyze.

SOURCE: Olsen, L., & Jaramillo, A. (1999). *Turning the tides of exclusion: A guide for educators and advocates for immigrant students* (pp. 299–300). Oakland, CA: California Tomorrow.

- Middle School Student Questionnaire (Figure 8.4, pages 187–188)
- Middle School Parent-Guardian Questionnaire (Figure 8.5, pages 189–190)
- Senior's Application to College Survey (Figure 8.6, page 190)

The Middle School Student Questionnaire and the Middle School Parent-Guardian Questionnaire could be modified for use at the elementary level. The staff should review the questions, then make additions or modifications. These questionnaires will need to be completed well in advance of staff planning so that the summary data are available when the school staff begins to engage in intense discussion about reforms in the institutional culture. If possible, complete these before administering instruments such as Perceptions of Attitudes, Readiness, and Commitment to Reform (Figure 7.1a) and other culture surveys. The timing will depend on the culture of the school and the staff's readiness for reform. These data can be used to trigger a commitment to reform, to validate or dispute common assumptions, and to provide baseline data. A retreat or an off-site setting is a good environment for these kinds of discussions.

The Senior's Application to College Survey (Figure 8.6) can be used several times during each year to catch seniors who may be falling through the cracks. November, January, and March may be the best times. The survey could be expanded to include information on acceptances, but it should not be too lengthy and should only be used to gather essential information for quick interventions by counselors and teachers. The Senior's Application to College Survey is useful to gauge which seniors have filed applications, what their aspirations are, and if they need assistance. This is particularly important information for students who may be first-generation college goers. There may not be anyone at home with knowledge of steps that students need to take to meet college requirements and deadlines.

The Senior's Application to College Survey should be administered to every senior. Some schools select a class or classes that every senior is taking and ask the teachers to collaborate and cooperate in getting the data. When teachers understand the purpose, they are usually very glad to help out. This approach has been quite successful for quick turnaround. This should not take more than 10 minutes to fill out. Students must fill in their names so counselors or others can follow up with them.

(text continues on page 188)

Figure 8.2 High School Student Questionnaire

School: _____

Date: _____

Directions: We want to improve the quality of your education. Therefore, we are asking you to take part in a survey that includes students from our high schools. Please answer all questions by checking your answer, by circling the number that corresponds to your choice, or by filling in the blank. There are no right or wrong answers. You do not need to put your name on the survey.

1. How far in school do you think your parents/guardians want you to go?
   ____ Graduate from high school but go no further.
   ____ Attend vocational, trade or business school after high school.
   ____ Attend and graduate from a 2-year college.
   ____ Attend and graduate from a 4-year college or university.
   ____ Attend graduate school.
   ____ Don't know.

2. What are your plans after graduation from high school?
   ____ Attend a 2-year college.
   ____ Attend a 4-year college or university.
   ____ Get vocational or technical training.
   ____ Work full-time.
   ____ Military service.
   ____ Other (please specify _____)

3a. Do you have a career goal?   ____ Yes   ____ No

3b. If yes, describe your career goal.
   _____

4. Which of the following best describes the focus of your high school classes?
   ____ Preparation for college.
   ____ Vocational or technical education.
   ____ General or regular education (without a focus on college preparation or vocational education).
   ____ Other (please specify _____)

5. Which of the following best describes your average high school grades?
   ____ A– to A+
   ____ B– to B+
   ____ C– to C+
   ____ Below C

6. Indicate the course that best describes the mathematics course you are taking this year or the last mathematics course you have taken.
   ____ Basic/General Math
   ____ Pre-Algebra
   ____ Algebra II
   ____ Geometry
   ____ Trigonometry/Math Analysis
   ____ Other (please specify _____)

(continued)

Figure 8.2   Continued

7. Indicate the course title that best describes the science class you are taking this year or the last science course you have taken.
    _____ Life or Physical Science
    _____ Earth Science
    _____ Biology
    _____ Advanced Biology
    _____ Chemistry
    _____ Other (please specify _____)

8. Do you have a plan for the courses you will take throughout high school?   _____ Yes   _____ No

9. When was this plan made for you?
    _____ 9th Grade
    _____ 10th Grade
    _____ 11th Grade
    _____ 12th Grade

10. How frequently do you ask the following people for information regarding what courses to take?

	Never Ask	Ask Occasionally	Ask Frequently
Teachers	1	2	3
Counselors	1	2	3
Parents or guardians	1	2	3
Other students	1	2	3
Others (for example, principal, counselor assistants); Specify _____	1	2	3

11. How helpful are the following people in providing information regarding what courses to take?

	Not Helpful	Somewhat Helpful	Very Helpful
Teachers	1	2	3
Counselors	1	2	3
Parents or guardians	1	2	3
Other students	1	2	3
Others (for example, principal, counselor assistants); Specify _____	1	2	3

12. During this school year has your *school counselor* done the following?

	Yes	No
• Met with you to plan the courses you will take during the remainder of high school?	1	2
• Encouraged you to take courses which are challenging for you?	1	2
• Assisted you in getting the appropriate and/or necessary help so you could be successful in courses that were challenging for you?	1	2
• Discussed going to college or applying for scholarships?	1	2
• Discussed career opportunities or your career goals?	1	2
• Met with you to review your educational plans and your progress toward them?	1	2

13. How many times have you met with your counselor this year?
    _____ Once
    _____ Twice
    _____ Three times
    _____ Four times
    _____ Five or more times
    _____ Not at all

Figure 8.2 Continued

14. Since the beginning of this school year, how often have you talked about the following with your parents or guardians?

	Never	Once or Twice	Three or More Times
• Selecting courses at school.	1	2	3
• School activities or events of particular interest to you.	1	2	3
• Your career goals.	1	2	3
• Going to college or applying for scholarships.	1	2	3
• Your plans following high school such as work or college.	1	2	3

15. Since the beginning of this school year, how often have your parents or guardians done any of the following?

	Never	Once or Twice	Three or More Times
• Had a discussion with one of your teachers.	1	2	3
• Had a discussion with a high school counselor.	1	2	3
• Attended a school meeting.	1	2	3

16. Please indicate your agreement or disagreement with the following statements.

	Strongly Disagree	Disagree	Neutral	Agree	Strongly Agree
• I understand the relationship between the courses I take and the options I have after high school.	1	2	3	4	5
• I am getting a good education at this school.	1	2	3	4	5
• My high school counselor has helped me select courses.	1	2	3	4	5
• Most of my classes are interesting to me.	1	2	3	4	5
• I like to take classes where I have to work hard.	1	2	3	4	5

17. What grade are you in?   9   10   11   12

18. Are you male or female?   _____ Male   _____ Female

19. What is your ethnic background?

_____ American Indian or Alaskan Native	_____ African American
_____ Pacific Islander/Filipino/Asian	_____ White
_____ Latino	_____ Other

Revised by The Achievement Council with permission from the California Department of Education.

Figure 8.3   High School Parent-Guardian Questionnaire

Your Child's School: _____

Grade: _____

We are engaged in a process to improve our school. We need imput from parents as well as students, counselors, teachers and administrators. Your opinion is valued and we appreciate your taking the time to complete this survey.

Completed surveys need to be returned in the attached envelope by _____.

Directions: We are asking you to take part in a study that includes parents with children in all high schools. Please answer all questions by checking your answer, by circling the number that corresponds to your choice, or by filling in the blank. There are no right or wrong answers. You do not need to put your name on the survey.

1a. Do you belong to a parent group(s)?   _____ Yes   _____ No

1b. If yes, please list which ones.

_____

_____

2. How far in school do you think you want your child to go?
    _____ Graduate from high school but go no further.
    _____ Attend vocational, trade or business school after high school.
    _____ Attend and graduate from a 2-year college.
    _____ Attend and graduate from a 4-year college or university.
    _____ Attend graduate school.
    _____ Don't know.

3a. Does your child have a career goal?   _____ Yes   _____ No

3b. If yes, describe your child's career goal.

_____

4. Which of the following best describes the focus of your child's high school classes?
    _____ Preparation for college.
    _____ Vocational or technical education.
    _____ General or regular education (without a focus on college preparation or vocational education).
    _____ Other (please specify _____)

5. Which of the following best describes your child's average high school grades?
    _____ A– to A+
    _____ B– to B+
    _____ C– to C+
    _____ Below C

6. What is your ethnic background?
    _____ American Indian or Alaskan Native
    _____ Pacific Islander/Filipino/Asian
    _____ Latino
    _____ African American
    _____ White
    _____ Other

Revised by The Achievement Council with permission from the California Department of Education.

Figure 8.4   Middle School Student Questionnaire

School: _____

Date: _____

Directions: We want to improve the quality of your education. Therefore, we are asking you to take part in a survey that includes students from our middle schools. Please answer all questions by checking your answer, by circling the number that corresponds to your choice, or by filling in the blank. There are no right or wrong answers. You do not need to put your name on the survey.

1.   What grade are you in?   6   7   8

2.   How far in school do you think your parents/guardians want you to go?
      _____ High school graduate.
      _____ Attend a 2-year college.
      _____ Attend a 4-year college or university.
      _____ Work full-time.
      _____ Military service.
      _____ Other (please specify _____)

3.   What are your plans after graduation from high school?
      _____ High school graduate.
      _____ Attend a 2-year college.
      _____ Attend a 4-year college or university.
      _____ Work full-time.
      _____ Military service.
      _____ Other (please specify _____)

4a. Do you have a career goal?   _____ Yes   _____ No

4b. If yes, describe your career goal.

      _____

      _____

5.   Which of the following best describes your average middle school grades?
      _____ A– to A+
      _____ B– to B+
      _____ C– to C+
      _____ Below C

6.   How often have you discussed your career goals with your parents or guardians?
      _____ Never   _____ Once or Twice   _____ Three or More Times

7.   How often have you discussed going to college with your parents or guardians?
      _____ Never   _____ Once or Twice   _____ Three or More Times

8.   How often have you discussed your plans after high school with your parents or guardians?
      _____ Never   _____ Once or Twice   _____ Three or More Times

9.   Have any of your teachers met with you to plan the courses you will take during high school?
      _____ Yes   _____ No

10. Have any of your teachers encouraged you to take courses which are challenging to you?
      _____ Yes   _____ No

11. Have any of your teachers helped you succeed in courses which are challenging for you?
      _____ Yes   _____ No

(continued)

Figure 8.4 Continued

---

12. Have any of your teachers discussed career opportunities or your career goals?
    _____ Yes   _____ No

13. Are you male or female?   _____ Male   _____ Female

14. What is your ethnic background?
    _____ American Indian or Alaskan Native
    _____ Pacific Islander/Filipino/Asian
    _____ Latino
    _____ African American
    _____ White
    _____ Other

15. How far in school did your mother go?
    _____ Not a high school graduate.
    _____ High school graduate.
    _____ Some college.
    _____ College degree.
    _____ Advanced college degree.
    _____ Don't know.

16. How far in school did your father go?
    _____ Not a high school graduate.
    _____ High school graduate.
    _____ Some college.
    _____ College degree.
    _____ Advanced college degree.
    _____ Don't know.

Revised by The Achievement Council with permission from the California Department of Education.

Administering the Questionnaires

Schools may choose to have all students fill out the High School Student Questionnaire (Figure 8.2) and the Middle School Student Questionnaire (Figure 8.4). Sufficient staff must be assigned to input all the data. A school may also choose to survey a random sample, but only with the assistance of an experienced evaluator. The student questionnaires should be administered in classrooms during a regular class period. It is important to brief all personnel who will be responsible for administration. Both students and adults will need to understand the purpose and how the results will be used. Do not ask for student names, only demographic data, so students will feel free to answer questions without any fear that the information might somehow be used in a negative way. Terminology should be explained, and students should be given the opportunity to ask for clarification during administration. The purpose is to find out information, not to penalize students for lack of understanding.

The High School Parent-Guardian Questionnaire (Figure 8.3) and the Middle School Parent-Guardian Questionnaire (Figure 8.5) can be sent to a random sample of parents. Some kind of coding will be useful so second mailings can be sent if necessary. If feasible, self-addressed stamped envelopes should be included for more

Figure 8.5   Middle School Parent-Guardian Questionnaire

Your Child's School: _____

Grade: _____

We are engaged in a process to improve our school. We need imput from parents as well as students, counselors, teachers and administrators. Your opinion is valued and we appreciate your taking the time to complete this survey.

Completed surveys need to be returned in the attached envelope by _____ .

Directions: We are asking you to take part in a study that includes parents with children in all middle schools. Please answer all questions by checking your answer, by circling the number that corresponds to your choice or by filling in the blank. There are no right or wrong answers. You do not need to put your name on the survey.

1.   What is the name of your child's school?   _____

2.   What grade is your child in?   6   7   8

3a. Do you belong to a parent group(s)?   _____ Yes   _____ No

3b. If yes, please list which ones.
     _____
     _____

4.   How far in school did you go?
     _____ Not a high school graduate.
     _____ High school graduate.
     _____ Some college.
     _____ College degree.
     _____ Advanced college degree.
     _____ Don't know.

5.   How far in school do you think you want your child to go?
     _____ Graduate from high school but go no further.
     _____ Attend vocational, trade or business school after high school.
     _____ Attend and graduate from a 2-year college.
     _____ Attend and graduate from a 4-year college or university.
     _____ Attend graduate school.
     _____ Don't know.

6a. Does your child have a career goal?   _____ Yes   _____ No

6b. If yes, describe your child's career goal.
     _____
     _____

7.   Which of the following best describes the focus of your child's middle school classes?
     _____ Preparation for college.
     _____ Vocational or technical education.
     _____ General or regular education (without a focus on college preparation or vocational education).
     _____ Other (please specify _____)

8.   Which of the following best describes your child's average middle school grades?
     _____ A– to A+
     _____ B– to B+
     _____ C– to C+
     _____ Below C

(continued)

Figure 8.5   Continued

9. Is your child taking courses that lead into a college-preparatory program?
    (Example: Algebra, Foreign Language)
    _____ Yes   _____ No

10. Since the beginning of this school year, how often have you done any of the following?

	Never	Once or Twice	Three or More Times
• Had a discussion with one of your child's teachers.	1	2	3
• Had a discussion with a counselor.	1	2	3
• Attended a school meeting.	1	2	3

11. What is your ethnic background?
    _____ American Indian or Alaskan Native
    _____ Pacific Islander/Filipino/Asian
    _____ Latino
    _____ African American
    _____ White
    _____ Other

Revised by The Achievement Council with permission from the California Department of Education.

Figure 8.6   Senior's Application to College Survey

School/District: _____
Student Name: _____
Counselor: _____
Date: _____

Information is needed from all seniors who have filed admission applications to colleges or universities, or who need to do so. Please check as many of the following that apply to your situation so that we can assist you with your plan after high school.

_____ Yes, I filled out a college application.
_____ No, I did not fill out a college application, but I would like to go to college.
_____ I need assistance on the financial aid application.
_____ I need assistance in selecting a 2-year college.
_____ I need assistance in selecting a 4-year college or university.
_____ I need assistance in getting a job after college.
_____ Other needs.

rapid returns. Also parents should be sent an explanatory letter that states the goals, the purpose for the information, and how it will be used and shared. Parents should be given the option to fill this out anonymously or to sign their names. Parents should also be notified that they have the opportunity to see the summary data and the plans for improving outcomes.

The High School Student and Parent-Guardian Questionnaires and the Middle School Student and Parent-Guardian Questionnaires should be administered about every three years to assess progress over time.

Data Analysis and Presentations

The data from the High School Student and Parent-Guardian Questionnaires (Figures 8.2 and 8.3) and the Middle School Student and Parent-Guardian Questionnaires (Figures 8.4 and 8.5) can be summarized in a variety of ways, depending on what questions are to be answered. They first can be used to establish baseline information. They can be disaggregated by grade, race, ethnicity, gender, and so forth to tell the story of access, opportunity, and aspirations. The data also identify whom students go to for information and what types of opportunity, access, and aspirations they and their parents possess regarding postsecondary education.

This chapter also includes some possible data presentations. The students' voices in this setting inform us that students most frequently ask their parents or guardians about what courses to take (see Figure 8.7a, Whom Do Students Ask for Help About What Courses to Take?). Counselors rate second. Also, students ask other students for assistance more than they ask teachers. Students have daily contact with teachers, yet Figure 8.7b (What Kind of Assistance With Planning Courses Did Students Receive From Teachers?) shows that teachers do not spend a lot of time discussing future options with students, and only 38% of students indicated that teachers encouraged them to take courses that are challenging to them. Interestingly, in Figure 8.7c (Who Do Students Say Gave Them the Most Helpful Information Regarding Which Courses to Take?), students consider information gained from counselors to be the most useful, but they also named their peers as a source of information. What are some possible implications? For example, should the school consider training some students to counsel their peers? Also, parents need access to information. These data raise questions about practices, expectations, and roles of teachers and counselors. They might have more meaning if they were disaggregated to see if some groups have different types of distributions.

The Senior's Application to College Survey presentations (Figure 8.8, page 193) can provide a year-to-year or a within-year look at how a school is doing regarding the numbers and percentage of students filling out applications to college and for financial aid.

This was administered in an actual high school in the spring, and the results helped to challenge existing practices. Figure 8.8 shows a baseline from the first administration and year 2 data after the school altered some of its practices. Although there is an increase in the percentage of students filling out applications, there is still a sizable percentage of seniors (33%) who have aspirations for college who did not fill out applications. The school needs to continue to improve. Are the adults aware of the students' desires, and how does this get leveraged to improved academic performance?

Although these are summarized data, the information comes from surveys filled out by individual students. The counselors and other advisers can then use this to monitor individual students. The data also can be disaggregated by counselor, student groups, and so forth. The full school staff should see all of the data from this survey. This raises questions about access to information: Are these students eligible for college? Which students had access, and which did not? Looking at individual students and gathering more data can give a fuller picture. The students have the aspirations, but how do they begin to make them reality?

Figure 8.7   Student and Parent-Guardian Questionnaires: Sample Presentation of a School's Summarized Data

a.   Whom Do Students Ask for Help About What Courses to Take?

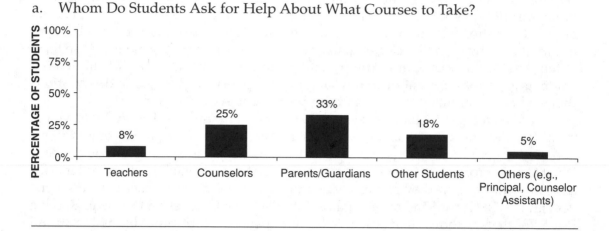

b.   What Kind of Assistance With Planning Courses Did Students Receive From Teachers?

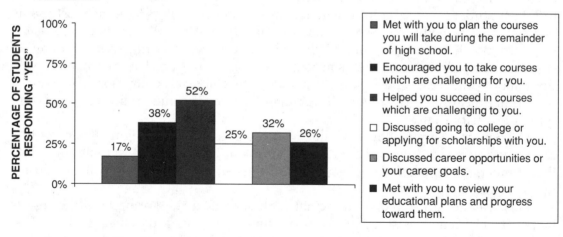

c.   Who Do Students Say Gave Them the Most Helpful Information Regarding Which Courses to Take?

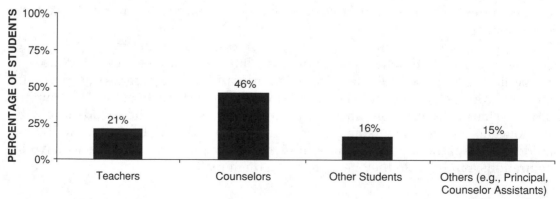

SOURCE: An urban school district.

Figure 8.8 Senior's Application to College Survey: Sample Presentation of a School's Summarized Data

	School/District:			
	Year One: Total Number of Students Responding: 336		**Year Two: Total Number of Students Responding: 336**	
	#	%	#	%
1) Yes, I filled out a college application.	115	34	148	44
2) No, I did not fill out a college application, but I would like to go to college.	140	42	111	33
3) I need assistance on the financial aid application.	63	19	60	18
4) I need assistance in selecting a 2-year college.	53	16	47	14
5) I need assistance in selecting a 4-year college or university.	32	10	27	8
6) I need assistance in getting a job after college.	61	18	60	18
7) Other needs.	62	19	57	17

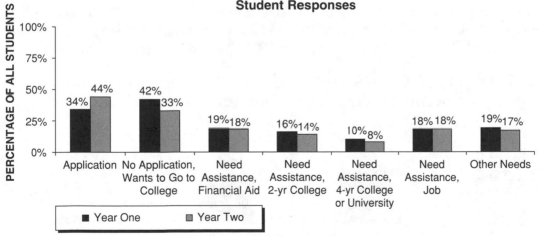

Discussion and Cautionary Notes

Some of these questionnaires require extensive input of data and the skills to manipulate the data in meaningful ways. School leaders must commit to gather, analyze, and share these data and to see them as valuable in decision making and reform. Computer capability is important, although the Senior's Application to College Survey (Figure 8.6) can be administered quickly without the use of technology. Once the questionnaires are in the system, the subsequent input should take a much shorter time. Schools and districts that have personnel or others in the community with expertise in sampling techniques might suggest approaches that would greatly reduce the numbers taking the High School Student and Parent-Guardian Questionnaires (Figures 8.2 and 8.3) and the Middle School Student and Parent-Guardian

Questionnaires (Figures 8.4 and 8.5). Each senior must take the Senior's Application to College Survey, however, because it seeks individual rather than whole-school data.

Because so much information will be generated, it might be wise to present different pieces at different times, rather than asking the school community to try digesting it all at once. The data might well leave more questions than they might answer, and follow-up discussions with students and parents will be critical. Be sure to share with parents and students the results of these surveys and to include them in the analysis of the data.

ASPIRATIONS AND REALITY

Figure 8.9 shows combined data to describe the disparities in student aspirations for four-year colleges and actual enrollments. These data are disaggregated by race/ethnicity. The combined pieces of information suggest that school processes are leading to inequitable outcomes. Students and their parents who want college careers are not being steered toward their goals. These presentations can be used to question underlying assumptions about different racial/ethnic groups' aspirations. Again, these can serve as baseline indicators to describe present conditions and to provide the impetus for improvement.

Figure 8.9 shows that when African American and Latino parents and students were asked about their desires to attend a four-year institution of higher education (baccalaureate degree-granting institution), a high percentage (55%) of African American parents and 49% of African American students desired four-year college enrollment. However, only 8% enrolled in a four-year college. Similarly, 39% of Latino parents and 38% of Latino students expected to go to a four-year college. The actual

Figure 8.9   Comparison of Students' and Parents' Expectations for College Enrollment to Percentage of June Graduates Enrolled in College

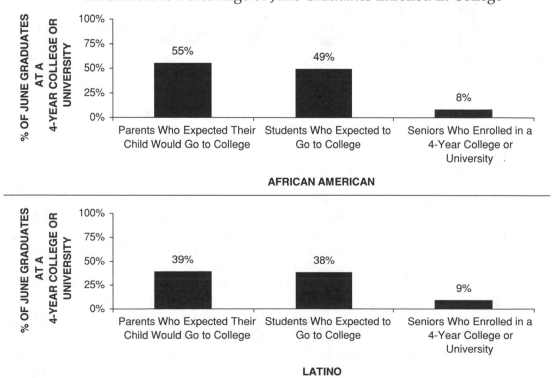

SOURCE: An urban school district.

college rate was a mere 9%. Are we hearing the voices of parents and students? If so, what actions need to be taken to close gaps between expectations and reality?

LISTENING TO STUDENTS' VOICES REGARDING THE ACADEMIC CULTURE OF THE SCHOOL

Students have often-overlooked insights and knowledge about the school and its culture. Students' views about their school are important, not only because they can inform reform decisions, but also because they affect the quality of students' educational experiences. With this in mind, one middle school adapted the instrument Assessing Institutional Reforms in the Academic Culture of Schools (Figure 7.2a, pages 144–147) for students. In order to ensure that the language would be meaningful to students, a teacher and a reform consultant from The Achievement Council in Los Angeles, a nonprofit public interest organization whose mission is to address equity issues for urban and low-income students, sought assistance from a student to revise each area of the instrument.

This instrument, Students Assessing the Academic Culture of Schools (Figure 8.10), should be administered to students at the same time the adults in the school community are assessing the culture. The middle school team that developed this revision administered it during extended class periods. After the results were charted, members of the school leadership team visited classes to discuss their possible meanings with students; teachers were on hand to listen to what the students had to say.

A risk-free environment must be fostered so students are not fearful of expressing their opinions about the culture and climate of their school. As with adults,

Figure 8.10   Students Assessing the Academic Culture of Schools

Name (optional): _____   Room: _____
         Grade: _____   Date: _____

(Fill in for postassessment *only*.)
Filled out instrument in 200____?   Yes ____   No ____

Directions: Please fill in the circle under the number that you believe best represents your school. One (1) is the lowest rating and five (5) is the highest.

Area	Underachievement		Rating		Higher Achievement
Planning/Decision Making	* Little or no discussion between administrators and teachers about how to raise student achievement.	1 2 3 4 5 -O- -O- -O- -O- -O-			* Lots of discussion about how to raise student achievement.
	* Mostly the principal is in charge.	1 2 3 4 5 -O- -O- -O- -O- -O-			* Teamwork among teachers, administrators, and parents to make decisions.
	* No vision for the future.	1 2 3 4 5 -O- -O- -O- -O- -O-			* Everyone agrees on a vision for the school.

(continued)

Figure 8.10 Continued

Area	Underachievement	Rating	Higher Achievement
Professionalism/ Responsibility	* No one takes responsibility and everyone blames everyone else for low achievement at school.	1 2 3 4 5 -O- -O- -O- -O- -O-	* Everyone takes responsibility for improving achievement at the school.
	* Most teachers don't know their subject.	1 2 3 4 5 -O- -O- -O- -O- -O-	* Most teachers know their subject and teach well.
	* Teachers don't take the opportunity to improve their teaching skills and methods.	1 2 3 4 5 -O- -O- -O- -O- -O-	* Teachers take the opportunity to improve their teaching skills.

Area	Underachievement	Rating	Higher Achievement
Curriculum	* Subjects are too easy.	1 2 3 4 5 -O- -O- -O- -O- -O-	* Subjects are challenging and make students work hard.
	* Students are taught below grade level.	1 2 3 4 5 -O- -O- -O- -O- -O-	* All students are taught at or above grade level.
	* No technology used in the classroom.	1 2 3 4 5 -O- -O- -O- -O- -O-	* Students use technology in the classroom.

Area	Underachievement	Rating	Higher Achievement
Instruction	* Mostly the teacher talks at students.	1 2 3 4 5 -O- -O- -O- -O- -O-	* Teachers use many different ways to teach and involve students.
	* Teachers use lots of workbooks and handouts.	1 2 3 4 5 -O- -O- -O- -O- -O-	* Students are taught to think and work out problems in different ways.
	* Students are taken out of class for special teaching.	1 2 3 4 5 -O- -O- -O- -O- -O-	* All students are taught all subjects that lead to college.
	* Students take a lot of multiple-choice tests.	1 2 3 4 5 -O- -O- -O- -O- -O-	* Students show what they've learned with portfolios and projects.

Area	Underachievement	Rating	Higher Achievement
Expectations	* Some students are seen as unable to learn.	1 2 3 4 5 -O- -O- -O- -O- -O-	* All students are seen as able to learn and able to go on to college.
	* Teachers disrespect students regularly.	1 2 3 4 5 -O- -O- -O- -O- -O-	* Teachers encourage students and help them to achieve.

Figure 8.10 Continued

Area	Underachievement	Rating	Higher Achievement
Learning Opportunities Grouping/ Tracking/ Labeling	* Students are grouped by how well they learn.	1 2 3 4 5 -O- -O- -O- -O- -O-	* Students are mixed in groups.
	* Only smart kids get to use computers.	1 2 3 4 5 -O- -O- -O- -O- -O-	* All students get to use computers.
	* Students who get low grades don't have many choices at school.	1 2 3 4 5 -O- -O- -O- -O- -O-	* All students have choices at school.
	* Students do not help each other with schoolwork.	1 2 3 4 5 -O- -O- -O- -O- -O-	* Students get together to study and help each other learn.
	* Students have little opportunity to learn.	1 2 3 4 5 -O- -O- -O- -O- -O-	* All students have lots of opportunities to learn.

Area	Underachievement	Rating	Higher Achievement
Parent Involvement	* School staff believes that parents don't care about their child's grades.	1 2 3 4 5 -O- -O- -O- -O- -O-	* School staff believes that parents care about the school and their child's education.
	* Parents are not involved in school.	1 2 3 4 5 -O- -O- -O- -O- -O-	* Parents are involved in school, including their child's homework and talking with teachers.
	* Information does not go home in the language the parents speak.	1 2 3 4 5 -O- -O- -O- -O- -O-	* School communicates with parents in their language.

Area	Underachievement	Rating	Higher Achievement
Support Services for Students	* Few support services for students.	1 2 3 4 5 -O- -O- -O- -O- -O-	* Lots of support services.
	* No one gets in trouble for breaking school rules.	1 2 3 4 5 -O- -O- -O- -O- -O-	* Everyone knows the school rules and follows them.

students should be encouraged to give reasons and examples explaining why they feel the way they do. Ask them not to name people, but to share information. This dialogue should be used as a time to talk to students about what they feel is working at the school, what they feel needs to be reformed, and what role they might play in improving their school. Finally, the data and analysis from the student survey should be discussed in conjunction with the results of the adult instrument—making sure students are ongoing participants in the dialogue and analysis.

This instrument is an innovative example of how one school saw the possibilities for taking a tool in this book to a level that met their specific inquiry needs. It should inspire school communities to consider the critical importance of student voices in the reform process.

9

Evaluating Programs and Interventions

A high school principal complained that there were so many programs in her school that she could not keep up with them. The principal was constantly calling in substitutes for teachers going through new training programs. Although all of the programs had the greatest of intentions, she was not sure specifically what each was supposed to achieve, how, and for which students. There seemed to be overlap in many of the goals and activities, but the teachers involved in the different initiatives rarely communicated, much less collaborated.

Frankly, the principal felt that many of the programs had been forced on her by central administration. She wished the school could focus in more depth on improvement efforts already begun before adding on new programs. A colleague asked her, "Why don't you tell them that you don't want any more programs?" Her reply was, "Oh, I can't do that, they would think that I don't want to improve my school!" Still, the principal wondered whether there was any way to determine which programs were best for her school and which were not particularly effective.

Subsequently, the principal and some staff members attended an institute where they were challenged to analyze the disparate programs at their school. The principal realized it was the first time in a while that she had been encouraged to think solely in terms of what was best for her students. The principal, with the assistance of the data team, began analyzing program impact at the school, getting familiar with all of the efforts, collecting data, and finding out how others evaluated the programs—including students and parents. They presented this research in a coherent way to support whether particular improvement efforts should be kept, modified, or eliminated.

Some of the findings from the team were the following:

- ISS Class. The in-school detention class keeps students who are tardy out of class for a whole period. During that time, no academic work is given or expected to be completed. No provisions are made for missed academic work. Modifications are needed to address the stated academic goals.
- Academic Study Hall. This class is for students to complete homework and to get academic assistance with concepts and test preparation. There is no guidance for the teacher, little collaboration with the students' teachers, and no evidence as to whether this class is working to raise student achievement. This program needs modifications and evaluation of impact on student achievement.
- Double Periods. This was designed to give students extra math periods. It cuts across the lunch period. Many students are cutting, and there is no mechanism to monitor attendance or impact. Again, program monitoring, evaluation, and modification are necessary.
- College Preparatory Programs. Many programs that were formally labeled "college prep" had had a remedial label until the district eliminated remedial courses. However, the course content did not change. Classes must reflect college preparatory content. Curriculum upgrading and teacher development is necessary.
- English Language Learner Programs. These programs reveal that students are being underserviced and that there is a large attrition rate. Immediate and serious attention to these programs is necessary.

With the participation of the leadership team, the data team, and the school community, this evaluation had a major impact on how the school progressed. Over time, the school reformed the content and the way the programs were implemented in order to devote concentrated energy on the efforts that showed the best promise of raising achievement for all students. Data were always used to defend decisions. The central administration did not entirely change its views, but the principal's immediate supervisor supported the new direction of the school.

Overview

Many low-performing schools suffer from program overload combined with a fragmentation of efforts. Although the goals of the programs appear to be good, they may exacerbate the problems of low achievement. All kinds of "silver bullet" type programs are adopted, often out of desperation to raise test scores. Many individuals are unaware of the different programs at the site. Some programs that are operating simultaneously may be incompatible philosophically. Sometimes there are contradictory approaches in curriculum areas, teachers are asked to implement more efforts than they can handle, and the staff does not have the opportunity to learn new approaches before another one is piled on.

When these efforts are initiated from outside the school, there may be little understanding from external sources about the school's culture and program fit. On the other hand, the school community may not have the slightest clue about the new program or initiative and the theoretical or conceptual underpinnings on which the program is based. One middle school that conducted a program analysis found 38 separate programs and initiatives running on campus. They have few clues about program effectiveness.

There is little coordination or collaboration among improvement efforts in districts and schools. Some are burdened with rigid administrative structures (Winfield, Johnson, & Manning, 1993). This results in a lack of coherence and unfocused approaches. There is little analysis as to how new efforts will strengthen good school practices or replace poor practices. Resource allocations are scattered, and time and energy are wasted on activities that do not make a difference in student academic achievement.

A report of the Steering Committee Consortium on Chicago School Research (Bryk, Easton, Kerbow, Rollow, & Sebring, 1993) described the add-on program mentality as "Unfocused Academic Initiatives." Two of the categories they identified paint a vivid picture of fragmentation and add-on efforts:

1. "Peripheral Academic Changes"
   - Add-on accrual programs with little innovation
   - Limited focus on improving core teaching
   - Absence of coherent planning
   - Little active resource seeking

2. "Christmas Tree Schools"
   - Showcase schools with many new programs
   - Multiple "add-ons" with little coordination
   - Little attention to strengthening organizational core
   - Entrepreneurial principals actively seeking resources (p. 15)

This book urges schools to constantly assess the effectiveness of their programs and practices; efforts that are not leading to higher academic outcomes for all students need to be reevaluated. Check the Bibliography at the end of the book for resources on evaluation and data collection.

ANALYSES OF EFFORTS TO RAISE STUDENT ACHIEVEMENT

To assist schools in focusing on what they are accomplishing with their improvement activities, the Analysis of Efforts to Raise Student Achievement (Table 9.1a) was developed. This has been a real "eye-opener" for schools. They realize why, in spite of their many improvement efforts, they are working hard but getting few meaningful long-term results. They also realize that they have little knowledge of program impact on student achievement. "Criteria" for keeping or abandoning programs and policies often take the form of someone in power saying, "Kids like it," "It's a good program," "The director/teacher is great!" "Parents like it," "We have always done it that way," "The materials are great!" "This is a board member's pet project," or "We can't get rid of that program because so-and-so might lose his or her position."

When to Use

The Analysis of Efforts to Raise Student Achievement (Table 9.1a) provides a framework to analyze the school through the assessment of the various improve-

Table 9.1a Analysis of Efforts to Raise Student Achievement

School: _____
Date: _____
Position: _____

Based on your knowledge, please fill in the information below about efforts at your school to raise student achievement.

Programs/Initiatives	Who's Involved	Initiated by Whom	Impact on Student Achievement				Documentation (Multiple Indicators)
			High	Med	Low	Don't know	

ment plans and programs taking place. This form should be used at the beginning of the reform process, when assessing whether to add new programs, and to monitor ongoing programs.

Administering the Form

The entire school community can participate in this analysis, or it can be administered to a cross section of members of the school who have knowledge of all of the efforts. It might also be administered by grade level or department. It will require about a two-hour time block to complete the analysis and discussion. Participants should have some knowledge of all of the programs in the school, and they should be asked to bring data about program results to the session. Participants should first look at all of the components of the instrument, making sure they understand what to do.

- Each participant fills out the form individually. This should take approximately 20 to 30 minutes.
- Tally the number of improvement efforts identified at the school. Tallying can be done right away, or it can be summarized and brought back for fuller discussion at a different session. The following steps can be done at either time.
- Discuss where there appears to be overload, fragmentation, and gaps. Are the efforts philosophically compatible? Are they focused on high achievement outcomes? How broad is the impact?
- Ask for volunteers in each group to share one of the efforts they rated high and to explain the reason and evidence for the rating. If they don't have immediate evidence, this will underscore the need for data to substantiate and document the impact of various programs. If others give low ratings to the same effort, discuss discrepancies.
- Ask volunteers to share the one effort they rated the lowest and why, again including evidence. The blame for the low ratings for various programs may focus on external causes. It is important to focus on issues that can be substantiated in some way. Some issues may require further information, discussion, and data gathering about institutional practices. Discuss discrepancies.
- Identify and discuss program overload, unfocused efforts, and fragmentation. Discuss in depth the implications for student achievement. The school may need to engage in a more rigorous evaluation of the impact and effectiveness of the various programs in order to decide which ones to continue and which ones to end or phase out. This has implications for use of resources, especially staff time and energy.

Data Analysis and Presentations

Once all of the separate programs and efforts are identified, the data can be summarized. One way to disaggregate the data is by the sources of the initiation of the efforts. It can be interesting to find out whether staff perceptions about program effectiveness are related to whether the source of the program was internal or external to the school (see Table 9.1b).

The next step is to gather documentation to see if perceptions match reality. This may take some time, but it will prove invaluable. The staff should work together to

Table 9.1b Analysis of Efforts to Raise Student Achievement: Sample Data

School: _____
Date: _____
Position: _____

Based on your knowledge, please fill in the information below about efforts at your school to raise student achievement.

Programs/Initiatives	Who's Involved	Initiated by Whom	Impact on Student Achievement				Documentation
			High	Med	Low	Don't Know	
Increase of College Prep Classes	All students	Principal			✓		Overall increase in number of students, course rigor low, little change in test scores
Math/Reading Professional Development for Teachers	All					✓	None
Math Lab	Low achievers	Chapter 1				✓	None
Reading Lab	Low achievers	Chapter 1				✓	None
In-School Detention	Tardy students	School				✓	None
Academic Support Class	Math/English	District				✓	None
English Language	English learners	State			✓		Low scores, GPAs, and attrition data
Double Lunch	Students needing math assistance	School				✓	Class cutting
AVID/Score Program	Teachers, students	District	✓				Attendance, self-esteem, GPA, college enrollment
Parent Center	Parents, teachers, administrators	District	✓				Participation, parent education classes/training; increased school visitations

look at program goals and identify indicators needed to document impact. Once those indicators are gathered, the information should be compared to perceptions. Discussions will need to continue to inform decisions about systemic reform.

Discussion and Cautionary Notes

Although some staff members will welcome the elimination of projects, many projects and programs will have staunch advocates who will not want to see their favorites criticized or dropped. Elimination may affect not only the school program but also jobs. Therefore, it will be important to use data to support or challenge the need for certain programs. How programs are phased out or eliminated also requires careful thought and action. The parents and community will need to be informed of any such reforms and the reasons. If a staff member favored by the community or the administration heads up a program, he or she can rally others to retain it regardless of the impact on student outcomes. However, the focus must be fixed on students and decisions informed by their best welfare.

The Analysis of Efforts to Raise Student Achievement (Table 9.1a) can provide an opportunity to discuss the optimal use of resources—time, money, and people. The exercise also raises issues fundamental to systemic reform. Districts and schools must develop ways to systematically analyze how improvement efforts are implemented in schools and must routinely make links between these improvement efforts and their intended outcomes.

ASSESSING ELEMENTARY PROGRAMS AND PRACTICES

In the Elementary Collection Form: Student Progress (Table 9.2a), several student and school characteristics are indicated to trace progress over a three-year period for racial/ethnic and gender groups. These indicators—retention, promotion, special education placement, gifted and talented placement, and bilingual reclassification—were selected because they are frequently cited as areas in which high levels of inequities exist. What types of progress and placements occur for different groups of students? Do groups improve over time as they progress through school? Which ones? Are there patterns by grades, teachers, and so forth?

This form can also be used to disaggregate data further by such important student characteristics as income background and language proficiency. Schools that serve primarily one racial/ethnic group should certainly be looking at these kinds of trends. Schools within schools and magnets within regular schools should also disaggregate data. These collection and presentation formats can be adapted for middle and high school use.

Elementary School Progress and Program Information

Table 9.2b shows a sample of how a K-6 school might fill out the form. Some findings and representations of the data that might flow from this are shown in Figures 9.1a and 9.1b, which show a triple bar graph representation of the percentage of students in certain categories over a three-year period. If goals are set to increase or

Table 9.2a Elementary Collection Form: Student Progress

		M – Male F – Female				AA – African American A – Asian				L – Latino W – White T – Total			
Indicators		*June 200__*				*June 200__*				*June 200__*			
		AA	A	L	W	T	AA	A	L	W	T	AA	A	L	W	T
Total Number of Students:																
Promotion	M																
	F																
Retention	M																
	F																
Bilingual	M																
	F																
Redesignated to Regular Program From Bilingual	M																
	F																
Special Education	M																
	F																
Redesignated to Regular Program From Special Ed	M																
	F																
Gifted & Talented	M																
	F																

Source of Data: _____   Date: _____

Person Responsible for Collecting Data: _____

Table 9.2b Elementary Collection Form: Student Progress—Grades K-6 Sample

M – Male F – Female
AA – African American A – Asian
L – Latino W – White
T – Total

Indicators		June 2000					June 2001					June 2002				
		AA	A	L	W	T	AA	A	L	W	T	AA	A	L	W	T
Total Number of Students:		188	112	194	120	614	190	114	192	118	614	203	148	207	147	705
Promotion	M	80	56	80	53	269	85	62	85	59	291	98	78	99	71	346
	F	82	42	85	52	261	91	47	89	55	282	98	70	98	75	341
Retention	M	17	7	19	8	51	10	3	14	2	29	6	0	8	1	15
	F	9	7	10	7	33	4	2	4	2	12	1	0	2	0	3
Bilingual	M	0	10	44	0	54	0	9	46	0	55	0	6	48	0	54
	F	0	10	20	0	20	0	10	22	0	32	0	8	24	0	32
Redesignated to Regular Program From Bilingual	M	0	5	12	0	17	0	6	10	0	16	0	6	12	0	18
	F	0	6	14	0	20	0	6	12	0	18	0	7	14	0	21
Special Education	M	15	0	12	2	29	16	0	14	2	32	15	0	12	1	28
	F	3	0	2	1	6	4	0	3	1	8	4	0	2	0	6
Redesignated to Regular Program From Special Ed	M	0	0	0	0	0	0	0	0	0	0	0	0	0	1	1
	F	0	0	0	0	0	0	0	0	0	0	0	0	0	0	0
Gifted & Talented	M	1	10	1	6	18	1	10	1	7	19	4	12	6	8	30
	F	1	8	2	8	19	1	9	2	8	20	2	7	4	8	21

Source of Data: _____   Date: _____

Person Responsible
for Collecting Data: _____

Figure 9.1 Elementary School Progress and Program Information: Sample Presentation of a School's Summarized Data

a. Elementary School Progress Information

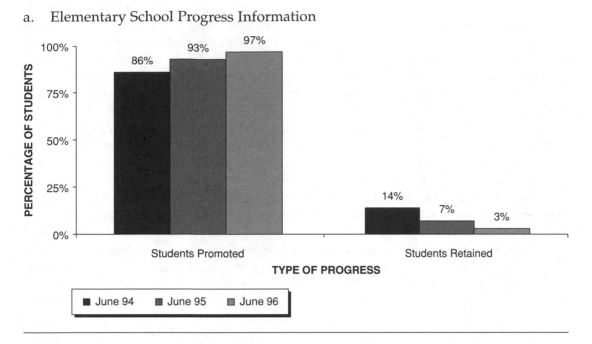

b. Elementary School Program Information

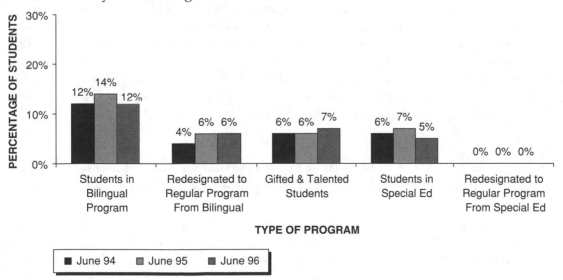

NOTE: Sample data.

decrease the percentage of students in each category, that goal should be known to all who engage in discussion and to all who are responsible for implementing the reforms when they look at this graph. This puts the information in a context so progress or lack of progress toward goals can be assessed. Goals can be written on the figure.

Percentage of Students in Special Education and Gifted and Talented Programs

Sample illustrations of disaggregated data regarding placement patterns for racial, ethnic, and gender groups for a three-year period are shown in Figure 9.2. What we can see is that there are differential placements by racial, ethnic, and gender groups. This was cited earlier in the text as a national pattern. Startling contrasts are shown in particular for African Americans and Latinos versus Asians and whites in the percentage of placements in gifted and talented programs and special education programs. African Americans and Latinos show a high percentage of placement in special education and a low percentage in gifted and talented compared to their representation in the student population. Males have higher rates of placement than females in special education. Asians and whites show the opposite patterns, with higher percentages of placement in gifted and talented and negligible placement in special education compared to their representation in the school population. The changes between 2000 and 2002 seem to indicate that some efforts might have been made to reduce the inequities. Data such as these show the need for continual monitoring.

The form What Do We Want to Find Out About Our Reform Initiative? (Tables 9.3a and 9.3b, pages 210–212) presents a plan to evaluate a mathematics reform initiative in 20 K-8 schools. The form includes questions, criteria for success, indicators for analyzing progress, when and how the information will be collected, and how the data will be analyzed and interpreted. Additional columns can be added as necessary. Dialogue will be essential to identify how different stakeholders in the school or district communities perceive success. Some may want to eliminate all remedial groupings, whereas others may consider any decrease to be satisfactory; some may want all children placed in algebra, whereas others may be satisfied with incremental increases. These perceptions have an impact on how the reforms are implemented and can also affect the levels of commitment to the reform. Although these discussions can produce some conflict, the problem solving that ensues can be healthy for the process. If this open dialogue does not occur—or is not allowed to occur—problems from differential expectations will surface later in ways that may not be possible to mediate.

ASSESSING THE IMPROVEMENT OF COLLEGE PREPARATION AND COLLEGE-GOING RATES

Table 9.4 (pages 213–216) measures a district or school's goals toward increasing college eligibility and enrollment. The numerical goal that would define success should be stated, for example, (a) all graduating seniors will be college eligible, and (b) 90% will enroll in college. This form shows a way that a district assessed processes, test scores, and actual college-going rates for each high school in a district by race/ ethnicity and gender. It was initially designed by a cross section of teachers, administrators, and counselors from high schools in the process of reform. Involving the implementers of reform in the monitoring process is essential so that they can examine the impact of their work.

The form specifies the inquiries to be answered, the indicators, collection dates, who is responsible for collecting, and the data sources. Other items could be added such as presentation dates, audiences, and so forth. Although specific collection dates

(text continues on page 216)

Figure 9.2 Percentage of Students in Special Education and Gifted and Talented Programs

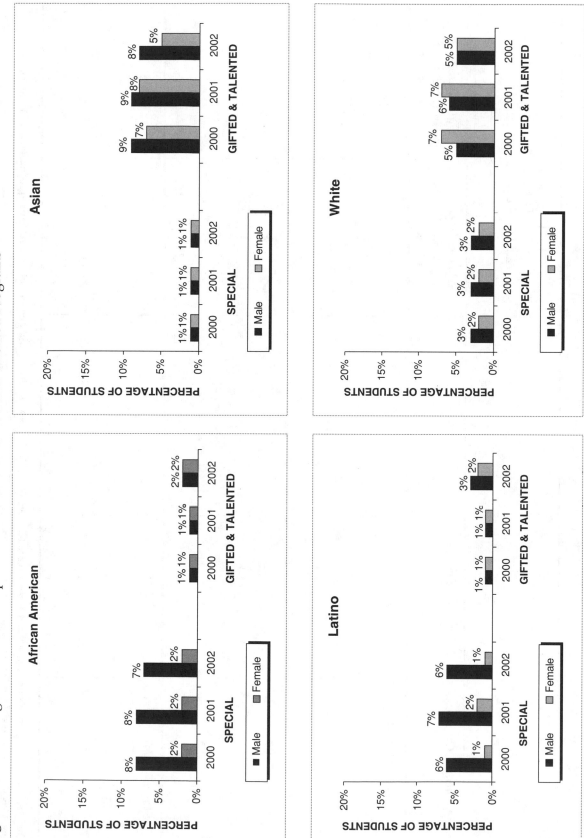

NOTE: Sample data.

Table 9.3a What Do We Want to Find Out About Our Reform Initiative?

School/District: _____

Date: _____

Planning Team Members: _____

Component & Questions	Criteria for Success	Indicators	When & How the Information Will Be Collected	Data Analysis & Interpretation Procedures
A. Classroom Practice				
B. School Culture				
C. Student Achievement				

Table 9.3b What Do We Want to Find Out About Our Reform Initiative? Sample

School/District: _____

Date: _____

Planning Team Members: _____

Component & Questions	Criteria for Success	Indicators	When & How the Information Will Be Collected	Data Analysis & Interpretation Procedures
A. Classroom Practice				
1) To what degrees do classroom practices of teachers who attended the academies change?	• Teachers use multiple representations when introducing concepts • Teachers use open-ended questions • Teachers participating in other learning experiences • Teachers use multiple strategies • Teachers use cooperative groups	• Use of replacement units over time • Inclusion of manipulatives • Types of questions implied/asked • Multiple representation used • What gets taught to *all students* • Attendance at workshops dealing with replacement units (math) • Use of cooperative groups	2000–2002 • Observation • Survey • Interview (Collected by data team and site facilitator)	• By school • By grade • Level of participation by teachers • Content analysis of anecdotal to be written by data team
2) How do academies change expectations about Latino and African American children's capacity to learn higher-level mathematics?	• Perceptions of students' and teachers' capabilities change	• Teaching strategies • Discussion of issues of equity and college going • Wait time • Teacher expectations changed/raised • Use of authentic assessment tools	2000–2002 • Observation • Survey • Interview (Collected by data team and site facilitator)	• By school • By grade • By classroom

(continued)

Table 9.3b Continued

Component & Questions	Criteria for Success	Indicators	When & How the Information Will Be Collected	Data Analysis & Interpretation Procedures
3) What is the profile of participating and nonparticipating teachers?	• Representation of all groups	• Race, ethnicity, gender, years of experience, credential, economic background	2000–2002 • Attendance records of all staff development	• By school • By grade
B. School Culture 1) How has the initiative helped administrators better support mathematics reform at the school?	• Support for release time for teachers to engage in dialogue • Changes in teaching behavior that reflect an equitable teaching environment	• Broadness of change (middle school across department; outside) • Role groups meet • Release time • Classroom observations increase • Peer coaching implemented • Tracking eliminated	• Summer • Observations by teacher/data team • Site facilitators/administrators responsible for administering surveys collect observation data and resource teacher reports	• Meetings with data team project director, facilitator, and resource teachers to discuss and analyze summary data, draft reports • Data team writes final report to share with school community
C. Student Achievement 1) To what extent has the initiative had an impact on student achievement?	• Increase in all student achievement indicators as stated in our annual goals	• Test scores • Performance assessments • Grades • College course enrollments	• Principal and site facilitators will collect and summarize data with data team	• Scores, grades, enrollments by grade, race, ethnicity, gender

Table 9.4a   Assessing the Improvement of College Preparation and
College-Going Rates

Data Team Members: _____		Data Team Members: _____	
		_____	
Goal:			
Monitoring Activity	*Collection Dates*	*Responsible Person*	*Data Source*

NOTE: All data are to be disaggregated by race/ethnicity and gender.

Table 9.4b　Assessing the Improvement of College Preparation and
College-Going Rates: Sample

Data Team Members: _____	School/District: _____
_____	Date: _____
_____	

Goal: To increase college preparation and actual college-going rates.

Monitoring Activity	Collection Dates	Responsible Person	Data Source
1) What are parent and student interests and expectations? What are teacher, counselor, and administrator expectations? *Methods/Indicator Tools:* • Student Survey—6th to 8th, 9th to 12th grade • Parent Questionnaire • Teacher Survey—all high school and middle school faculty • Counselor survey—all high school and middle school • Administrator survey—all high school and middle school	Spring every year	Assistant Superintendent of Curriculum, Director of Guidance, Director of Research & Evaluation, middle and high school principals	School, District
2) Do all students have a four-year plan? *Indicators:* Four-year plan review	Twice a year	Assistant Principal, High School	School Counselors
3) What are the actual college-going rates? What is the distribution by two-year and four-year public/private institutions? *Indicators:* • Actual college-going rates for Fall 2000 and beyond by high school and district (disaggregated by race/ethnicity and gender) • # of students by ethnicity & gender • Two-year public colleges • Two-year private colleges • Four-year public colleges & universities • Four-year private colleges & universities	2000 & future years— every March	Assistant Superintendent of Curriculum, Director of Guidance, Assistant Superintendent	California Postsecondary Education Commission (CPEC) & high school performace reports Possible source: District graduate follow-up study and private colleges (for private college students)

Table 9.4b Continued

Monitoring Activity	Collection Dates	Responsible Person	Data Source
4) Who has applied to colleges and for financial aid? *Indicators:* • *Senior's Application to College Survey* This data needs to be collected annually by high school and submitted to district in June in the Principal's report to the Superintendent.	3 times yearly Nov. 15th, Dec. 15th, and May 15th	Assistant Principal & Head Counselor in cooperation with Counselors and Teachers	Scholarship Office Counselors High School Counselors
5) What percentage of students are taking and passing courses they need to enter four-year postsecondary institutions? *Indicators:* • Annual transcript evaluation for college eligibility—9th to 12th graders.	Spring every year/Fall and Spring for 9th graders	Head Counselor	High School Counselors
6) How many students are applying for and receiving financial aid? *Indicators:* • Senior financial aid and scholarship information by high school and by race/ethnicity and gender. • # of students who applied for financial aid and scholarships • # of students who received state grants and scholarships • # of students who received Pell Grants • # of students who received local scholarships	June every year	Head Counselor, Clerk, Scholarship Counselor	High School Counselors

(continued)

Table 9.4b Continued

Monitoring Activity	Collection Dates	Responsible Person	Data Source

7) **What percentage of students are prepared for and taking the necessary tests for college entrance?**
 	
Indicators:
• College-related tests by high school and by race/ethnicity and gender.
 	
    # of   %   mean
    students   score
PSAT _____ ___ _____
PACT _____ ___ _____
SAT _____ ___ _____
ACT _____ ___ _____
AP _____ ___ _____
     (% of students
     who score 3, 4, 5)
	August	Head Counselor, Counselors, Assistant Superintendent of Curriculum	Performance reports and College Board

8) **What percentage of students are enrolling in college preparatory by level? What percentage are enrolling in Advanced Placement courses?** *Indicators:* • All college preparatory course enrollments by grade level, school, district, race/ethnicity, and gender. • Standardized tests.	Twice a year— October & March	Assistant Superintendent of Curriculum, Middle & High School Principals	Middle and High Schools, Districts, Performance reports

NOTE: All data are to be disaggregated by race/ethnicity and gender.

are designated, there might be interim times that are also important for documentation. The data team or others will need to keep track of the collection times and periodically remind key individuals of their responsibilities.

PROFESSIONAL DEVELOPMENT

I often get questions about measuring the impact of professional development on achievement. This is often a difficult area in which to measure direct impact because teachers may be involved in more than one type of development or the school may have many initiatives. However, it is important to come as close as possible to measuring impact because of the large sums of money that are being directed to professional development and the assumptions about its impact on teacher development and hence student achievement. The instrument What Do We Want to Find

Out About Our Reform Initiative? (Table 9.3, pages 210–212, and Figure 11.4, page 266) offers some guidance under the Classroom Practice section. In designing the measures schools and districts may need the assistance of those with evaluation skills.

In designing and developing the inquiry, first the leadership should be clear about the expectations and outcomes for the professional development. Professional development is often rushed into without much forethought. Some of the questions that you might want to ask are the following: What are the types and natures of the behaviors that you expect to be exhibited after the development? Are there baseline data for each teacher on these indicators prior to the professional development? How can you say behaviors changed if you don't know what they looked like at the beginning? How do you expect the professional development will affect student achievement? Is it intended to affect some student groups more than others? What levels of implementation are considered successful? This must be a thoughtful rather than a haphazard process.

In measuring impact, use multiple approaches and indicators, such as the following:

- Questionnaires administered to participants and significant others
- Observations
- Interviews
- Multiple indicators of student achievement for measuring impact
- Levels of participation and implementation to assess whether those who had higher or lower levels of implementation affected the desired outcomes

The professional development inquiries can be designed using forms such as What Do We Want to Find Out About Our Reform Initiative (Table 9.3) and Assessing the Improvement of College Preparation and College-Going Rates (Table 9.4).

Schools and districts need to assess the amount of money spent and types of professional development to begin to assess whether there are any links to student achievement. This information gathering needs to be carefully crafted so the information is used for improving the quality of professional development and not for personal attacks.

Table 9.5 is only one suggested example of what could be used to gather data. Districts and schools should develop ways that will best meet their needs. The important issue is to link the information gathered to changes in practices and ultimately to student achievement.

Table 9.5 Professional Development Activities, 2002–2004

Teacher	Type	Hrs	Type	Hrs	Cost	Student Achievement Gains
A						
B						
C						
D						
E						

10

Using School Indicators to Answer Critical Questions

As the data team met and looked at the information in front of them, they realized that they had limited information about why African American, Latino, and Native American students had low enrollments in algebra. They only had enrollment statistics. They said, "Many pieces of the puzzle are missing, and all we have are the edges." They began to think about what other kinds of indicators they needed and who they needed to get information from. They subsequently looked at multiple indicators such as test scores, placement, and race and ethnicity; they interviewed students and parents; they looked at placement policies. They compiled and combined the indicators to fill in pieces of the puzzle. The picture that emerged showed that there were institutional biases in placements: students and parents lacked important information about the need to take higher-level math courses, and faculty realized that they needed to revamp policies and practices. Using multiple indicators deepened their knowledge and vastly improved their decision making.

Overview

What can we learn when we analyze combinations of "indicators" about our school or district? For example, what would be the implications of realizing we have 50 computers at our school, but two thirds of our students rarely get their hands on them? Or what might it mean to discover that 80% of our faculty meeting time is spent on administrative matters and routines, and only 20% of the time is spent discussing curriculum and raising student achievement? First, you need the distinct pieces of data. This chapter suggests some ways schools and districts can collect and analyze the data for many helpful purposes. Benefits include gaining a clearer understanding of our students and teachers, our practices, how resources are utilized, and our results.

The units of information needed to piece together these puzzles are called indicators. A well-organized and updated "bank" of school indicators can serve many critical reform and equity needs, such as (a) for creating district, school, and student profiles; (b) for developing comprehensive progress reports for accountability purposes; and (c) for reflecting, planning, and decision making. Although the first two are important, the third is paramount, because decisions related to practices and uses of resources must be fully informed by accurate and current data on our students, staff, and school community.

Detailed and accurate indicators help us answer questions related to equity, such as these: Does the distribution of resources correspond to our improvement priorities? How do the data change—or not change—from year to year? How are opportunities for students to learn higher-level knowledge distributed across racial/ethnic groups?

Gathering and analyzing indicators helps the school community to focus on goals, to establish outcomes, and to determine benchmarks of progress. When school staffs consider themselves responsible for the education of young people, they will consider it necessary to determine clear and creative ways for the school community and others to judge the results.

Indicators suggested in this book include the following:

- Student characteristics
- School characteristics, culture, programs, and policies
- Administrator and teacher characteristics
- Student outcome information and aspirations
- Parent involvement
- Resources

HOW AND WHEN TO GATHER INDICATORS

A coherent system for gathering and analyzing indicator data should be developed at the outset of the reform effort, or the process can become fragmented and ineffective. Therefore, discussions about what might indicate the relative "goodness" or "weakness" of the school need to begin early on (see Chapters 3 and 4). Engaging the staff in thinking about these issues from the beginning will pave the way for openness to reflecting on what the data may reveal. The staff should look at the high-stakes indicators of progress, such as test scores, and decide which ways to present those data. In addition, it is important to determine other indicators that might describe how students are achieving. Schools that have established performance standards and assessments should include these. It is critical to think carefully about both what data are needed to describe current conditions and what data will be needed to monitor ongoing progress and outcomes. After all, data should not be collected just for the sake of it. Planning will help avoid chasing after numbers that serve little purpose in helping to raise student achievement.

The data should be collected in ways that use minimum amounts of staff time. This capability will depend on the level of technology accessible to staff. If specific desired data are not available locally, it may be possible to download them from a central source. The data team should find out where the data are located and the timelines for when they are available. Archival data should be readily available. Specific pieces of data should be collected, analyzed, and reported each year, using the same sources at the same time of year. This is important for comparing year-to-year progress.

It is important to check the accuracy of the data. Having more than one person checking and recording the data helps to minimize errors. Errors many occur with the best procedures, but they need to be minimized or your credibility will be doubted. Don't mix "apples and oranges." For instance, don't compare different portrayals of the data, such as drop-out rates, which are often calculated differently. If data are going to be compared from year to year, look at the same sources, at the same time of year, using the same statistical procedures.

In addition to disaggregating the data by race, ethnicity, and gender, it is equally important to analyze data by programs and projects, especially those that are related to income (Title I); so-called "special needs" (bilingual, gifted, special education); and by school-within-a-school programs, such as magnets. When this is done, in addition to disparities in achievement, many schools have found inequitable distribution of resources (such as equipment, teaching talents, etc.) and disparities in opportunity to learn high-level knowledge. Samples of these kinds of explorations appear in the following section.

The data and leadership teams should create suitable collection forms to record the summary and disaggregated data (either on the computer or by hand) and create graphics to display information. A blank School Indicator Planning Form (Figure 10.1a) is provided. The three right columns are left blank; here the data team can begin planning which data are readily available, who will be responsible for collecting the data, and when. Following are a series of sample tools for gathering and utilizing indicators. First are Figures 10.1b (pages 222–223) and 10.1c (page 224), Suggested School Indicators; Part 1 of this form (Figure 10.1b) lists sample cross cutting issues, and Part 2 (Figure 10.1c) lists unique issues for elementary, middle, and high schools. This form also guides in the assessment of indicator availability and location and of which indicators need further research or development.

Next is Figure 10.2 (pages 225–238), the Sample Indicator Summary Form. This form provides a suggested way to lay out a five-year summary of information collected. It is intended as a model. Schools can create their own summary form based on the data they choose to collect. Summaries of the analysis of student and school outcome process indicators should also be attached and considered along with these indicators.

COMBINING INDICATORS TO ANSWER CRITICAL QUESTIONS

The most powerful possibilities for uses of data exist in combining indicators to reveal patterns, practices, and processes of schools and districts. These combinations can provide insights and access to knowledge that would otherwise go undiscovered.

The data team should explore the possibilities of combining indicator data such as student characteristics and placements in order to paint the most deeply descriptive picture of the school and to answer critical questions. Disaggregated student data should be analyzed to see what student achievement patterns emerge, how

Figure 10.1a School Indicator Planning Form

| School: _____ |
| Date: _____ |
| Filled out by: _____ |

Indicators	Source	When to Collect	Responsible Person

Figure 10.1b Suggested School Indicators: Part 1

Sample of Crosscutting Indicators for Elementary, Middle, and High School	Available Now Location	Research Required
Student Characteristics: • Number and percentage of students by: – Racial/ethnic group. – Gender breakdown. – Languages represented. – Country of origin. – English language proficient. – Family mobililty. – Parent socioeconomic status (SES). **School Staff Characteristics:** *Teachers, counselors, coordinators, principals, paraprofessionals* • Number of teachers. • Number of administrators. • Number of coordinators. • Number of paraprofessionals. • Number of counselors. • Racial composition. • Ethnic composition. • Percentage bilingual. • Languages spoken. • Teacher status: – Number and percentage tenured/nontenured. – Number and percentage probationary. – Number and percentage emergency, provisional and intern. – Number and percentage extended substitutes and temporary. – Number and percentage of mentor teachers. – Percentage of teachers evaluated annually. – Teacher and administrator certification. – Assignments by certification and years taught to programs/courses. – Professional development and involvement. – College coursework. – Continuing education. – Absences per teacher and types of absences. • Distribution of Administrators: – Number by category. – Number of years experience. – Number of years at location. **School Characteristics:** • Pupil-teacher, administrator, counselor ratio/class size. • Number and percentage of students in gifted programs disaggregated by race, ethnicity, and gender. • Number and percentage of students in special education disaggregated by race, ethnicity, and gender. • Number and percentage of students by Title I and Special Education, Magnets by race, ethnicity, and gender. • Promotion/retention rates for students by race, ethnicity, and gender. • Suspension/expulsion/truancy/tardy rates by race, ethnicity, and gender. • In-seat attendance by race, ethnicity, and gender. • Curriculum time allocations for instruction. • Nature and type of support programs for students. • Professional development (opportunities, nature and type). • School policies: tracking, grouping, student placement, homework, suspension, retention, promotion, discipline, teacher assignment and placement. • Archival: master schedules, calendars, lesson plans, etc. • Instructional Culture: – Perceptions of change. – Academic culture. – Classroom practice.		

Figure 10.1b Continued

Sample of Crosscutting Indicators for Elementary, Middle and High School	Available Now Location	Research Required

Measures of Student Aspirations and Achievement Disaggregated by Race, Ethnicity, Gender, and Cohort:
• Student aspirations for career and college.
• Percentage and number of students tested/not tested, broken down by programs students are placed in, i.e., special education.
• Test scores by quartile, grade, class, program.
• Course enrollments and completion.
• Grades by subject, department, grade, teacher.
• Performance assessments.
Parent Involvement Disaggregated by Race, Ethnicity, and Gender:
• Percentage advocacy.
• Percentage advisory (type).
• Opportunities for decision making, leadership roles.
• Aspirations for children.
• Attendance at conferences.
• Volunteer work.
• Time on campus/in classrooms.
Resources:
• Number and status of classrooms, labs, meeting rooms.
• Number and location and level of technology programs and computers.
• Adult/student ratio compared to teacher/student ratio.
• Number and kind of separate programs.
• Per pupil expenditures by program. How are the resources distributed?
• Budget breakdown.
• Time allocations:
  – Percentage of administrator time focused on instruction.
  – Meetings: percentage of time discussing routines and operations compared to percentage of time discussing instruction (in department, faculty, leadership team meetings).
  – Time for planning school reforms/professional development.		

students are sorted into groups, which teachers are assigned to which groups, and so on.

Indicator combinations help crystallize the equity of practices at the school. For example, one school realized that magnet school students had the opportunity to use computers featuring high-quality software programs, while students in the rest of the school rarely had opportunities to use the computers or to learn the high-level program content. This caused the school to look more closely at the distribution of resources as well as student outcomes. It is important to identify equity issues, to determine what indicators you need to address the issue, and to state your inquiry. Depending on the inquiry, the team should consider the following multiple sources for authentic data:

- What existing information do we already have available?
- How and what do we need to query from students about this issue?
- How and what do we need to query from teachers about this issue?
- How and what do we need to query from administrators about this issue?
- How and what do we need to query from parents about this issue?
- How and what do we need to query from central administration about this issue?

Figure 10.1c Suggested School Indicators: Part 2

Unique Indicators for the Elementary Level	Available Now Location	Research Required
• Program enrollment in Special Education; Title I; Bilingual Programs disaggregated by race, ethnicity, and gender. • Exit rates from programs disaggregated by race, ethnicity, and gender. • Within-class groupings disaggregated by race, ethnicity, and gender.		
Unique Indicators for the Middle and High School Grades	**Available Now Location**	**Research Required**
Student Characteristics Disaggregated by Race, Ethnicity, Gender, and Cohort: • Course enrollments by program/track, i.e., college preparatory, vocational. • Attendance: by class, course enrollment. • Drop-out rates. • Percentage leaving middle school overage for grade. • Grades by courses, departments. • Participation in extracurricular clubs and community activities. **Measures of Student Achievement Disaggregated by Race, Ethnicity, and Gender:** • Grade distribution. • Graduation rates. • Actual college enrollment by 2-year, 4-year, public, private. • Number of courses (college preparatory, general). • Percentage of students enrolled and completing college preparatory courses, vocational courses, etc. • Students' knowledge of college preparatory requirements/steps for enrollment, financial aid, etc. • Meeting of college course entrance requirements. • Number of scholarships. • Number of students with 4-year plans. • Number of students tested and scores on college tests [Advanced Placement (AP); SAT; SAT II; ACT; PSAT].		

- What existing documents (artifacts, archival materials) do we need, such as policies, schedules, program placements, teacher placements, master schedule, and so forth?
- What do we need to know about curriculum, pedagogy, and opportunity to learn?

Remember, however, that indicator analysis is not always simple. As an example, data on the percentage of teachers with emergency credentials in a school may have many implications. Usually, such teachers are woefully underprepared for the classroom, and there is high turnover of these teachers, resulting in a lack of stability at the school. But in schools with good supports and visionary leadership, emergency teachers may form a core of energetic new teachers, willing to develop student-responsive strategies. Working along with more senior teachers with a common belief system, they can be a formidable force for reform. Knowing who our emergency-credentialed teachers are, which students they are teaching, and the supports we are providing them is a first step toward working to prevent negative effects.

The displays in the final section of this chapter (Sample Indicator Combinations) and those in preceding chapters are only a small sampling of the kinds of pictures

(text continues on page 238)

Figure 10.2 Sample Indicator Summary Form

School: _____ Principal Name: _____

Note: This form does not include all possible indicators. Each school/district should design a form to meet its individual needs.

ENROLLMENT

	Enrollment by Grade and Total						
Year	Grade ___ # of Students	Grade ___ # of Students	Grade ___ # of Students	Grade ___ # of Students	Grade ___ # of Students	Grade ___ # of Students	Total
2002							
2003							
2004							
2005							
2006							

Source of Data: _____ Date Collected and Collector: _____

STUDENT CHARACTERISTICS

	Students by Race/Ethnicity									
	African American		Native American/ Alaskan		Asian/Pacific Islander		Latino		White	
Year	#	%	#	%	#	%	#	%	#	%
2002										
2003										
2004										
2005										
2006										

Source of Data: _____ Date Collected and Collector: _____

	Students by Gender			
	Male		Female	
Year	#	%	#	%
2002				
2003				
2004				
2005				
2006				

Source of Data: _____
Date Collected
and Collector: _____

Students on Reduced/Free Lunch Program		
Year	#	%
2002		
2003		
2004		
2005		
2006		

Source of Data: _____
Date Collected
and Collector: _____

(continued)

Figure 10.2   Continued

STUDENT CHARACTERISTICS (continued)

	Students' Language											
	Chinese		French		Hmong		Japanese		Spanish		Vietnamese	
Year	#	%	#	%	#	%	#	%	#	%	#	%
2002												
2003												
2004												
2005												
2006												

Source of Data: _____   Date Collected and Collector: _____

	Students' English Language Proficiency							
	English Only		English Language Learner		Redesignated		Fluent English	
Year	#	%	#	%	#	%	#	%
2002								
2003								
2004								
2005								
2006								

Source of Data: _____   Date Collected and Collector: _____

SCHOOL STAFF CHARACTERISTICS

	School Staff				
Year	# of Teachers	# of Administrators	# of Coordinators	# of Counselors	# of Paraprofessionals
2002					
2003					
2004					
2005					
2006					

Source of Data: _____   Date Collected and Collector: _____

Figure 10.2 Continued

SCHOOL STAFF CHARACTERISTICS (continued)

Ethnic and Language Composition of Professional Staff (Teachers, Administrators, Coordinators, Counselors)												
	African American		Native American/ Alaskan		Asian/Pacific Islander		Latino		White		Bilingual	
Year	#	%	#	%	#	%	#	%	#	%	#	%
2002												
2003												
2004												
2005												
2006												

Source of Data: _____

Date Collected and
Collector: _____

Ethnic and Language Composition of Support Staff (Paraprofessionals, Clerical, Custodial)												
	African American		Native American/ Alaskan		Asian/Pacific Islander		Latino		White		Bilingual	
Year	#	%	#	%	#	%	#	%	#	%	#	%
2002												
2003												
2004												
2005												
2006												

Source of Data: _____

Date Collected and
Collector: _____

Status of Teachers												
									Absences			
	Tenured		Probationary		Emergency		Long-Term Substitutes		Illness		Other	
Year	#	%	#	%	#	%	#	%	#	%	#	%
2002												
2003												
2004												
2005												
2006												

Source of Data: _____

Date Collected and
Collector: _____

(continued)

Figure 10.2 Continued

SCHOOL STAFF CHARACTERISTICS (continued)

	# of Years Experience in Administration			# of Years at Location		
Year	Principal	Assistant Principal I	Assistant Principal II	Principal	Assistant Principal I	Assistant Principal II
2002						
2003						
2004						
2005						
2006						

Status of Administrators

Source of Data: _____

Date Collected and Collector: _____

Professional Development Participation
(Nature and type, i.e., peer coaching, workshops)
* Can be done by grade, years of teaching, etc.

	Type A		Type B		Type C		Type D		Type E	
Year	#	%	#	%	#	%	#	%	#	%
2002										
2003										
2004										
2005										
2006										

Source of Data: _____

Date Collected and Collector: _____

SCHOOL CHARACTERISTICS

Student Attendance

	Average Daily Attendance		Actual In-Seat		Truancy	
Year	#	%	#	%	#	%
2002						
2003						
2004						
2005						
2006						

Source of Data: _____

Date Collected and Collector: _____

Figure 10.2 Continued

SCHOOL CHARACTERISTCS (continued)

	African American		Native American/ Alaskan		Asian/Pacific Islander		Latino		White	
Promotion										
Year	#	%	#	%	#	%	#	%	#	%
2002										
2003										
2004										
2005										
2006										

Source of Data: _____   Date Collected and Collector: _____

	African American		Native American/ Alaskan		Asian/Pacific Islander		Latino		White	
Retention										
Year	#	%	#	%	#	%	#	%	#	%
2002										
2003										
2004										
2005										
2006										

Source of Data: _____   Date Collected and Collector: _____

	African American		Native American/ Alaskan		Asian/Pacific Islander		Latino		White	
Suspension										
Year	#	%	#	%	#	%	#	%	#	%
2002										
2003										
2004										
2005										
2006										

Source of Data: _____   Date Collected and Collector: _____

(continued)

Figure 10.2 Continued

SCHOOL CHARACTERISTCS (continued)

	African American		Native American/ Alaskan		Asian/Pacific Islander		Latino		White	
Gifted										
Year	#	%	#	%	#	%	#	%	#	%
2002										
2003										
2004										
2005										
2006										

Source of Data: _____

Date Collected and Collector: _____

	African American		Native American/ Alaskan		Asian/Pacific Islander		Latino		White	
Special Education *Can be done by Special Education Designation.*										
Year	#	%	#	%	#	%	#	%	#	%
2002										
2003										
2004										
2005										
2006										

Source of Data: _____

Date Collected and Collector: _____

	African American		Native American/ Alaskan		Asian/Pacific Islander		Latino		White	
Title I										
Year	#	%	#	%	#	%	#	%	#	%
2002										
2003										
2004										
2005										
2006										

Source of Data: _____

Date Collected and Collector: _____

Figure 10.2 Continued

SCHOOL CHARACTERISTCS (continued)

Course Enrollment (Middle–High School): College Preparatory Math * Can be done by course and grade level.										
	African American		Native American/ Alaskan		Asian/Pacfic Islander		Latino		White	
Year	#	%	#	%	#	%	#	%	#	%
2002										
2003										
2004										
2005										
2006										

Source of Data: _____   Date Collected and Collector: _____

Course Enrollment (Middle–High School): General Math * Can be done by course and grade level.										
	African American		Native American/ Alaskan		Asian/Pacific Islander		Latino		White	
Year	#	%	#	%	#	%	#	%	#	%
2002										
2003										
2004										
2005										
2006										

Source of Data: _____   Date Collected and Collector: _____

Course Enrollment (Middle–High School): College Preparatory Science * Can be done by course and grade level.										
	African American		Native American/ Alaskan		Asian/Pacific Islander		Latino		White	
Year	#	%	#	%	#	%	#	%	#	%
2002										
2003										
2004										
2005										
2006										

Source of Data: _____   Date Collected and Collector: _____

(continued)

Figure 10.2 Continued

SCHOOL CHARACTERISTCS (continued)

Course Enrollment (Middle–High School): General Science *Can be done by course and grade level.*										
	African American		Native American/ Alaskan		Asian/Pacific Islander		Latino		White	
Year	#	%	#	%	#	%	#	%	#	%
2002										
2003										
2004										
2005										
2006										

Source of Data: _____ Date Collected and Collector: _____

Course Enrollment (Middle–High School): Foreign Language *Can be done by course and grade level.*										
	African American		Native American/ Alaskan		Asian/Pacific Islander		Latino		White	
Year	#	%	#	%	#	%	#	%	#	%
2002										
2003										
2004										
2005										
2006										

Source of Data: _____ Date Collected and Collector: _____

Group Patterns by Reading Groups (Elementary School) *Do for math also—can be done by grade level and teacher.*										
	Top		Middle		Low		Pull-Out		Other	
Year	#	%	#	%	#	%	#	%	#	%
2002										
2003										
2004										
2005										
2006										

Source of Data: _____ Date Collected and Collector: _____

Figure 10.2   Continued

STUDENT ASPIRATIONS AND ACHIEVEMENT

Career Choice—Needs College										
	African American		Native American/ Alaskan		Asian/Pacific Islander		Latino		White	
Year	#	%	#	%	#	%	#	%	#	%
2002										
2003										
2004										
2005										
2006										

Source of Data: _____ Date Collected and Collector: _____

Expects to Attend College										
	African American		Native American/ Alaskan		Asian/Pacific Islander		Latino		White	
Year	#	%	#	%	#	%	#	%	#	%
2002										
2003										
2004										
2005										
2006										

Source of Data: _____ Date Collected and Collector: _____

Enrolled in College Courses * For elementary, can be modified, i.e., to reflect level of curriculum taught, group placement, etc.										
	African American		Native American/ Alaskan		Asian/Pacific Islander		Latino		White	
Year	#	%	#	%	#	%	#	%	#	%
2002										
2003										
2004										
2005										
2006										

Source of Data: _____ Date Collected and Collector: _____

(continued)

Figure 10.2 Continued

STUDENT OUTCOMES

	Standardized Test Scores * Should be disaggregated by race/ethnicity, grade.											
	Reading				Math				Language			
Year	Q1	Q2	Q3	Q4	Q1	Q2	Q3	Q4	Q1	Q2	Q3	Q4
2002												
2003												
2004												
2005												
2006												

Source of Data: _____   Date Collected and Collector: _____

	Standardized Test Scores * Should be disaggregated by race/ethnicity, grade.											
	PSAT						SAT					
	Verbal			Math			Verbal			Math		
Year	# Tested	% Tested	Avg. Score	# Tested	% Tested	Avg. Score	# Tested	% Tested	Avg. Score	# Tested	% Tested	Avg. Score
2002												
2003												
2004												
2005												
2006												

Source of Data: _____   Date Collected and Collector: _____

Advanced Placement Tests * Should be disaggregated by race/ethnicity, grades/subjects.			
Year	# Enrolled	# Tested	3 or Better Score
2002			
2003			
2004			
2005			
2006			

Source of Data: _____   Date Collected and Collector: _____

Figure 10.2   Continued

STUDENT OUTCOMES (continued)

	Standards Assessments * *Should be disaggregated by race/ethnicity, gender, grade, course, etc.*									
	Level One Far Below Basic		Level Two Below Basic		Level Three Basic		Level Four Proficient		Level Five Advanced	
Year	#	%	#	%	#	%	#	%	#	%
2002										
2003										
2004										
2005										
2006										

Source of Data: _____   Date Collected and
Collector: _____

	Grades * *Should be disaggregated by race/ethnicity, gender, grade, course, etc.*									
	A's		B's		C's		D's		F's	
Year	#	%	#	%	#	%	#	%	#	%
2002										
2003										
2004										
2005										
2006										

Source of Data: _____   Date Collected and
Collector: _____

	Graduation **Can also be done by cohorts that entered in Grade 9 or 10.*									
	African American		Native American/ Alaskan		Asian/Pacific Islander		Latino		White	
Year	#	%	#	%	#	%	#	%	#	%
2002										
2003										
2004										
2005										
2006										

Source of Data: _____   Date Collected and
Collector: _____

(continued)

Figure 10.2 Continued

PARENT PARTICIPATION

	Type of Participation *Should be disaggregated by race/ethnicity, grade.*									
	Parent-Teacher Conference		Advisory		Advocacy		Leadership		Classroom Observation	
Year	#	%	#	%	#	%	#	%	#	%
2002										
2003										
2004										
2005										
2006										

Source of Data: _____ Date Collected and Collector: _____

PARENT ASPIRATIONS

	Expects Child to Attend 2-Year College, 4-Year College/University, or Graduate School									
	African American		Native American/ Alaskan		Asian/Pacific Islander		Latino		White	
Year	#	%	#	%	#	%	#	%	#	%
2002										
2003										
2004										
2005										
2006										

Source of Data: _____ Date Collected and Collector: _____

	Not Expecting Child to Attend 2-Year College, 4-Year College/University, or Graduate School									
	African American		Native American/ Alaskan		Asian/Pacific Islander		Latino		White	
Year	#	%	#	%	#	%	#	%	#	%
2002										
2003										
2004										
2005										
2006										

Source of Data: _____ Date Collected and Collector: _____

Figure 10.2 Continued

SCHOOL RESOURCES

Year	Average # of Students per Classroom			Adult/Student Ratio			Ratio of Computers to Students		
	Regular	Magnet	Special Ed.	Regular	Magnet	Special Ed.	Regular	Magnet	Special Ed.
2002									
2003									
2004									
2005									
2006									

Source of Data: _____   Date Collected and Collector: _____

Institutional Culture
Perceptions of Attitudes, Readiness, and Commitment to Reform
The results from several of the surveys in Chapter 7 can be reported annually or within other seasonal time frames. The data can be displayed similarly to the representations in Chapter 7.

Year	Beliefs and Practices	Perceptions of Support	Current School Status
2002			
2003			
2004	* Attach summary data using percentages in tables, graphs, etc.		
2005			
2006			

Source of Data: _____   Date Collected and Collector: _____

Institutional Culture
Assessing Changes in the Academic Culture of School
The results from several of the surveys in Chapter 7 can be reported annually or within other seasonal time frames. The data can be displayed similarly to the representations in Chapter 7.

Year	
2002	
2003	
2004	* Include baseline and post data information on the areas assessed, e.g., expectations, instructional practices.
2005	
2006	

Source of Data: _____   Date Collected and Collector: _____

(continued)

Figure 10.2 Continued

Institutional Culture
Characteristics of High- and Low-Performing Counselling Programs
* The results from several of the surveys in Chapter 7 can be reported annually or within other seasonal time frames.
The data can be displayed similarly to the representations in Chapter 7.

Year	Counseling Services Rating	Student Support Rating	Counselor Functioning	Coordinated Planning	Use of Data	Progress of Underrepresented Students
2002						
2003						
2004		** Include baseline and post data information on the areas assessed, e.g., expectations, instructional practices.*				
2005						
2006						

Source of Data: _____   Date Collected and Collector: _____

that can evolve out of indicator data. Although they were created for illustrative purposes only, all reflect information from the real world of schools and districts. Some are descriptors of student and teacher characteristics, and others describe differential patterns and outcomes. Some address opportunity-to-learn concerns and the distribution of resources.

Each presentation poses an initial question(s) for the school or district community to answer. These presentations offer only a glimpse of what can be portrayed. The capability to combine applications via computer will be very important to the process.

The team should make decisions about what pieces of data are priorities for discussion and which sets seem linked to each other. Review Chapter 3 on the need to develop questions. Are there some data that appear to explain some student outcomes? If so, they need to be looked at simultaneously. It will be important to link some of the findings to current research and literature on implications for reform. Keeping up with the research will also inform schools and districts about what and how indicators can inform their decision making. Some group should be charged with this major responsibility for keeping the educational community informed. Again, a reminder: Assess your technology capability at the beginning stages of the process.

Although sophisticated technology can raise your capacity to another level, don't let the lack of this stop you from trying to piece together the answers to critical questions. Many of the indicators can be hand counted and tallied with a calculator, and many of the displays can be hand drawn—the important thing is to get the data out there so the school can begin analyzing their implications.

This section is intended to show some of the possibilities, but readers are urged not to limit their own indicator selections, analyses, and representations. This text would be too cumbersome if all possible approaches were presented. Ideally, these will inspire readers to design more and better ways of looking at measures of progress.

Data Analysis and Presentations

Different staff members should have the opportunity to analyze indicator data, particularly data that look at issues close to their own work. The staff must devote time and close attention to the data and discuss the implications. Suggested ways to create and frame the conversations from the data findings can be found in Chapter 5. Parents, students, and staff should all have the opportunity to review and discuss what the data mean to them and what implications for action are suggested.

Discussion and Cautionary Notes

Engaging the educational community in determining indicators is important in building the capacity of the institution to look critically inward. Time must be provided so the staff and others can think deeply about the issues and also have time to revise, add, or delete. An outsider with expertise in this area may be needed to set the framework and guidelines. The purpose should be established ahead of time. Hollow indicators will be of no use in improving the educational program. There must be a commitment to continue the process and to establish its value. This should become a part of the way the school does business.

It is especially difficult, but not impossible, to get broad student progress data at the elementary school level. There may be distribution by program. Report card data are usually hard to aggregate. For the middle and high school levels, course enrollment data, such as enrollment in higher-level courses, are usually available to be disaggregated by subgroups. Course grades are also usually more readily available. However, the meaning of letter grades may vary from teacher to teacher. Schools need to develop performance standards and rubrics for measuring progress. Again, indicators of opportunities to learn are critical. Who gets access to which curricula? Who has the opportunity to learn high-status knowledge?

SAMPLE INDICATOR COMBINATIONS

How Do the Racial and Ethnic Characteristics of the Teachers and Students Compare?

The literature (Darder, 1991; Irvine, 1990; Olsen et al., 1994; Rice & Walsh, 1996; Spring, 2000) often suggests that the mismatch between student and teacher characteristics may affect teachers' expectations of students, their approaches with students, and their relationships with parents. When student and teacher characteristics are vastly different, there is probably reason to try to find out if the differences are affecting the teaching and learning process. This basic information—such as faculty and student ethnicity characteristics—begins to describe the school environment but will not address qualitative issues. Figure 10.3 shows that at this school, the majority of students are people of color and the majority of the staff is white. There is a need to dig deeper, using qualitative methods such as observations, to observe the interactions between teachers and students regarding opportunity to learn, expectations, and whether culturally relevant teaching is occurring. Ladson-Billings (1994) states, "Specifically, culturally relevant teaching is a pedagogy that empowers students

Figure 10.3   How Do the Racial and Ethnic Characteristics of the Teachers and Students Compare?

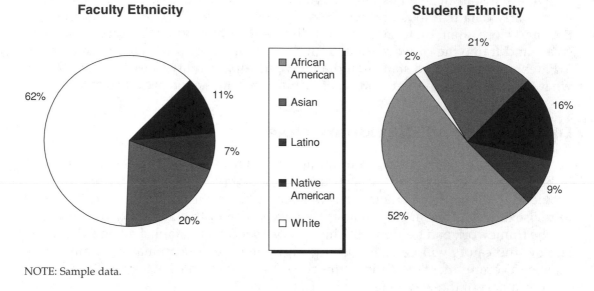

NOTE: Sample data.

intellectually, socially, emotionally, and politically by using cultural referents to impart knowledge, skills and attitudes" (pp. 17–18).

Which Teachers Have the Most Years of Experience, by Race/Ethnicity?

Figure 10.4 shows that if we disaggregate the data further by teacher classification, we find that the majority of the experienced teachers are white and that the teachers most newly hired and probationary are African American, Asian, and Latino. This has significant implications for professional development, support, and mentoring of new teachers.

Which Teachers Have the Most Proficiency in a Second Language, by Years of Experience?

In Figure 10.5a, further disaggregation of the data by years of teaching experience shows us that the newer teachers have the highest percentage of second language proficiency—a critical need, because 40% of current students are Limited English Proficient (Figure 10.5b). Again, this points to the importance of efforts to retain new teachers. Note: There are qualitative indicators of the teaching and learning process, regardless of teacher characteristics, that also need to be reported, such as content presented and the time teachers spend on subject matter. Other questions will relate to instructional strategies. What types of learning opportunities are students experiencing? Are there differential patterns by race, ethnicity, and gender?

Figure 10.4   How Are Teacher Characteristics Related to Number of Years Teaching Experience?

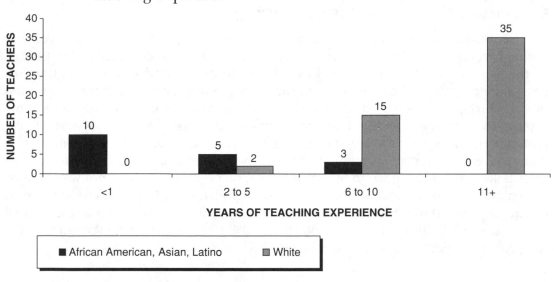

Figure 10.5a   Percentage of Teachers Proficient in a Second Language by Years of Experience

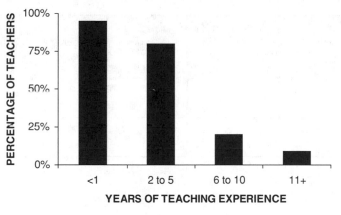

Figure 10.5b   Percentages of Limited English Proficient and Fluent English Proficient Students

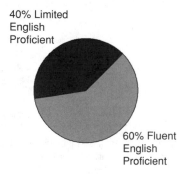

NOTE: Sample data.

Are Eligible Students From Different Racial and Gender Groups Receiving the Same Opportunities for Higher Learning?

Combination data can be used to measure which students are gaining access to higher-level courses. One way is to look at the proportions of different ethnic groups in the school and the proportion in different programs and courses. Figure 10.6 shows the proportion of each group in the school's eighth grade and the proportion of each group in algebra. It clearly shows the imbalance of placements of some groups to their representation in the population. African Americans and Native Americans/Alaskans have lower representations, Asian/Pacific Islander and white students have higher representations, and Latino students have almost matched representation to their proportion of the eighth-grade population. A school would need to explore why the data look like this. These data also need to be looked at in terms of equity goals, standards, and expectations for students at the school. The school and district could also choose the option of 100% access to all students and provide the proper support for those students who need it.

Figure 10.6a   Eighth-Grade Course Enrollment in Algebra

	African American		Native American/ Alaskan		Asian/Pacific Islander		Latino		White		Total	
	#	%	#	%	#	%	#	%	#	%	#	%
In Grade 8	176	24	56	8	102	14	256	35	136	19	726	100
In Algebra	50	14	10	3	90	23	132	34	101	26	383	100

SOURCE: An urban school.

Figure 10.6b   Middle School Algebra Placement

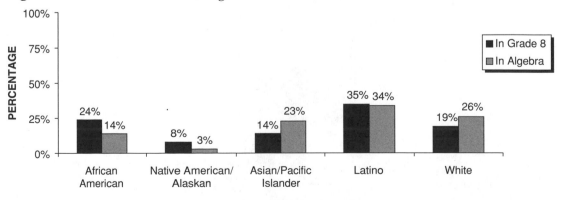

Are Placements Based on Meritocracy?

Many times schools and districts will say they use merit to place students, and they consider the process fair and color-blind. Figure 10.7a shows data gathered from a district that espoused "fairness in placement." When this district was asked why there were gaps among the student racial/ethnic groups in placement in algebra, they explained that they used test scores for placement and that students had to be in the top quartile to be placed in algebra. (I am by no means endorsing this as the criterion for placement, but I am using it as an example to measure the public statements vs. the reality of what takes place in a school or district.)

The data come from an urban middle school and show the distribution of top-quartile students in eighth-grade algebra. An alarming pattern emerges. For African Americans and Latinos who score high on tests, it appears that they are not afforded the opportunity to learn algebra at the same rates as their Asian and white counterparts. For example, barely more than 40% of all Latino and 51% of all African American top-quartile performers were actually placed in college preparatory math, compared to 64% of all Asian and 61% of all white top-quartile performers. What does this say about the school's assumptions regarding their African American and Latino students' capabilities?

Figure 10.7b takes the inquiry further by disaggregating these racial groups by gender. For African American top scorers, there is little discernible difference between the placement of males and females in algebra—all are placed around the very low rate of 50%. Latino females are placed at the abysmally low rate of 40%, with their male counterparts placed only slightly higher, at 44%. For Asian groups, qualified males are placed at a far higher frequency than qualified females are. Why? Why are white males placed at lower levels than their female counterparts—the only group showing this trend? The school community should find much to discuss regarding data of this striking nature. This data picture is not unique to this district. I have encountered many other instances of this occurring in schools and districts.

What Proportion of Students Who Enroll Actually Complete Selected Mathematics Courses With a Grade of C or Better, by Race/Ethnicity?

Usually schools keep enrollment data, but they do not look at course completion data. Or, if they do look at course completion data, they do not monitor students' grades in those courses. How many students are barely passing their courses? Enrolling students in the "right courses" is necessary, but not sufficient. It is essential to closely monitor what happens to students in courses. The data in Figure 10.8 are disaggregated by student characteristics. These are examples of only a few courses, but this type of information is needed on other courses as well. The figure highlights not only low completion rates with a grade of C or better for all students, but alarmingly low rates for African American and Latino students in all three courses and for white students in calculus, chemistry, and physics. If there is a belief system that these students are capable of mastering these courses, the school community must tackle issues of approaches used, support systems for teachers and students, and monitoring of students' and teachers' progress. If there are belief systems operating that influence perceptions about who is capable of learning higher-level knowledge, then these must also be tackled. If the school or district is truly committed

Figure 10.7a Are Eligible Students From Different Racial Groups Receiving the Same Opportunities for Higher Learning?

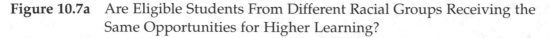
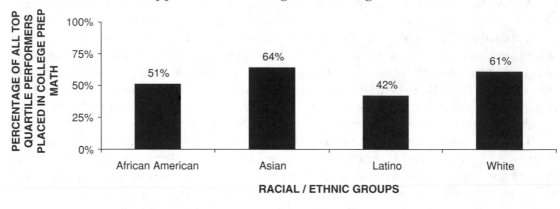

Figure 10.7b Middle School Algebra Placement

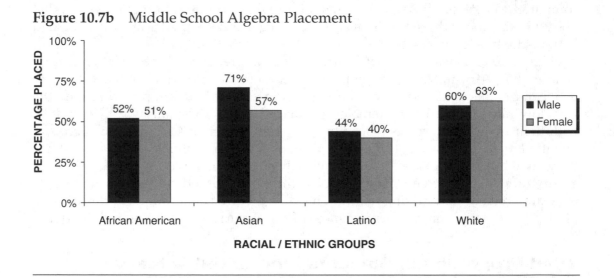

Figure 10.8 Proportion of High School Seniors Completing Selected Courses With a Grade of C or Better

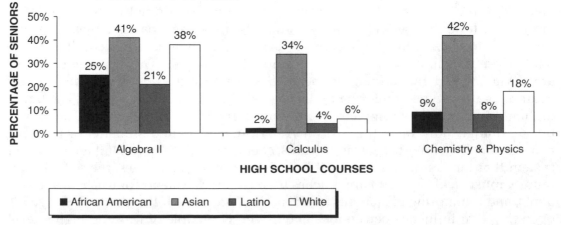

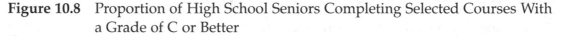

SOURCE: An urban high school.

Figure 10.9   Number of Students on "Grade Level": Comparison of Grade Point Averages and SAT9 Performance

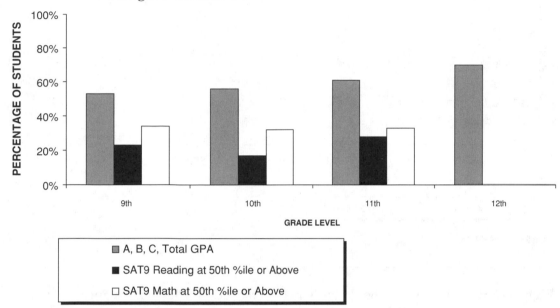

SOURCE: The Principals Exchange.

to fundamental reform in student outcomes, these data provide compelling information and an opening for discussions about practices and processes. Data of this nature can also be reported among indicators of achievement.

Comparison of Test Scores and Grades

Figure 10.9 shows data from a low-income urban school. Test scores in mathematics and reading and grades A to C in mathematics and reading were combined to analyze if students who received these grades scored at or above the 50th percentile on the test. The 50th percentile was considered average. This combination of indicators clearly shows that there is probably grade inflation. Many students are receiving grades higher than what is reflected for the test scores. This reflects a similar picture to the national NAEP data presented in Chapter 2. The school needs to dig deeper and do analysis of the curriculum and instructional practices.

The Price of "High-Stakes" Test Scores: Are There Patterns Between the Placement of Students in Special Education, the Grade Retention of Students, and Rising Test Scores Reported by Schools?

"High-stakes" (standardized and state) testing puts pressure on schools to raise scores. Sometimes they respond by retaining certain students or placing other students in special education so that they will not be tested and their scores will not be factored into the school's performance. Several studies have found that, as retention rates and placements in special education accelerate, test scores rise (Allington & McGill-Franzen, 1992a, 1992b; McGill-Franzen & Allington, 1993).

Figure 10.10a Median Percentile Test Scores

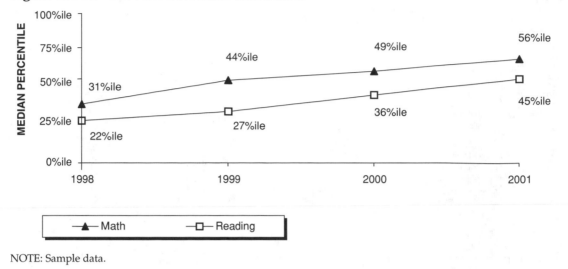

NOTE: Sample data.

Figure 10.10b What Are the Patterns Between Student Placements and Rising Test Scores?

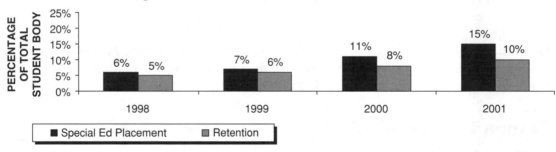

NOTE: Sample data.

This practice of increasing test scores by re-sorting students comes with a high price for the young people, and it misleads adults into thinking that the school is really improving. There may be no fundamental reforms, no attack on inequities—in fact inequities may increase—and yet there is the appearance of improvement.

Every school and district would do well to conduct an analysis such as the one that follows. Although not shown in this analysis, the data should also be disaggregated to find out if some racial/ethnic groups are re-sorted in special education or retained at higher rates than others. It can also be very revealing to disaggregate data by grade level and classroom.

Figure 10.10a shows that this school's standardized test scores increased over a period of four years. This might be cause to celebrate . . . until we look at some other data (see Figure 10.10b).

Figure 10.10b shows that over a four-year period, the same school showed an increasing trend in the retention of students and the placement of students in special education. The bar graph shows that in fact from 1999 to 2001, special education placement doubled from 6% to 15%, and retention doubled from 5% to 10%.

Figure 10.11   What Percentage of All Students Are Tested?

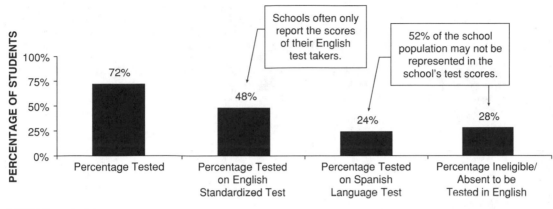

NOTE: Sample data.

Meanwhile, it is also apparent that the percentage of students taking the standardized test decreased. Is raising test scores worth this price—sacrificing students' educational opportunities?

Do the Test Scores Reflect How All Students Are Achieving? What Percentage of Students Take the Test, and What Percentage Are Tested in English?

Many big city school districts' test scores do not represent the entire population —in some schools a large proportion of students may not be tested. Therefore, it is important to make sure we know the percentage of students tested. Some schools with large populations of students who are not fluent in English also test very low percentages of students, and only the scores of the English test takers are reported. Reviewing the disaggregated data on testing in Figure 10.11 shows that only 48% of the students in this school were tested in English on the standardized test; if this school is typical, only the scores of these students will be reported to the school community and the public. Meanwhile, 52% of the school population—the students tested in Spanish and the students who were not tested at all—would not even be represented in the data. It is unproductive to base decisions regarding a school's achievement on such a distorted sample of the entire school population. This is not to say that the scores of English test takers should not be taken seriously—it's just that the picture is incomplete.

How Are Resources Distributed? Who Has Access to Computers? For What Amount of Time Do Individual Students Actually Have Their Hands on Computers?

Although schools and districts have budget information available, it is important to assess the type and nature of resource distribution, particularly to address issues of equity. Table 10.1 is a sample illustration of how a resource such as computers gets allocated. It is clear that technological capability will be a basic skill in the 21st century and that students who are denied access to this type of knowledge will be handicapped (Buschwaller & Fatemi, 2001; Kohl, 2001, cited in Scoon & Reid, 2001; Scoon

Table 10.1   How Are Computer Resources Distributed?

Program	Total Number of Students in School	Total Number of Computers Available	Average Number of Hours per Week Each Student Spends on Computers	Type of Computer Program
Regular Classrooms	225	20	1.00	75% Drill, practice, test taking, 25% Web site and problem solving
Gifted	55	25	6.50	100% Multimedia, Web site, and problem solving
Magnet Program	125	60	6.00	100% Multimedia, Web site, and problem solving
Special Education	42	2	0.25	100% Drill, practice, test taking

NOTE: Sample data.

& Reid, 2001). Table 10.1 reflects the kind of data that are being found in districts. According to the table, there is one computer for every two magnet students, and every magnet student uses the computers three to five times a week. Students in the gifted program have similar access and use levels. The greatest disparity exists for students in special education. Not only do they have limited access, but their use levels are very low. Students in regular classrooms have more access and use than students in special education, but they still have much less than students in the magnet and gifted programs. The type of programs different groups of students use is also illustrated. Students in higher-level programs get more problem-solving time on the computer, whereas others use the computer for more drill and practice. This information should spur discussions about why this is occurring. Some other questions may need to be answered, such as these: Where are the computers located? How are they funded? Do teachers have the skills to engage students with the technology? What types of computer programs do students in different groups use?

As the school or district goes through the reform process, some of the information like the samples presented in this chapter will be gathered on a regular basis. Other information might be gathered to answer questions that arise at other times. Once decisions are made based on the data, there needs to be monitoring to find out what the outcomes are. This process should be dynamic and continuous and should result in building the capacity of the institution to make decisions that result in positive, deep-level reforms for students.

11

Will We Know It When We See It?

Visioning, Planning, and Implementation

When the school reform team was asked if there was a vision for the school, they were not sure. Most did not really know what a school vision looked like or why it was important. The members also realized they didn't know if they shared similar ideas about what they expected to happen for the children at their school. The school community had never discussed what they would like to see taking place in three to six to nine years. Business as usual continued day after day, week after week, year after year.

When school plans were devised, they were mostly for the benefit of external sources, such as central administration or funders. These plans were usually crafted by a small group with few contributions from the wider school community. Most staff members had no idea what was in the plan, what the expectations were, or what the school was accountable for doing. No one seemed to check whether what was promised actually happened. The plans were based on activities and rarely mentioned clearly stated goals for student achievement or for reforms in the organization's academic culture. This school community clearly needed to channel its energies in more productive ways. They were working hard, but not smart. It was time to break the cycle of meaningless planning.

The school then spent substantial time examining their beliefs about children's learning capability and their sorting and grouping practices. They had pored over the data that gave them clues to practices that might be enhancing or detracting from achievement. Many parents and community stakeholders were involved in looking at the data and were part of the decision-making process.

As a result of all this time, effort, and reflection, teachers, parents, and administrators came to a consensus that they needed to make changes. Plans were made, resources were reallocated, priorities were established, and new initiatives were launched. The leadership teams, staff, students, and parents were anxious for implementation.

The data teams were aware that, with all of these changes, it would be critical to monitor student academic progress and changes in the institutional culture. How would they know what was working? Did they need to make midcourse corrections? What indicators would suggest that they were achieving their goals? What information did they need to report?

The data teams designed a monitoring plan. The information they collected was consistently used in the evaluation and decision-making process. It was not always easy. Many did not want to take the time to gather information; they wanted to make decisions based on impressions. The data and leadership teams held firm and remained committed to the process of monitoring. As a result, the school and district were able to communicate effectively about outcomes and the changes that led to them. They were able to discuss pluses and minuses of different approaches and were able to adjust plans as needed. As a result, student achievement improved, and they were able to institutionalize reforms.

Overview

This chapter suggests ways to

- Keep your "eyes on the prize"
- Develop a vision for reform based on the data you have gathered and a way to describe what reform will look like when you accomplish your vision
- Craft a Plan for Schoolwide Reform (see Figure 11.2a, page 258) that includes built-in ways to measure how well each aspect of the vision is accomplished
- Look at resources for implementation
- Monitor progress

When a school community reflects on the information it has gathered, participants will begin to ask: What is our vision? Where do we want to go? How do we develop a plan for reform that includes goals based on the information and data we have collected? How can we use what we have learned about mapping and measuring so far to develop our vision and plans?

Real reform requires school staffs and parents to assume control of designing the plan for reform and to feel accountable for both the process and outcomes. For example, if the goal is to eliminate remedial curricula, then a plan is needed that expresses specifically how this will be done, who will do it, and the timelines for accomplishing it. The plan for reform must be understood and agreed upon by all key participants. The plan should also include a feedback mechanism for monitoring effectiveness in improving student outcomes, so that midcourse corrections or revisions can be accomplished.

Many times, schools and districts begin a reform effort by developing a vision. The literature emphasizes the importance of a vision, and simple observation makes it clear that dramatic improvements in student achievement require both personal vision on the part of leaders and shared vision on the part of the school or district staff. Once a vision is articulated, the next early step is usually to develop an action plan for reform in the school setting.

If this is the norm, why are the discussions about visions and action planning occurring this late in this book? Because it is critical for the education community to have first done the kind of deep reflection and assessment suggested throughout this book. Most educators are at best resigned and at worst cynical when—once again—they are asked to go through a visioning or planning exercise. But when educators have already invested great time and thought in truly understanding their teaching habits, expectations, and outcomes for students, there will be much greater chance for reform to be lasting.

Often at the initiation of the reform process, school communities hear motivational speeches about the need for a vision. They typically participate in one or two workshops with a flurry of vision-building activity. Questions that emerge from participants, such as, "How many pages does our vision have to be?" speak for themselves. The exercise can feel hollow, especially when perceived as the only time allotted for vision building.

Unfortunately, the resulting visions usually end up very general, littered with vague language. This is particularly common in schools and districts with low achievement patterns. In the end, then, the exercise is purely symbolic, mostly because there was very little reflection prior to the development of the vision. Slogan-like language—such as, "All children will achieve to their highest potential" or "All of our graduates will be successful in postsecondary endeavors"—doesn't accomplish very much. When questioned, participants often give very different definitions of what such statements mean. They are glad the task is over and hope not to have to talk about visions any further. They have been through this process too many times.

For these reasons, vision-building work should begin only after serious thought and dialogue have taken place about issues of equity, assumptions about who can learn high-level knowledge, and what kinds of reforms are possible. By now, the school or district should have very important data gathered through its inquiry process; it should have assessed its academic culture and commitment to reform; staff members should have measured the equity of current practices in relationship to the school experiences and outcomes for different kinds of students; and they should have analyzed the effectiveness of current efforts to raise student achievement. There should be an awareness of the school community's strengths and weaknesses related to equity because indicators have been examined in combinations.

According to Michael Fullan (1993),

> Vision emerges from, more than it precedes action. Even then it is always provisional. Second, shared vision, which is essential for success, must evolve through the dynamic interaction of organizational members and leaders. This takes time and will not succeed unless the vision building process is somewhat open-ended. A vision coming later does not mean that they are not worked on. Just the opposite is true. They are pursued more authentically while avoiding premature formalizations. (p. 28)

If there is a vision created at the beginning of a reform process, it should be considered a working vision, one that must be revisited. The working vision will be revised through the reform process, informed by the data and dialogue encouraged throughout this book. Then the vision becomes the engine that pulls the train, the living document that has deep roots and real ownership to guide future work. Stakeholders will feel passionate about accomplishing this kind of vision—not often the case for some quickly written statement buried in a pile of plans.

Stop! Before You Start

The school community will benefit from reading and discussing in depth the following literature: "Acquiring and Using Resources" (Parker, 1993); *Change Forces: Probing the Depths of Educational Reform*, Chapter 2 (Fullan, 1993); "Establishing the Mission, Vision and Goals" (Stout, 1993); *Improving Schools From Within*, Chapters 11 and 12 (Barth, 1990); "Managing Instructional Diversity" (Winfield et al., 1993); and *Prisoners of Time* (National Education Commission on Time and Learning, 1994).

In cultures resistant to the reform process, a highly skilled external facilitator-coach may need to assist with or lead the process. The staff will need at least two one-hour blocks to read and discuss the writings in both small and large groups. Don't rush this process or squeeze it in between agenda items at a faculty meeting. The optimal environment would be off-site, where the school community can be free of distractions.

WE WANT OUR SCHOOL TO LOOK LIKE THIS

Following is a suggested approach to help school communities really think about what they want their school to look like in three to six to nine years. The visioning imagines future educator practices and behaviors as well as student outcomes. This can be used as an ongoing reminder of the desired future. A prose-type vision can be crafted from this document.

We Want Our School to Look Like This (Figure 11.1a) was developed to help education communities focus on their vision for reform and on outcomes that go beyond test scores. It was developed so schools could envision an organizational culture that was different from the one that currently existed, and so that schools could look at behaviors and practices of the key players. We Want Our School to Look Like This can present challenges for discussions that dig below the surface. A completed sample of this template is presented in Figure 11.1b (page 254).

When to Use

As discussed earlier, the visioning process is meant to follow review of data, reflection, and dialogue. The school should have identified what it wants to do differently and should have made the commitment to working toward long-term equitable reform. The visioning exercise itself may take several sessions of a minimum of two hours each, allowing plenty of time for discussion.

Administering the Form

A team that is representative of the school community, including parents and students, can develop a draft of the vision, or the entire school community can be

Figure 11.1a   In 200_, We Want Our School to Look Like This

School policies to promote equity will be evident in:

-
-
-
-
-

Student achievement will be evident in:

-
-
-
-
-

Counselors will:

-
-
-
-
-

Teachers will:

-
-
-
-
-

Administrators will:

-
-
-
-
-

Students will:

-
-
-
-
-

Parents and communities will:

-
-
-

Figure 11.1b   In 2006, We Want Our School to Look Like This: Sample High School Vision

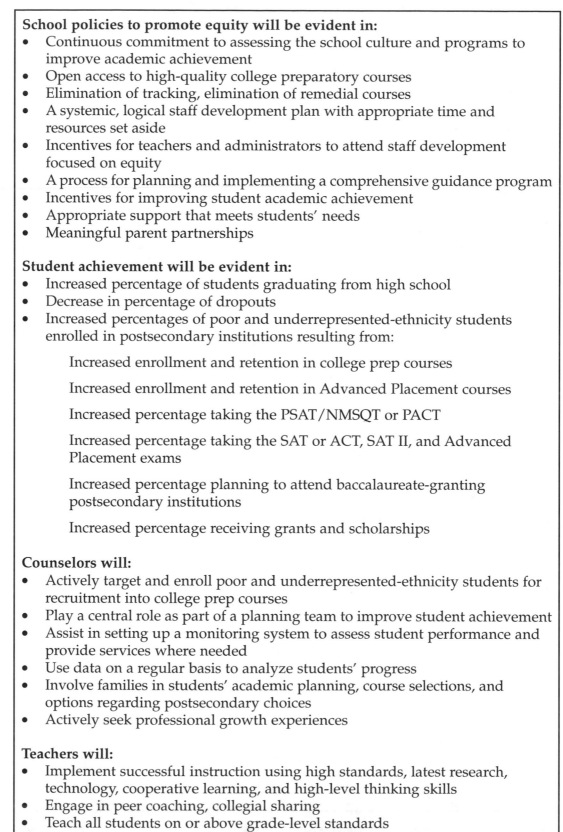

School policies to promote equity will be evident in:
- Continuous commitment to assessing the school culture and programs to improve academic achievement
- Open access to high-quality college preparatory courses
- Elimination of tracking, elimination of remedial courses
- A systemic, logical staff development plan with appropriate time and resources set aside
- Incentives for teachers and administrators to attend staff development focused on equity
- A process for planning and implementing a comprehensive guidance program
- Incentives for improving student academic achievement
- Appropriate support that meets students' needs
- Meaningful parent partnerships

Student achievement will be evident in:
- Increased percentage of students graduating from high school
- Decrease in percentage of dropouts
- Increased percentages of poor and underrepresented-ethnicity students enrolled in postsecondary institutions resulting from:

> Increased enrollment and retention in college prep courses
>
> Increased enrollment and retention in Advanced Placement courses
>
> Increased percentage taking the PSAT/NMSQT or PACT
>
> Increased percentage taking the SAT or ACT, SAT II, and Advanced Placement exams
>
> Increased percentage planning to attend baccalaureate-granting postsecondary institutions
>
> Increased percentage receiving grants and scholarships

Counselors will:
- Actively target and enroll poor and underrepresented-ethnicity students for recruitment into college prep courses
- Play a central role as part of a planning team to improve student achievement
- Assist in setting up a monitoring system to assess student performance and provide services where needed
- Use data on a regular basis to analyze students' progress
- Involve families in students' academic planning, course selections, and options regarding postsecondary choices
- Actively seek professional growth experiences

Teachers will:
- Implement successful instruction using high standards, latest research, technology, cooperative learning, and high-level thinking skills
- Engage in peer coaching, collegial sharing
- Teach all students on or above grade-level standards

Figure 11.1b   Continued

- Have increased higher expectations for students, including open access and retention in college prep courses
- Actively seek professional growth experiences
- Strive for partnerships with parents regarding students' academic experience
- Use assessments and other data on a regular basis to analyze and improve students' learning

Administrators will:
- Play a key role in setting the climate for successful implementation of a plan to strengthen teaching and learning, educational guidance and counseling services, and support services for students
- Set up a system to monitor progress toward increasing the numbers of poor and underrepresented-ethnicity students who enter postsecondary institutions
- Evaluate teachers and counselors in ways that recognize these improved strategies
- Create structures to provide ongoing communication to facilitate better use of resources
- Facilitate structuring time for staff development related to the plan's objectives
- Promote collaboration between teachers, counselors, administrators, students, and parents to meet the plan's objectives
- Analyze student achievement data with staff and use data for improvement of student learning

Students will:
- Demonstrate increased awareness of and enrollment in the required college preparatory courses needed to meet their future career aspirations
- Use vehicles to express their voices regarding the school culture and program —and know that their opinions are weighed seriously in decision making
- Feel capable of achieving at high levels and know that their individual aspirations are important
- Show increased awareness of the connection between education, income level, and future quality-of-life possibilities
- Increase completion of homework assignments
- Attend school regularly and on time
- Participate more in school activities
- Decrease involvement in incidents that lead to suspensions, expulsions, and other disciplinary actions

Parents and communities will:
- Play a role in the collection, analysis, and presentation of data—and decision making based on the data
- Use a variety of vehicles to voice their ideas and concerns in the school reform process
- Show an increase in knowledge of courses their children should be enrolled in to reach their college and career aspirations
- Become informed advocates for closing the achievement gap
- Participate in and encourage their child's educational growth

involved from the outset, first working in small groups and then all together. This will depend on what works best in your school culture. The sample vision in Figure 11.1b can be used to provoke thought relevant to the circumstances of the individual school or district. A knowledgeable facilitator may be brought in to guide the process.

Prior to discussing a vision for the future, the individuals and groups in the school community should be challenged to complete the following (Barth, 1990):

"I want my school to become a place where . . ."

"The kind of school I would like my own children to attend would . . ."

"The kind of school I would like to teach in . . ."

It is important to ask, "Is the kind of school envisioned good enough for my family, or are we thinking only of what is good enough for 'other people's children'?" This will help get to the bottom of the values and beliefs of those in the school community.

Discussion and Cautionary Notes

If this vision-building exercise is to lead to real reform, it must take place at a time when participants can give it their full attention. This work may take several months and should not be relegated to one or two sessions.

Although revisions may be necessary, keep expectations high. It is better to aim for the stars than to aim low just to succeed. The vision should be considered a working document that guides and becomes the conscience for the reform process over the long haul.

The school vision must be referred to constantly to assess whether practices, strategies, behaviors, and data outcomes are consistent with where the school wants to be. When activities begin to detract from realization of the vision, then the vision must be brought back into focus. About everything we must ask, "How does this help us achieve our vision?" This is a continuous process so that behaviors and practices become institutionalized.

PLAN FOR SCHOOLWIDE REFORM

As with visions, school communities have typically developed plan after plan, often at the direction of governmental or district officials. It is not uncommon to see more than one of these documents, as thick as telephone directories, abandoned on the shelves of school administrators. Although public and private funding sources recently have called for more collaborative processes to produce the work plans in funding proposals, expediency still often results in the work's being done primarily by a couple of individuals with the time and skills to follow the guidelines.

This undermines broad ownership and commitment to any plan. Even when staff and parents have worked jointly on a plan, its long-term manageability and practical benefits may come into question once the writing exercise is complete. For schools with multiple plans—some with schoolwide application and others targeting particular segments—it is unusual for the plans to be coordinated or cross-referenced with respect to compatibility of focus, goals, and implementation strategies. Schools can analyze and prioritize their array of efforts, using the suggestions in the directions for administering the Analysis of Efforts to Raise Student Achievement (Table 9.1a, page 201). This exercise could easily be adapted to analyze the impact of school plans.

The Plan for Schoolwide Reform (Figure 11.2a) is designed to avoid dead-end planning. The action plan should be thought of simply as a road map that leads us toward our vision. What do our data say about where we are? Where do we want our students to be? How are the adults going to help them get there? Who is going to be primarily responsible? What supports will it take? What is the time frame? How will we know if we are making progress?

The intent of the Plan for Schoolwide Reform is to establish the general areas of focus and action for moving toward a schoolwide culture of high achievement. A comprehensive framework listing critical dimensions of school practice, such as that provided in Assessing Institutional Reforms in the Academic Culture of Schools (Figure 7.2a, pages 144–147), can suggest specific areas of focus for a first year of planning. Focus areas may be addressed simultaneously, perhaps by different teams, as long as the process for each is comprehensive and the efforts are not completely fragmented and isolated. This instrument is particularly helpful as a baseline self-assessment that will generate data about the school's relative strengths and limitations. Following are questions you should ask as you choose focus areas:

- Have you limited the focus to a maximum of three areas for any one year?
- Does at least one of those areas build off current plans or priorities?
- Does the proposed activity address concerns raised in the assessment? Is it likely to help achieve the desired result?
- Are we really changing the core instructional program, or are we "adding on" programs while conducting business as usual in our classrooms?
- Is the expectation sufficiently high to be challenging for all students?
- Is this strategy likely to be the most effective leverage point for improving the instructional program?
- Are we prepared to implement this activity, or do we need additional training?

Planning for reform also requires attention to needed resources and their availability. Funding and time are equally critical. The absence of these often contributes to difficulties and frustrations in reform work. If these resources are not available, then strategies for acquiring them should be considered. Nevertheless, the influence of resources on the scope of reform merits discussion. An important and often overlooked resource is human support.

It is important to stop and think about incentives—and disincentives—for individuals to engage in reform efforts. Consider, for example, that some individuals will participate in curriculum reform for the rewards attached, such as new lab equipment and time off for weeklong trips to New York for training. Some will become involved because of a strong desire to improve student achievement and a belief that it is possible. On the other hand, some will not become involved in reform work for fear of the risk of exposing professional inadequacies or because they do not believe that their students can achieve.

An external reform agent can assist in the development of a plan that realistically matches resources available with needs. Multiple sources of funding and other resources should be dedicated to create the best chances of accomplishing a goal. Figure 11.2 can help schools assess needs in this area.

Figure 11.2a Plan for Schoolwide Reform—Stage One: Year One in Review

Note: Use annually

School:

Goal (only 1 goal per sheet):	What the condition looked like prior to September 200_	What the condition looks like in June 200_

Implementation Strategies	Timeline	Who Was Involved/Responsible?	Resources	Evidence That This Effort Is Making a Difference	Next Steps for 200_ –200_

Figure 11.2b Plan for Schoolwide Reform—Stage One: Year One in Review—Sample of an Elementary School

Note: Use annually

School: Elementary School

Goal (only 1 goal per sheet)	What the condition looked like prior to September 2001	What the condition looks like in June 2002
To restructure Staff Development Program for improved student achievement	*Staff Development Program fragmented—too many unrelated topics; little or no follow-up or evidence of implementation*	*Staff Development Program focused with related topics; ongoing provisions for follow-up and the beginning of collegial plans.*

Implementation Strategies	Timeline	Who Was Involved/Responsible?	Resources	Evidence That This Effort Is Making a Difference	Next Steps for 2002–03
• Selected two major academic thrusts (language arts, math) around which staff development calendar was developed; selections made on assessment of needs.	October 2001	• Staff development subcommittee; principal & representatives from the School Leadership Teams and Data Teams in language arts & math.	• General/Bilingual and Title 1 funds. • Release time/substitutes for on- and off-site in-services.	• End-of-year grade level surveys indicate that more than half of the staff are seeing improved student performance and interest in reading, writing, and mathematical problem solving.	• Continue focus on language arts and math. • Continue planning staff development sessions that deepen staff understanding of new strategies—emphasis on sharing classroom implementation and student outcomes.
• Coordinated staff development series in language arts and math focusing on curriculum frameworks and delivered using the following: (a) whole group sessions, (b) grade level follow-up, (c) interactive hands-on activities throughout, (d) grade level sharing of classroom implementations, and (e) site visits	October–June 2002	• Presenters from on- and off-site. • All teachers/paraprofessionals and administrators received staff development.	• Purchase of language arts and math-based materials.	• Teacher self reports, observations, minutes from meetings indicate that 80% of teachers are implementing the curriculum: 20% on a minimal, 40% on a moderate, and 20% on an intensive level.	• Expand collegial program to include more grade levels. • Share successes. • Implement peer coaching. • Monitor and collect data on levels of implementation.
• Requested and received plans/schedules of collegial observations/demonstrations from interested grade level.	October–June 2002	• Teachers and administrators	• General funds. • Principal/coordinator substitute for teachers.	• Observations show that 50% of teachers' instructional behaviors have changed positively.	• Continue focus.
• Set up monitoring plans.	October 2001	• Data Team	• Release time. • External facilitator/coach.	• Reports, decision making.	• Review monitoring plan, make necessary revisions.

Figure 11.2c Plan for Schoolwide Reform—Stage One: Year One in Review—Sample of a Middle School

Note: Use annually

School: Middle School

Goal (only 1 goal per sheet):	What the condition looked like prior to September 2001	What the condition looks like in June 2002
To untrack math department	*10 sections of basic or remedial 9th grade math*	*Eliminated 8 remedial sections and added 8 algebra sections*

Implementation Strategies	Timeline	Who Was Involved/Responsible?	Resources	Evidence That This Effort Is Making a Difference	Next Steps for 2002–03
• Chose department most ready for reform.	August 2001	• School Leadership Team met with Head Counselor and Math Chair to plan.	• District paid teachers to come during intersession—worked on curriculum.	• 65% of students who wouldn't have taken algebra before are getting A's, B's, and C's.	• Continue staff development with Math Department.
• Principal and Math Chair met with teachers to discuss issue, get buy-in, and determine their needs.	September 2001	• Principal and Math Chair	• Planning time by principal.	• Of the 200 new students in algebra, 65% were Latinos/25% African American.	• Provide student study groups and tutoring to develop student skills and reduce D's and F's.
• Set up staff development with Math Chair on strategies to teach algebra and higher-level math to heterogeneous groups.	October 2001–March 2002	• Principal, Head Counselor, and Math Chair	• Release time, after school videos, conferences and coaching,	• Observation of teachers' practices using multiple approaches.	• Add algebra sections.
• Gather and collect baseline data. • Collect data to monitor progress.	August 2001	• Math Chair, Math Project Director, and selected teachers	• Planning time.	• Teachers engage in dialogue about the data. • Data collected.	• Share and discuss data with all teachers, parents, students, district, and community. • Provide opportunities for dialogue for teachers to talk about data and to suggest data to collect. • Continue data collection and monitoring.

The Plan for Schoolwide Reform is intended to be a user-friendly guide that members of the leadership and planning team consult regularly to help them to stay on course as members carry out their responsibilities in a logical, systematic, and co-ordinated manner. Referring to the plan during team meetings will help ensure that members follow through on their assignments and thus will help build the credibility and confidence of the team.

When to Use

After the school community has made some decisions about where they want to be, they must begin to plan how to get there. The prioritizing will have taken place. Timelines for implementation strategies may vary. These kinds of decisions will have to be made based on the school's culture and resources. The vision, crafted as proposed in this chapter, should be referred to closely through this process, along with the other data and indicators the school has worked hard to collect.

Administering the Form

There are a variety of approaches that can be used to plan, and most school communities know them. The bottom line is that those who are going to implement the plans should be involved in designing them. A plan should also incorporate time for troubleshooting barriers to progress as they arise.

A representative cross section of the school community can draft a plan, with the leadership team taking responsibility for presenting the draft to the entire school or district. Or small groups by area, grade, or department might develop implementation plans. In any case, timelines and responsibilities should be established at the outset.

During the planning process, the key data needed for making decisions must be available, including information about resources. Other plans that are already supposedly operating at the site should be assessed. Will they be merged under a comprehensive umbrella plan? How will all the efforts be coordinated and integrated?

Stage One of the Plan for Schoolwide Reform (Figure 11.2) focuses on a goal and establishes baseline and outcome indicators. The planning team must also look at implementation strategies, responsibilities, and resources. This would be used at the end of a time period to assess what happened and should provide data for future planning.

Stage Two of the Plan for Schoolwide Reform (Figure 11.3) involves forward planning. The school community is asked to focus on the practice being addressed, goals, and future indicators. The planners also must decide on strategies, responsibilities, and resources. A reminder: When resources are discussed, not only allocation but also reallocation of time, people, facilities, and money should be considered. Are resources currently being allocated according to priorities? Are they in alignment with the vision?

These conversations can become uncomfortable and conflicted. This is where the use of information from data gathered is important. How resources are distributed will reflect values, priorities, and issues of power and control. One of the indicators of reform will be a shift in how time, money, and people are allocated. The decisions must always lead back to what is best for achieving the desired outcomes for students.

Once the plans are completed, structures and timelines are needed to monitor progress. Review, discussion, modifications, and revisions should be ongoing.

Figure 11.3a Plan for Schoolwide Reform—Stage Two: Year Two Declaration of Focus for Schoolwide Reform

Note: Use annually

School:

Goal (only 1 goal per sheet):	What norm/practice is being addressed?	What will it look like in June 200_

Condition:

Implementation Strategies	Timeline	Who Will Be Involved/Responsible?	Resources to Be Utilized (human, material, & time)	Evidence That This Effort Is Making a Difference

Figure 11.3b Plan for Schoolwide Reform—Stage Two: Year Two Declaration of Focus for Schoolwide Reform—Sample of a Middle School

Note: Use annually

School: Middle School

Goal (only 1 goal per sheet):	What norm/practice is being addressed?	What will it look like in June 2003
To untrack math department	Majority of staff supports tracking	50% of staff in favor of eliminating tracking as indicated on the survey

Condition: Grouping/Tracking/Labeling

Implementation Strategies	Timeline	Who Will Be Involved/Responsible?	Resources to Be Utilized (human, material, & time)	Evidence That This Effort Is Making a Difference—June 2003
• Professional development with Math Department teachers—how to teach heterogeneous classes. • Gather, present, and discuss data (research and local data). • Visit sites where successful practices are being implemented. • Plan for elimination of remedial courses; institution of higher-level courses.	September–November 2002 September, October 2002 October–December 2002 January–April 2003	• Title I Coordinator and Math Department Chair to set up staff development; all math teachers will participate in staff development. • Teachers, counselors, administrators, parents, students.	• HUMAN: Math Project Director will meet with Math Department Chair to discuss needs. • MATERIAL: Title I funding will help support professional development costs. • TIME: Time set aside for planning, professional development, and evaluation—covered by substitutes.	1. Elimination of all remedial math. 2. 75% of students in algebra earning C or better. 3. Increase of geometry sections from one to three.

Discussion and Cautionary Notes

The planning process, like the creation of a vision, can turn into an exercise to meet someone else's needs. It will be meaningless unless the implementers are seriously committed. Leaders must monitor the process to demonstrate their own commitment. Incentives for implementation should be ongoing and public. The entire school community must be aware of what is being planned and envisioned, perhaps through regular public meetings. It is important for everyone to know how progress will be measured and reported.

When the status quo is being challenged, expect criticism and conflict. It is wise to anticipate in advance questions from members of the school community and public and to prepare answers to foreseen questions as thoughtfully as possible.

WILL WE KNOW IT WHEN WE SEE IT? MONITORING FOR PROGRESS

Enthusiasm often reigns at the beginning of change initiatives. Leaders exude confidence that the changes are going to work and rush headlong to implement plans. But in this fervor, a critical piece of the change design is often bypassed—that is, building in plans from the outset to monitor the progress and impact of the reform.

There is much discussion about the development of indicators to monitor school reform nationally. However, schools and districts need customized measures to assess progress that will help them in decision making, as well as in presenting accurate information to audiences.

What indicators are important to measure? How, where, and from whom do we get the information? When do we collect it? Who is responsible for this?

In addition to outcomes, changes in the academic culture of the institution or district need to be monitored. How are opportunities to learn, expectations, curriculum, and instructional practices changing?

To answer these questions, school staff must start developing instruments to measure progress during the early stages of reform initiatives. The instruments elsewhere in this book as well as the suggestions in this chapter should be of help in this process.

What follows are examples of ways to plan for and actually monitor progress in schools. These examples are not designed to be comprehensive, but merely suggestive. Above all, it will be necessary to supplement formal monitoring with informal approaches to what students and parents have to share about the changes. If institutional norms are truly changing, students should be getting a different message—one that tells them they are expected to excel academically and are perfectly capable of doing so. Schools and district may need to consider using the assistance of others with expertise in designing how to monitor progress. This can help in setting up the framework.

Stop! Before You Start

Review Chapter 3 on data in the change process and the data and presentations in Chapters 2 and 6 through 10.

PLANNING FOR MONITORING

An effective system for monitoring progress should be institutionalized into the way the school or district does business. Monitoring cannot be approached as a once-in-a-while activity. The initial start-up will take substantial time, because, as in all the data processes described in this book, it requires thinking about what information you need to gather; identifying the sources and times that the information needs to be collected; and pinpointing who will be responsible for gathering, analyzing, and designing the data presentations. It also requires deciding who, how, and when you will share the information and determining persons to make sure that all steps are completed. The data team should be central to or lead the process. In addition, the school might want to institute study-action research teams to focus on the progress of specific change initiatives. Whatever the structure, there must be a strong committed leadership that believes in the power of monitoring to enhance the change process. This means supporting the process with time, money, and human resources! Building strong technological capacity also will be critical.

Indicators of progress should be linked to vision and goals. By now, the school community, with the guidance of the leadership and data teams, should have developed sets of indicators such as those described in Chapter 10, which can greatly help to guide monitoring work. However, as the change work evolves, stakeholders should be on the lookout for new data and information that may not have been part of original plans but will be useful to collect and analyze. For example, one school was focusing on increasing access to college prep courses when they discovered that they needed to analyze drops and retention in those courses at certain intervals during the school year. At another school, the goal was to improve daily attendance, but as educators began to implement changes, they realized they needed to monitor both student and teacher absences, the days and periods (by instructor) that experienced the most class cutting, and the instructional approaches in classes with higher and lower attendance. If monitoring is a continuous process, layers of issues will surface, a sign that the school or district is tackling fundamental issues of change and that the implementers of change are not basing decisions on superficial information.

Monitoring means tracing progress over time. Therefore, baseline data must be established; then the same sources must be used from year to year in order to prevent "comparing apples to oranges." For instance, drop-out rates are calculated many different ways; college-going rates are sometimes based on students planning to attend and other times based on students actually attending; and ethnic categories can vary in whom they encompass. Therefore, data must be gathered at consistent times to ensure accurate comparisons. If the data are to be used for reporting purposes, report timelines also need to be established.

The form What Do We Want to Find Out About Our Reform Initiative? (Figure 11.4) presents a monitoring design that was created for a mathematics change initiative in 20 K-8 schools. The form includes questions, criteria for success, indicators for analyzing progress, when and how the information will be collected, and how the data will be analyzed and interpreted. (See Table 9.3b, pages 211–212, for a sample of a completed form.) Additional columns can be added as necessary. Dialogue will be essential to identify how different stakeholders in the school or district community perceive success. Some may want to eliminate all remedial groupings, whereas others may consider any decrease to be satisfactory; some may want all children placed in algebra, whereas others may be satisfied with incremental increases. These

Figure 11.4 What Do We Want to Find Out About Our Reform Initiative?

School/District: _____
Date: _____
Planning Team Members: _____

Component & Questions	Criteria for Success	Indicators	When & How the Information Will Be Collected	Data Analysis & Interpretation Procedures
A. Classroom Practice				
B. School Culture				
C. Student Achievement				

perceptions have an impact on how the changes are implemented and can also affect the levels of commitment to the change. Although these discussions can produce some conflict, the problem solving that ensues can be healthy for the process. If this open dialogue does not occur—or is not allowed to occur—problems from differential expectations will surface later in ways that may not be possible to mediate.

PLAN FOR MONITORING THE IMPROVEMENT OF COLLEGE PREPARATION AND COLLEGE-GOING RATES

Figure 11.5 is a sample of a monitoring plan measuring the processes, test scores, and actual college-going rates for each high school in a district by race/ethnicity and gender. (See Table 9.4b, pages 214–216, for a sample of a completed form.) It was initially designed by a cross section of teachers, administrators, and counselors from high schools in the process of reform. Involving the implementers of change in the monitoring process is essential so that they can examine the impact of their work.

The form specifies the questions to be answered, the indicators, collection dates, who is responsible for collecting, and the data sources. Other items could be added, such as presentation dates, audiences, and so forth. Although specific collection dates are designated, there might be interim times that are also important for documentation. The data team or others will need to keep track of the collection and periodically remind key individuals of their responsibilities.

THE ROLE OF THE EXTERNAL RESOURCE PERSON

Chapter 1 began to describe the role of the external resource person. That role is revisited here, because the school community can greatly benefit from appropriate external assistance as they begin to design their vision, plan, implementation, and monitoring strategies for reform. The teams in particular will probably need the assistance of an external resource person at various times during the reform process. The external resource person can

- Facilitate the work of the team and school
- Keep the group focused on the task at hand
- Guide the group in examining issues in depth, and in facing, rather than avoiding, the most difficult issues and thorniest problems such as beliefs, access, equity, sorting, and labeling practices
- Assist in developing greater levels of comfort and trust among members, ensuring meaningful participation by all and resolving conflicts when necessary
- Assist in building the leadership team's capacity to develop school and community ownership in improving student achievement
- Help the leadership team develop the skills to continue successfully leading the reform effort without the assistance of the external facilitator-coach

Figure 11.5 Plan for Monitoring the Improvement of College Preparation and College-Going Rates

Data Team Members: _____		School/District: _____	
_____		Date: _____	
_____			
Goal:			

Monitoring Activity	Collection Dates	Responsible Person	Data Source

NOTE: All data are to be disaggregated by race/ethnicity and gender.

Copyright © 2002 by Corwin Press. All rights reserved. Reprinted from *Using Data to Close the Achievement Gap* by Ruth S. Johnson. Reproduction authorized only for the local school site that has purchased this book.

When to Use and Administer Instrument

Team Priorities for Assistance From External Resource Person (Figure 11.6, page 270) works very well at an early off-site team planning meeting, where there is most likely an external resource person guiding the process. The facilitator should encourage the team to use the form to evaluate exactly what kind of future assistance they believe will help them work successfully in collaboration to achieve their objectives. This would ideally take place after the team has finished developing its plan. The form can also be used at other intervals and should be kept as an ongoing record of the types of development that the team has received and still requires.

The team should first review the form, discussing each of the categories and clarifying any ambiguities. Categories can be added—as always, participants should not be restrained by the form but should use it as a launching point. It might be useful to have each member fill out a copy, have everyone present his or her explanations for where each sees the strongest needs for assistance, and then work for consensus on prioritization. The external resource person should assist the team with this prioritization, helping team members to identify their areas of strength and weakness to date. An effective facilitator will push the team to higher expectations of themselves, especially in areas where they recognize need but hesitate to act because of lack of confidence that success can be realized. After the team has reached consensus on the areas of need listed on the form, the external resource person should make a revised copy for the team, help them set up timelines for meetings, and clarify who needs to do what to prepare for the activities, for example, securing substitutes, compensation for participants if needed, materials, meeting sites, times, and so forth. If more than one school is involved, such as in a K-12 cluster situation, the schedules should be coordinated—this is time-consuming but critical. The resource person should guide this process initially, and then others can take over. All should be clear about next steps before leaving this session.

Discussion and Cautionary Notes

There are some essential qualities of effective external facilitators. It is their responsibility to impress upon leadership teams and schools the reality of what the reform process is about—fundamental improvement in student achievement. They must emphasize that moving test scores by a few percentile points is not good enough. The objective is to create opportunities for students to achieve at levels that will greatly enhance their life opportunities in the 21st century. The external resource person has a major task to get the school to move beyond the barriers and make a real commitment to reform. For the school team, the opportunity to work with an effective external reform facilitator is the time to be real and honest and to focus on what is within the control of professionals.

A team must build its capacity to lead reform, with guidance and help. Members may need to learn the processes of problem solving and conducting meetings. External reform facilitators should recognize this and teach teams these skills. At the same time, they should not create dependency situations. They should consider the wise words of Lao Tzu as they assist teams and schools: "Give a man a fish and you feed him for a day; teach him how to fish, and you feed him for a lifetime."

Figure 11.6 Team Priorities for Assistance From External Resource Person

School: _____

Date: _____

Team Members: _____

Please prioritize your school's
needs on a scale of 1–3,
1 being the highest.

I. **Strengthening the School Site Leadership Team to Move the Student Achievement Agenda Schoolwide**

   A. Facilitation of off-site retreats for the team to further develop skills to implement schoolwide reforms to raise student achievement. _____

   B. Facilitation of cluster meetings/workshops around changing specific conditions at the school site.
Please check your school's focus for the coming year
(you may check more than one). _____
        ____Curriculum
        ____Instruction
        ____Learning Opportunities & Grouping/Tracking/Labeling
        ____Expectations
        ____Professionalism & Responsibility
        ____Planning/Decision Making
        ____Services for Students

   C. School site visits—Site visits to your school by the external faciltator/coach to provide more intensive assistance and feedback using such strategies as:
1) observing implementation strategies and debriefing with team members on their efforts, problem solving and reviewing progress; 2) observing and giving feedback on effectiveness of team meetings. _____

   D. Other _____

II. **Implementation of New Standards, Curriculum, and Strategies**

   A. Classroom visits to observe the implementation of standards and instructional strategies. Post-observation meetings with teachers at the school site for feedback and planning. _____

   B. Curriculum academies to focus on and learn how to implement new standards and instructional strategies. Follow-up workshops to maintain and build newly acquired curriculum and instructional skills. _____

   C. Standards and curriculum workshops for administrators. _____

   D. Other _____

III. **Monitoring, Assessment, and Institutionalization of Reform**

   A. Assistance with strategies for using data (identifying, gathering, summarizing, analyzing, presentation). _____

   B. Facilitation of collaborative planning, assessment meetings with representative groups of teachers, principals, and program coordinators. _____

   C. Summative and formative evaluation of classroom and schoolwide reform. _____

   D. Other _____

Resources for Equitable School Reform

This list is by no means exhaustive: Many listed Web sites have links to other organizations.

A World of Difference Institute and Anti-Defamation League
720 Market Street, Suite 800
San Francisco, CA 94102-2501
Phone: (415) 981-3500
or
10495 Santa Monica Boulevard
Los Angeles, CA 90025
Phone: (310) 446-8000
www.adl.org

Achieve, Inc.
8 Story Street, First Floor
Cambridge, MA 02138
Phone: (617) 496-6300
Fax: (617) 496-6361
www.achieve.org

Accelerated Schools Project
402 S. Ceras
Stanford University
Stanford, CA 94305
Phone: (415) 725-1676
www.acceleratedschools.net

The Achievement Council
3460 Wilshire Boulevard, Suite 420
Los Angeles, CA 90010
Phone: (213) 487-3194
Fax: (213) 487-0879
www.achievementcouncil.org

Achievement Network
Evanston Township High School
1600 Dodge Avenue
Evanston, IL 60204
Phone: (847) 424-7185
www.eths.k12.il.us

American Association for the Advancement of Science
1200 New York Avenue NW
Washington, DC 20005
Phone: (202) 326-6400
www.aaas.org

American Federation of Teachers
555 New Jersey Avenue NW
Washington, DC 20001
Phone: (202) 879-4400
www.aft.org

Annenberg Institute for School Reform
Brown University
Box 1985
Providence, RI 02912
Phone: (401) 863-7990
Fax: (401) 863-1290
www.annenberginstitute.org

Association of American Colleges and Universities
1818 R Street NW
Washington, DC 20009
Phone: (202) 387-3760
Fax: (202) 265-9532
www.aacu-edu.org

Association of Community Organizations for Reform Now
88 Third Avenue, Third Floor
Brooklyn, NY 11217
Phone: (718) 246-7900
Fax: (718) 246-7939
www.acorn.org

California Tomorrow
1904 Franklin Street
Suite 300
Oakland, CA 94612
Phone: (510) 496-0220
Fax: (510) 496-0225
www.californiatomorrow.org

Center for Applied Linguistics (CAL) and National Center for Research on Cultural
Diversity and Second Language Learning (NCRCDSLL)
4646 40th Street NW
Washington, DC 20016-1859
Phone: (202) 362-0700
www.cal.org/Archive/projects/ncrcdsll.htm

Center for Education Reform
1001 Connecticut Avenue NW, Suite 204
Washington, DC 20036
Phone: (800) 521-2118
Fax: (202) 822-5077
www.edreform.com

Center for Leadership in School Reform (CLSR)
950 Breckenridge Lane, Suite 200
Louisville, KY 40207
Phone: (502) 895-1942
Fax: (502) 895-7901
www.clsr.org

Center for Multilingual, Multicultural Research
Rossier School of Education
University of Southern California
Waite Phillips Hall, Suite 402
Los Angeles, CA 90089-0031
Phone: (213) 740-2360
Fax: (213) 740-7101
www.usc.edu/dept/education/CMMR/cmmrhomepage.html

Center for Research on Education, Diversity & Excellence
CREDE UCSC
1156 High Street
Santa Cruz, CA 95064
Phone: (831) 459-3500
www.crede.ucsc.edu/

Center for Research on the Education of Students Placed at Risk (CRESPAR)
Howard University
2900 Van Ness Street NW
Washington, DC 20008
Phone: (202) 806-8484
Fax: (202) 806-8498
www.founders.howard.edu/soe/programs/CRESPAR.HTM

Children's Defense Fund
25 E Street NW
Washington, DC 20001
Phone: (202) 628-8787
www.childrensdefense.org

The Civil Rights Project
Harvard University
444 Gutman Library
6 Appian Way
Cambridge, MA 02138
Phone: (617) 495-9139
www.law.harvard.edu/civilrights

The College Board
45 Columbus Avenue
New York, NY 10023
Phone: (212) 713-8000
www.collegeboard.org

The Consortium for Chicago School Research
1313 E. 60th Street
Chicago, IL 60637
Phone: (773) 702-3364
www.consortium-chicago.org

Consortium for Policy Research in Education (CPRE)
Graduate School of Education
University of Pennsylvania
3440 Market Street, Suite 560
Philadelphia, PA 19104-3325
Phone: (215) 573-0700
Fax: (215) 573-7914
www.gse.upenn.edu/cpre

Council of Great City Schools
1301 Pennsylvania Avenue NW, Suite 702
Washington, DC 20004
Phone: (202) 393-2427
Fax: (202) 393-2400
www.cgcs.org

Cross City Campaign for Urban School Reform
407 South Dearborn Street, Suite 1500
Chicago, IL 60605
Phone: (312) 322-4880
Fax: (312) 322-4885
www.crosscity.org

The Education Trust
1725 K Street NW, Suite 200
Washington, DC 20006
Phone: (202) 293-1217
Fax: (202) 293-2605
www.edtrust.org

Education Week and Editorial Projects in Education Inc.
6935 Arlington Road, Suite 100
Bethesda, MD 20814-5233
Phone: (800) 346-1834
Fax: (301) 280-3100
www.edweek.org

Educators for Social Responsibility
23 Garden Street
Cambridge, MA 02138
Phone: (800) 370-2515
Fax: (617) 864-5164
www.esrnational.org

ERIC Clearinghouse on Educational Management
University of Oregon
1787 Agate Street
Eugene, OR 97403-5207
Phone: (800) 438-8841
Fax: (541) 346-2334
www.eric.uoregon.edu

ERIC Clearinghouse on Urban Education
Institute for Urban and Minority Education
Box 40 Teachers College, Columbia University
New York, NY 10027
Phone: (800) 601-4868
eric-web.tc.columbia.edu/

Facing History and Ourselves National Foundation, Inc.
16 Hurd Road
Brookline, MA 02445
Phone: (617) 232-1595
Fax: (617) 232-0281
www.facinghistory.org

Intercultural Development Research Association (IDRA)
5835 Callaghan Road, Suite 350
San Antonio, TX 78228-1190
Phone: (210) 444-1710
Fax: (210) 444-1714
www.idra.org

Institute for Educational Leadership (IEL)
1001 Connecticut Avenue NW, Suite 310
Washington, DC 20036
Phone: (202) 822-8405
Fax: (202) 872-4050
www.iel.org

Kentucky Department of Education
500 Mero Street, 18th Floor
Frankfort, KY 40601
Phone: (502) 564-2256
Fax: (502) 564-7749
www.kde.state.ky.us/oaa

Mid-continent Research for Education and Learning (McREL)
2550 South Parker Road, Suite 500
Aurora, CO 80014
Phone: (303) 337-0990
Fax: (303) 337-3005
www.mcrel.org

National Alliance of Black School Educators
310 Pennsylvania Avenue SE
Washington, DC 20003
Phone: (800) 221-2654
Fax: (202) 608-6319
www.nabse.org

National Association for Asian and Pacific American Education (NAAPAE)
Phone and Fax: (650) 991-4676

National Association of Multicultural Education
Phone: (202) 628-6263
Fax: (202) 628-6264
www.nameorg.org

National Black Child Development Institute
1101 15th Street NW, Suite 900
Washington, DC 20005
Phone: (202) 833-2220
Fax: (202) 833-8222
www.nbcdi.org

National Center for Educational Statistics
1990 K Street NW
Washington, DC 20006
Phone: (202) 502-7300
www.nces.ed.gov

National Center for Restructuring Education, Schools, and Teaching
Teachers College, Columbia University
Box 110
525 W. 120th Street
New York, NY 10027
Phone: (212) 678-3432
Fax: (212) 678-4170
www.tc.columbia.edu/~ncrest

National Center on Education and the Economy and New Standards (Student Performance Standards and Assessment Systems)
700 11th Street NW, Suite 750
Washington, DC 20001
Phone: (202) 783-3668
www.ncee.org

National Center on Educational Outcomes (NCEO) (for students with disabilities)
University of Minnesota
350 Elliott Hall
75 E. River Road
Minneapolis, MN 55455
Phone: (612) 626-1530
Fax: (612) 624-0879
www.coled.umn.edu/NCEO

National Clearinghouse on Bilingual Education
The George Washington University
Center for the Study of Language & Education
2121 K Street NW, Suite 260
Washington, DC 20037
Phone: (800) 321-NCBE
Fax: (800) 531-9347
www.ncbe.gwu.edu

National Coalition of Advocates for Students (NCAS) and Clearinghouse for Immigrant Education (CHIME)
100 Boylston Street, Suite 737
Boston, MA 02116
Phone: (800) 441-7192
www.igc.org/ncas/

National Commission on Teaching and America's Future
Teachers College, Columbia University
525 W. 120th Street, Box 117
New York, NY 10027
Phone: (212) 678-4153
Fax: (212) 678-4039
www.nctaf.org

National Council of La Raza (NCLR)
1111 19th Street NW, Suite 1000
Washington, DC 20036
Phone: (202) 785-1670
or
Los Angeles Office
523 West Sixth Street, Suite 301
Los Angeles, CA 90014
Phone: (213) 489-3428

Fax: (213) 489-1167
www.nclr.org

National Education Association
1201 16th Street NW
Washington, DC 20036
Phone: (202) 833-4000
www.nea.org

National Middle School Association
4151 Executive Parkway, Suite 300
Westerville, OH 43081
Phone: (800) 528-NMSA
www.nmsa.org

The NETWORK, Inc.
136 Fenno Drive
Rowley, MA 01969-1004
Phone: (978) 948-7764
Fax: (978) 948-7836
www.thenetworkinc.org

New England Association of Schools and Colleges
The Office of School/College Relations
"Rural Partnership Project for Student Success"
209 Burlington Road
Bedford, MA 01703-1433
Phone: (617) 291-0022
www.neasc.org

Office of Bilingual Education and Minority Language Affairs
U.S. Department of Education
600 Independence Avenue SW
Washington, DC 20202-6510
www.ed.gov/offices/OBEMLA/index.html

Parents for Public Schools
1520 N. State Street
Jackson, MS 39202
Phone: (800) 880-1222
Fax: (601) 353-0002
www.parents4publicschools.com

Postsecondary Education Opportunity
P.O. Box 415
Oskaloosa, IA 52577-0415
Phone: (641) 673-3401
Fax: (641) 673-3411
www.postsecondary.org

The Principals Exchange
PMB B2
13502 Whittier Boulevard, Suite H
Whittier, CA 90605

Quality Education for Minorities Network
1818 North Street NW, Suite 350
Washington, DC 20036
Phone: (202) 659-1818
qemnetwork.qem.org/

Rethinking Schools
1001 E. Keefe Avenue
Milwaukee, WI 53212
Phone: (800) 669-4192
Fax: (414) 964-7220
www.rethinkingschools.org

Southern Regional Education Board
High Schools That Work Initiative
592 Tenth Street, NW
Atlanta, GA 30318-5790
Phone: (404) 875-9211
www.sreb.org/programs/hstw/hstwindex.asp

Teachers of English to Speakers of Other Languages (TESOL)
700 S. Washington Street, Suite 200
Alexandria, VA 22314
Phone: (703) 836-0774
Fax: (703) 836-7864
www.tesol.org

Urban Institute
2100 M Street NW, Suite 500
Washington, DC 20037
Phone: (202) 857-8617
www.urban.org

U.S. Department of Education
400 Maryland Avenue SW
Washington, DC 20202-0498
Phone: (800) USA-LEARN
www.ed.gov

Bibliography

	AAUW Educational Foundation. (1992). *The AAUW report: How schools shortchange girls.* Washington, DC: NEA Professional Library.	Adelman, C. (1999). *Answers in the tool box: Academic intensity, attendance patterns, and bachelor's degree attainment.* Washington, DC: U.S. Department of Education.	Ainsworth-Darnell, J. W., & Downey, D. B. (1998). Assessing the oppositional culture explanation for racial/ethnic differences in school performance. *American Sociological Review, 63,* 536–552.	Allington, R. L., & McGill-Franzen, A. (1992). Unintended effects of education reform in New York. *Educational Policy, 6,* 397–414.	American Association for the Advancement of Science, Project 2061. (1997). *Blueprints online: Equity.* Retrieved January 29, 2002, from http://www.project2061.org/tools/bluepol/Equity/text.htm	Anderson, G. L., Herr, K., & Sigrid Nihlen, A. (1994) *Studying your own school: An educator's guide to qualitative practitioner research.* Thousand Oaks, CA: Corwin.	Artiles, A. J., & Trent, S. C. (1994). Overrepresentation of minority students in special education: A continuing debate. *Journal of Special Education, 27,* 410–437.	Banks, J. A. (1988). *Multiethnic education: Theory and practice* (2nd ed.). Boston: Allyn & Bacon.
Teams								
School/Teacher/Counselor Practices	✓			✓		✓	✓	✓
Student Outcomes	✓	✓	✓	✓	✓		✓	✓
Sociocultural							✓	✓
Resources								
Racial/Ethnic Issues		✓	✓				✓	
Parents								✓
Leadership								
Language Issues								✓
Institutional Racism							✓	
Institutional Cultures				✓			✓	✓
Institutional Change							✓	
Immigrant Issues								✓
Higher Education		✓		✓				
Gender Issues	✓			✓				
Equity	✓	✓	✓			✓	✓	✓
District								
Data Use					✓			
Broader Societal Context	✓						✓	
Accountability				✓				

	Barth, R. S. (1990). Improving schools from within: Teachers, parents, and principals can make the difference. San Francisco: Jossey-Bass.	Beane, D. B. (1988). Mathematics and science: Critical filters for the future of minority students. Washington, DC: American University.	Beauboef-Lafontant, T., & Augustine, D. S. (Eds.). (1996). Facing racism in education (2nd ed.). Harvard Educational Review, reprint series no. 28.	Bell, J. (1993). Doing your research project: A guide for first-time researchers in education and social science. Buckingham, PA: Open University Press.	Blume, G. W., & Nicely, R. F., Jr. (Eds.). (1991). A guide for reviewing school mathematics programs. Reston, VA: National Council of Teachers of Mathematics.	California Tomorrow. (1995). The schools we need now: Action and information for parents, families and communities in school restructuring [also available in Spanish]. San Francisco: Author.	Campbell, P. B., & Hoey, L. (2000). Equity means all: Rethinking the role of special programs in science and math education (A commissioned paper for the National Institute for Science Education). Retrieved from http://www.wcer.wisc.edu/nise/News_Activities/Forums/campbellpaper.html
Teams	✓						
School/Teacher/Counselor Practices	✓	✓			✓	✓	✓
Student Outcomes		✓			✓	✓	✓
Sociocultural			✓			✓	
Resources							
Racial/Ethnic Issues		✓	✓			✓	
Parents						✓	
Leadership	✓						
Language Issues					✓	✓	
Institutional Racism		✓	✓			✓	
Institutional Cultures	✓	✓			✓	✓	
Institutional Change	✓				✓	✓	
Immigrant Issues						✓	
Higher Education		✓					
Gender Issues							
Equity		✓			✓	✓	
District							
Data Use		✓		✓	✓	✓	
Broader Societal Context					✓	✓	
Accountability					✓	✓	

	Charles A. Dana Center, University of Texas at Austin. (1999). *Hope for urban education: A study of nine high-performing, high-poverty, urban elementary schools.* Washington, DC: U.S. Department of Education, Planning and Evaluation Service.	Chavkin, N. F. (1989). Debunking the myth about minority parents. *Educational Horizons, 67(4),* 119–123.	Cicourel, A. V., & Kitsuse, J. I. (1963). *The educational decision-makers.* New York: Bobbs-Merrill.	College Board. (1999). *Projected social context for education of children: 1990–2015.* New York: Author.	College Board. (1999). *Reaching the top: A report of the National Task Force on Minority High Achievement.* New York: National Task Force on Minority Achievement.	Comer, J. P. (1988). Educating poor minority children. *Scientific American, 259(5),* 42–48.	Creighton, T. B. (2000). *Schools and data: The educator's guide for using data to improve decision making.* Newbury Park, CA: Corwin.	Cummins, J. (1989). *Empowering minority students.* Sacramento: California Association for Bilingual Education.	Darder, A. (1991). *Culture and power in the classroom: A critical foundation for bicultural education.* New York: Bergin and Garvey.
Teams									
School/Teacher/Counselor Practices	✓		✓	✓	✓	✓		✓	✓
Student Outcomes	✓			✓	✓	✓		✓	✓
Sociocultural			✓		✓	✓		✓	✓
Resources					✓	✓		✓	
Racial/Ethnic Issues					✓	✓		✓	✓
Parents		✓			✓	✓			
Leadership					✓	✓			
Language Issues								✓	✓
Institutional Racism		✓						✓	✓
Institutional Cultures			✓	✓	✓	✓		✓	✓
Institutional Change					✓	✓			
Immigrant Issues			✓					✓	✓
Higher Education			✓	✓	✓				
Gender Issues			✓	✓	✓				
Equity	✓		✓	✓	✓	✓		✓	✓
District									
Data Use							✓		
Broader Societal Context			✓	✓					
Accountability	✓				✓				

	Delgado-Gaitan (1991)	Delpit (1988)	Dentzer & Wheelock (1990)	Epstein (1984)	Fordham & Ogbu (1986)	Fullan (1993)	Fullan & Stiegelbauer (1991)
Teams							✓
School/Teacher/Counselor Practices	✓	✓	✓	✓		✓	
Student Outcomes		✓	✓	✓	✓		
Sociocultural		✓	✓			✓	
Resources				✓		✓	
Racial/Ethnic Issues	✓	✓	✓			✓	
Parents	✓			✓			
Leadership					✓	✓	
Language Issues		✓					
Institutional Racism		✓	✓				
Institutional Cultures		✓	✓		✓	✓	
Institutional Change		✓			✓	✓	
Immigrant Issues							
Higher Education							
Gender Issues							
Equity		✓	✓				
District			✓		✓		
Data Use			✓				
Broader Societal Context	✓				✓		
Accountability							

Column references:

1. Delgado-Gaitan, C. (1991). Involving parents in the schools: A process of empowerment. *American Journal of Education, 100*(1), 20–46.
2. Delpit, L. D. (1988). The silenced dialogue: Power and the pedagogy in educating other people's children. *Harvard Educational Review, 58,* 280–298.
3. Dentzer, E., & Wheelock, A. (1990). *Locked in/locked out: Tracking and placement practices in Boston public schools.* Boston: Massachusetts Advocacy Center.
4. Epstein, J. L. (1984). *Home and school connections in school of the future: Implications of research on parent involvement.* Baltimore: Johns Hopkins University, Center for the Social Organization of Schools.
5. Fordham, S., & Ogbu, J. (1986). Black students, school success: Coping with the burden of "acting white." *The Urban Review, 18,* 176–206.
6. Fullan, M. (1993). *Change forces: Probing the depths of educational reform.* Bristol, PA: Falmer.
7. Fullan, M., & Stiegelbauer, S. (1991). *The new meaning of educational reform.* New York: Teachers College Press.

	Gamoran & Hannigan (2000)	Gándara (1995)	Gibson & Ogbu (1991)	Goodale & Soden (1981)	Goodlad & Keating (1990)	Grayson & Martin (1997)	Haberman (1991)	Hart & Jacobi (1992)
Teams								
School/Teacher/Counselor Practices	✓	✓	✓	✓		✓	✓	✓
Student Outcomes	✓	✓	✓	✓		✓	✓	✓
Sociocultural		✓	✓			✓		✓
Resources	✓							
Racial/Ethnic Issues	✓	✓	✓	✓	✓			✓
Parents					✓			
Leadership								
Language Issues		✓	✓					
Institutional Racism		✓	✓		✓		✓	✓
Institutional Cultures		✓	✓		✓	✓	✓	✓
Institutional Change					✓		✓	✓
Immigrant Issues		✓	✓					
Higher Education	✓	✓			✓			
Gender Issues			✓		✓	✓		
Equity	✓	✓		✓	✓	✓	✓	✓
District								
Data Use				✓				
Broader Societal Context	✓							
Accountability								

Gamoran, A., & Hannigan, E. C. (2000). Algebra for everyone: Benefits of college-preparatory mathematics for students with diverse abilities in early secondary school. *Educational Evaluation and Policy Analysis, 22,* 241–254.

Gándara, P. (1995). *Over the ivy walls: The educational mobility of low-income Chicanos.* Albany: State University of New York Press.

Gibson, M., & Ogbu, J. (1991). *Minority status and schooling.* New York: Garland.

Goodale, R., & Soden, M. (1981). *Disproportional placement of black and Hispanic students in special education programs.* New Orleans, LA: Council for Exceptional Children Conference. (ERIC Document Reproduction Service No. ED 204 873

Goodlad, J. I., & Keating, P. (Eds.). (1990). *Access to knowledge: An agenda for our nation's schools.* New York: The College Board.

Grayson, D. A., & Martin, M. D. (1997). *Generating expectations for student achievement.* Canyon Lake, CA: GrayMill.

Haberman, M. (1991). The pedagogy of poverty versus good teaching. *Phi Delta Kappan, 73*(4), 290–294.

Hart, P. J., & Jacobi, M. (1992). *From gatekeeper to advocate.* New York: The College Board.

	Harvey, T. R., & Drolet, B. (1994). *Building teams, building people.* Lancaster, PA: Technomic.	Haycock, K. (1998). Good teaching matters: How well-qualified teachers can close the gap. *Thinking K-16, 3(2),* 3–7.	Haycock, K., Jerald, C., & Huang, S. (2001). Closing the gap: Done in a decade. *Thinking K-16, 5(2),* 3–21.	Henderson, A. T., Marburger, C. L., & Ooms, T. (1989). *Beyond the bake sale: An educator's guide to working with parents.* Columbia, MD: Committee for Citizens in Education.	Hilliard, A., III. (1990). Back to Binet: The case against the use of IQ tests in the schools. *Contemporary Education, 61,* 184–189.	Hilliard, A., III. (1991). Do we have the will to educate all children? *Educational Leadership, 49(1),* 31–36.	Holcomb, E. L. (1998). *Getting excited about data: How to combine people, passion, and proof.* Newbury Park, CA: Corwin.	Howard, J. (1991). *Getting smart: The social construction of intelligence.* Lexington, MA: Efficacy Institute.	Ingersoll, R. M. (1998). The problem of out-of-field teaching. *Kappan* (p. 773). Bloomington, IN: Phi Delta Kappa.	Irvine, J. J. (1990). *Black students and school failure: Policies, practices, and prescriptions.* New York: Greenwood Press.
Teams	✓									
School/Teacher/Counselor Practices		✓	✓	✓	✓	✓		✓	✓	✓
Student Outcomes		✓	✓		✓	✓			✓	✓
Sociocultural					✓			✓		
Resources										
Racial/Ethnic Issues		✓	✓		✓			✓		✓
Parents				✓						
Leadership	✓									
Language Issues										
Institutional Racism					✓			✓		✓
Institutional Cultures			✓					✓		✓
Institutional Change	✓					✓		✓		✓
Immigrant Issues										
Higher Education										
Gender Issues					✓			✓		✓
Equity		✓	✓		✓	✓		✓	✓	✓
District										
Data Use							✓			
Broader Societal Context								✓		✓
Accountability					✓					

Category	Johnson (1996)	Johnson (1995)	Johnston & Packer (1987)	Jones (1994)	Kinsler & Gamble (2001)	Kozol (1990)	Ladson-Billings (1994)	LEAP (1993)	Lee & Fradd (1998)
Teams									
School/Teacher/Counselor Practices	✓	✓		✓	✓		✓		✓
Student Outcomes		✓		✓	✓	✓	✓		✓
Sociocultural				✓	✓	✓	✓	✓	
Resources				✓	✓			✓	
Racial/Ethnic Issues	✓			✓		✓	✓	✓	
Parents				✓	✓				
Leadership				✓	✓				
Language Issues		✓					✓	✓	✓
Institutional Racism		✓			✓	✓			
Institutional Cultures	✓	✓		✓	✓	✓			
Institutional Change	✓			✓	✓				
Immigrant Issues									
Higher Education				✓			✓	✓	
Gender Issues							✓		
Equity	✓	✓		✓		✓	✓	✓	
District				✓	✓				
Data Use			✓	✓	✓		✓		
Broader Societal Context		✓	✓		✓			✓	
Accountability	✓				✓				

Johnson, R. (1996). Understanding the need for restructuring. In L. I. Rendon & R. Hope (Eds.), *Educating a new majority: Transforming America's educational system for diversity* (pp. 121–148). San Francisco: Jossey-Bass.

Johnson, S. T. (1995). Myths and realities: African Americans and the measurement of human abilities [Special issue]. *Journal of Negro Education, 64*(3).

Johnston, W. B., & Packer, A. H. (1987). *Workforce 2000: Work and workers for the 21st century.* Indianapolis, IN: Hudson Institute.

Jones, V. (1994). *Lessons from the Equity 2000 Educational Reform Model.* New York: The College Board.

Kinsler, K., & Gamble, M. (2001). *Reforming schools.* New York: Continuum Checkmark.

Kozol, T. (1990). *Savage inequalities.* Santa Monica, CA: RAND.

Ladson-Billings, G. (1994). *The dreamkeepers: Successful teachers of African American children.* San Francisco: Jossey-Bass.

LEAP Asian Pacific American Public Policy Institute and UCLA Asian American Studies Center. (1993). *The state of Asian Pacific America: Policy issues to the year 2020.* Los Angeles: Author.

Lee, O., & Fradd, S. H. (1998). Science for all, including students from non-English language backgrounds. *Educational Researcher, 27*(4), 12–21.

	Leitman, R., Bins, K., & Unni, A. (1995). Uninformed decisions: A survey of children and parents about math and science. *NACME, 5*(1), 1–9.	Love, N. (2002). *Using data/getting results: A practical guide for school improvement in mathematics and science.* Norwood, MA: Christopher-Gordon.	Lucas, T., Henze, R., & Donato, R. (1990). Promoting the success of Latino language-minority students: An exploratory study of six high schools. *Harvard Educational Review, 60,* 315–340.	Madaus, G. F., Madaus-West, M., Harmon, M. C., Lomax, R. G., & Viator, K. A. (1992). *The influence of testing on teaching math and science in grades 4–12* (Report of a study funded by the National Science Foundation (SPA 8954759) and conducted by the Center for the Study of Testing, Evaluation, and Educational Policy. Boston College). Boston: Boston College.	Maeroff, C. I. (1993). Building teams to rebuild schools. *Phi Delta Kappan, 74,* 512–519.	Mathematical Sciences Education Board & National Research Council. (1993). *Measuring what counts: A conceptual guide for mathematics assessment.* Washington, DC: National Academy Press.
Teams					✓	
School/Teacher/Counselor Practices	✓		✓		✓	
Student Outcomes	✓	✓	✓	✓		✓
Sociocultural			✓			
Resources						
Racial/Ethnic Issues			✓			
Parents	✓					
Leadership					✓	
Language Issues			✓			
Institutional Racism						
Institutional Cultures						
Institutional Change					✓	
Immigrant Issues			✓			
Higher Education						
Gender Issues						
Equity	✓	✓	✓			
District						
Data Use		✓		✓		✓
Broader Societal Context						
Accountability		✓		✓		

	McGill-Franzen, A., & Allington, R. L. (1993). Flunk 'em or get them classified: The contamination of primary grade accountability data. *Educational Researcher, 22*(1), 19–22.	Medina, N., & Neill, M. (1988). *Fallout from the testing explosion: How 100 million standardized exams undermine equity and excellence in America's public schools.* Cambridge, MA: FairTest.	Mitchell, R. (1996). *Front end alignment.* Washington, DC: Education Trust.	Morrow, R. D. (1989). Southeast-Asian parental involvement: Can it be a reality? *Elementary School Guidance and Counseling, 23,* 289–297.	National Center for Education Statistics. (2000). *NAEP 1999 long-term trends* (Calculations by the Education Trust). Washington, DC: U.S. Department of Education.	National Commission on the High School Senior Year. (2001). *Final report: Raising our sights: No high school senior left behind.* Princeton, NJ: Woodrow Wilson National Fellowship Foundation.	National Education Commission on Time and Learning. (1994). *Prisoners of time.* Washington, DC: U.S. Government Printing Office.
Teams							
School/Teacher/Counselor Practices	✓	✓	✓	✓		✓	✓
Student Outcomes	✓	✓	✓		✓	✓	
Sociocultural						✓	
Resources							✓
Racial/Ethnic Issues		✓				✓	
Parents				✓			
Leadership							
Language Issues							
Institutional Racism	✓					✓	
Institutional Cultures	✓					✓	✓
Institutional Change						✓	✓
Immigrant Issues							
Higher Education						✓	
Gender Issues							
Equity	✓	✓				✓	
District							
Data Use					✓		
Broader Societal Context					✓		
Accountability	✓	✓	✓		✓	✓	

	National School Public Relations Association. (1993). *The ABC complete book of school surveys.* Arlington, VA: Banach, Banach & Cassidy.	New York ACORN Schools Office. (1996). *Secret apartheid: A report on racial discrimination against black and Latino parents and children in the New York City public schools.* New York: Association of Community Organizations for Reform Now.	Nicholau, S., & Ramos, C. (1990). *Together is better: Building strong partnerships between schools and Hispanic parents.* New York: Hispanic Policy Development Project.	Nieto, S. (1992). *Affirming diversity: The sociopolitical context of multicultural education.* New York: Longman.	Oakes, J. (1985). *Keeping track: How schools structure inequality.* New Haven, CT: Yale University Press.	Oakes, J., & Lipton, M. (1990). *Making the best of schools.* New Haven, CT: Yale University Press.	Office of Education Research and Improvement. (1994). *What do student grades mean? Differences across schools* (Education Research Report). Washington, DC: U.S. Department of Education.
Teams							
School/Teacher/ Counselor Practices		✓	✓		✓	✓	✓
Student Outcomes				✓	✓	✓	✓
Sociocultural		✓	✓	✓	✓		
Resources							
Racial/Ethnic Issues		✓	✓	✓	✓	✓	
Parents		✓	✓			✓	
Leadership							
Language Issues				✓			
Institutional Racism		✓			✓		
Institutional Cultures		✓		✓	✓	✓	
Institutional Change						✓	
Immigrant Issues							
Higher Education				✓			
Gender Issues							
Equity		✓	✓	✓	✓	✓	
District							
Data Use	✓						
Broader Societal Context							
Accountability							

	Accountability	Broader Societal Context	Data Use	District	Equity	Gender Issues	Higher Education	Immigrant Issues	Institutional Change	Institutional Cultures	Institutional Racism	Language Issues	Leadership	Parents	Racial/Ethnic Issues	Resources	Sociocultural	Student Outcomes	School/Teacher/ Counselor Practices	Teams
Ogbu, J. U., & Matute-Bianchi, M. E. (1990). Understanding sociocultural factors: Knowledge, identity, and school adjustment. In *Beyond language: Social and cultural factors in schooling language minority students* (pp. 73–142; developed by the Bilingual Education Office, California State Department of Education, Sacramento, California). Los Angeles: California State University, Los Angeles, Evaluation, Dissemination and Assessment Center.		✓						✓		✓		✓			✓		✓	✓		
Olsen, L., Chang, H., De La Rosa Salazar, D., De Leong, C., McCall Perez, Z., McLain, G., & Raffel, L. (1994). *The unfinished journey: Restructuring schools in a diverse society*. San Francisco: California Tomorrow.	✓	✓		✓	✓			✓	✓	✓	✓	✓	✓	✓	✓	✓	✓	✓	✓	
Olsen, L., & Chen, M. (1988). *Crossing the schoolhouse border: Immigrant students and the California public schools*. San Francisco: California Tomorrow.		✓			✓			✓	✓			✓		✓	✓		✓	✓	✓	
Olsen, L., & Mullen, N. A. (1990). *Embracing diversity: Teachers' voices from California's classrooms*. San Francisco: California Tomorrow.		✓			✓			✓	✓			✓	✓		✓		✓		✓	
Padilla, R. V., & Benavides, A. H. (Eds.). (1992). *Critical perspectives on bilingual education research*. Tempe, AZ: Bilingual Press.					✓			✓		✓		✓			✓		✓	✓	✓	
Pelavin, S. H., & Kane, M. (1990). *Changing the odds: Factors increasing access to college*. New York: The College Board.					✓		✓		✓	✓					✓			✓	✓	

Category	Peters, W. (1987). *A class divided: Then and now.* New Haven, CT: Yale University Press.	Pine, G. J., & Hilliard, A. (1990). Rx for racism: Imperatives for America's schools. *Phi Delta Kappan, 71,* 593–600.	Rendón, L. I., & Hope, R. O. (1996). *Educating a new majority.* San Francisco: Jossey-Bass.	Rosenholtz, S. J. (1991). *Teachers' workplace: The social organization of schools.* New York: Teachers College Press.	Sanders, J. R. (2000). *Evaluating school programs: An educator's guide* (2nd ed.). Newbury Park, CA: Corwin.	Simons, J., & Jablonski, D. M. (1991). *An advocate's guide to using data.* Washington, DC: Children's Defense Fund.	Singham, M. (1999). The canary in the mine. *Phi Delta Kappan, 80,* 8–15.	Sleeter, C. E. (1991). *Empowering through multicultural education.* Albany: State University of New York Press.	Smith, J. B. (1996). Does an extra year make any difference? The impact of early access to algebra on long-term gains in mathematics attainment. *Educational Evaluation and Policy Analysis, 18,* 141–153.
Teams									
School/Teacher/Counselor Practices	✓	✓	✓	✓			✓	✓	✓
Student Outcomes	✓		✓				✓	✓	✓
Sociocultural		✓	✓				✓	✓	
Resources									
Racial/Ethnic Issues	✓	✓	✓				✓	✓	
Parents			✓						
Leadership			✓						
Language Issues			✓					✓	
Institutional Racism		✓					✓		
Institutional Cultures		✓	✓	✓			✓	✓	
Institutional Change			✓	✓					
Immigrant Issues								✓	
Higher Education			✓				✓		
Gender Issues								✓	
Equity	✓		✓				✓	✓	
District							✓		
Data Use	✓				✓	✓			
Broader Societal Context			✓						
Accountability									

Category	Spring (2000)	Stevens (1996)	Tate (1994)	Tewel (1995)	Thomas (1999)	Thompson (1994)	Urban Institute (1992)	U.S. Dept. of Education (1994)	Wang et al. (1988)
Teams									
School/Teacher/Counselor Practices	✓	✓	✓				✓		✓
Student Outcomes	✓	✓	✓				✓		✓
Sociocultural	✓						✓		
Resources									
Racial/Ethnic Issues	✓		✓				✓		
Parents	✓					✓		✓	
Leadership				✓					
Language Issues	✓								
Institutional Racism	✓								
Institutional Cultures	✓		✓						✓
Institutional Change				✓		✓			
Immigrant Issues									
Higher Education						✓			
Gender Issues	✓				✓				
Equity	✓		✓			✓	✓		✓
District				✓					
Data Use					✓				
Broader Societal Context	✓								
Accountability									

Spring, J. (2000). *American education*. White Plains, NY: Longman.

Stevens, F. I. (1996). *Opportunities to learn science: Connecting research knowledge to classroom practices* (LSS Publication). Retrieved January 29, 2002, from http://www.temple.edu/LSS/pub96-6.htm.

Tate, W. F. (1994). Race, retrenchment, and the reform of school mathematics. *Phi Delta Kappan, 75,* 477–484.

Tewel, K. J. (1995). Despair at the central office. *Educational Leadership, 52*(7), 65–68.

Thomas, S. J. (1999). *Designing surveys that work: A step-by-step guide.* Thousand Oaks, CA: Corwin.

Thompson, S. (Ed.). (1994). *New schools, new communities* (formerly *Equity and choice*). Newbury Park, CA: Corwin.

Urban Institute. (1992). *Nurturing young black males: Programs that work.* Washington, DC: Author.

U.S. Department of Education. (1994). *Preparing your child for college: A resource book for parents.* Washington, DC: U.S. Government Printing Office.

Wang, M. C., Reynolds, M. C., & Walberg, H. J. (1988). Integrating the children of the second system. *Phi Delta Kappan, 70,* 248–251.

	Weiss, L., & Fine, M. (1993). *Beyond silenced voices: Class, race, and gender in United States schools.* Albany: State University of New York Press.	Wheelock, A. (1992). *Crossing the tracks: How "untracking" can save American schools.* New York: The New Press.	Wheelock, A. (1995). *Alternatives to tracking and ability grouping.* Arlington, VA: American Association of School Administrators.	Williams, B. (Ed.). (1996). *Closing the achievement gap: A vision for changing beliefs and practices.* Alexandria, VA: Association for Supervision and Curriculum Development.	Willie, C. V., Garibaldi, A. M., & Reed, W. L. (Eds.). (1991). *The education of African-Americans.* New York: Auburn House.	Willis, S. (1995). Teachers as researchers. *ASCD Education Update, 37*(3), 1–5.	Winfield, L. F., & Woodard, M. D. (1994). Assessment, equity, and diversity in reforming America's schools. *Educational Policy, 8*(1), 3–27.	Wong-Fillmore, L. (1991). When learning a second language means losing the first. *Early Childhood Research Quarterly, 6,* 323–347.
Teams								
School/Teacher/ Counselor Practices	✓	✓	✓	✓	✓	✓		
Student Outcomes		✓	✓	✓	✓		✓	
Sociocultural	✓		✓	✓	✓		✓	✓
Resources			✓					
Racial/Ethnic Issues	✓		✓	✓	✓		✓	✓
Parents							✓	✓
Leadership								
Language Issues							✓	
Institutional Racism	✓		✓					
Institutional Cultures	✓	✓	✓	✓	✓			
Institutional Change		✓	✓	✓				
Immigrant Issues					✓			
Higher Education				✓				
Gender Issues	✓	✓						
Equity	✓	✓	✓	✓	✓		✓	✓
District		✓						
Data Use						✓		
Broader Societal Context	✓			✓	✓			✓
Accountability							✓	

References

Adelman, C. (1999). *Answers in the tool box: Academic intensity, attendance patterns, and bachelor's degree attainment.* Washington, DC: U.S. Department of Education.

Allington, R. L., & Cunningham, P. M. (1996). *Schools that work: Where all children read and write.* New York: HarperCollins.

Allington, R. L., & McGill-Franzen, A. (1992a). Does high-stakes testing improve school effectiveness? *ERS-Spectrum, 10*(2), 3–12.

Allington, R. L., & McGill-Franzen, A. (1992b). Unintended effects of education reform in New York. *Educational Policy, 6,* 397–414.

Anderson, G. L., Herr, K., & Sigrid Nihlen, A. (1994) *Studying your own school: An educator's guide to qualitative practitioner research.* Thousand Oaks, CA: Corwin.

Banks, J. A. (1988). *Multiethnic education: Theory and practice* (2nd ed.). Boston: Allyn & Bacon.

Barth, R. S. (1990). *Improving schools from within: Teachers, parents, and principals can make the difference.* San Francisco: Jossey-Bass.

A better balance: Standards, tests, and the tools to succeed: Quality Counts 2001 [Special issue]. (2001, January 11). *Education Week, 20*(17).

Blank, R., & Gruebel, D. (1995). *State indicators of science and mathematics education 1995.* Washington, DC: Council of Chief State School Officers.

Brophy, J. E., & Good, T. L. (1974). *Teacher-student relationships: Courses and consequences.* New York: Holt, Rinehart & Winston.

Brophy, J., & Good, T. (1986). Teacher behavior and student achievements. In M. Wittrock (Ed.), *Handbook of research on teachings* (pp. 328–375). New York: Macmillan.

Bryk, A. S., Easton, J. Q., Kerbow, D., Rollow, S. G., & Sebring, P. A. (1993). *A view from the elementary schools: The state of reform in Chicago: A report of the Steering Committee Consortium on Chicago School Research.* Chicago: Consortium on Chicago School Research.

Bureau of Labor Statistics. (2001). *Most new entrants to the labor force will be non-white and women.* Retrieved March 5, 2002, from ftp://ftp.bls.gov/pubnews.release/history/empsit.07062001.news

Bushweller, K., & Fatemi, E. (Eds.). (2001). Technology Counts 2001: The new divide [Special issue: 2001 Editorial Projects in Education]. *Education Week, 20*(35).

California Tomorrow. (1995). *The schools we need now: Action and information for parents, families and communities in school restructuring* [also available in Spanish]. San Francisco: Author.

Chavkin, N. F. (1989). Debunking the myth about minority parents. *Educational Horizons, 67*(4), 119–123.

Cicourel, A. V., & Kitsuse, J. I. (1963). *The educational decision-makers.* New York: Bobbs-Merrill.

Clark, R. M. (1983). *Family life and school achievement*. Chicago: University of Chicago Press.

Cohen, D. K. (1991). Revolution in one classroom (or, then again was it?). *American Educator: The Professional Journal of the American Federation of Teachers, 15*(2), 16–48.

College Board. (1987). *Keeping the options open: Final report of the Commission on Precollege Guidance and Counseling*. New York: College Entrance Examination Board.

College Board. (2001). 2001 college bound seniors are the largest, most diverse group in history: More than a third are minority, but the gap remains. *The College Board News 2000–2001*. Retrieved January 29, 2002, from http://www.collegeboard.org/press/senior01/html/082801.html

College Board's National Task Force on Minority Achievement. (1999). *Reaching the top: A report of the National Task Force on Minority High Achievement*. New York: Author.

Committee on Equal Opportunities in Science and Engineering. (2000). *Enhancing the diversity of the science and engineering workforce to sustain America's leadership in the 21st century: Executive summary of the 2000 Biennial Report to Congress*. Arlington, VA: National Science Foundation.

Crawford, M., & Dougherty, E. (2000). *Updraft/downdraft: Class, culture and academic achievement in high school*. Unpublished manuscript prepared for the National Association of System Heads.

Cummins, J. (1989). *Empowering minority students*. Sacramento: California Association for Bilingual Education.

Darder, A. (1991). *Culture and power in the classroom: A critical foundation for bicultural education*. New York: Bergin and Garvey.

Darling-Hammond, L., Berry, B., & Thoreson, A. (2001). Does teacher certification matter? Evaluating the evidence. *Educational Evaluation and Policy Analysis, 23*(1), 57–77.

Delpit, L. D. (1988). The silenced dialogue: Power and the pedagogy in educating other people's children. *Harvard Educational Review, 58*, 280–298.

Dentzer, E., & Wheelock, A. (1990). *Locked in/locked out: Tracking and placement practices in Boston public schools*. Boston: Massachusetts Advocacy Center.

Edmonds, R. (1979). Effective schools for the urban poor. *Educational Leadership, 37*(1), 15–23.

Education Trust. (2001). *Education in America 2001* [PowerPoint presentation]. Washington, DC: Author.

Elmore, R. F. (2000). *Building a new structure for school leadership*. Washington, DC: The Albert Shaker Institute.

Epstein, J. L. (1984). *Home and school connections in school of the future: Implications of research on parent involvement*. Baltimore: Johns Hopkins University, Center for the Social Organization of Schools.

Estler, S., & Boyan, N. J. (Eds.). (1988). *Handbook of research on educational administration*. White Plains, NY: Longman.

Evans, L., & Teddlie, C. (1995). Facilitating change in schools: Is there one best style? *School Effectiveness and School Improvements, 6*(1), 1–22.

Fine, L. (2001, March 14). Studies examine racial disparities in special education. *Education Week, 20*(27), 6.

Fine, M. (1993). [Ap]parent involvement. *Equity and Choice, 9*(3), 4–8.

Floden, R., Porter, A., Freeman, D., Schmidt, W., & Schwille, J. (1981). Responses to curriculum pressures: A policy-capturing study of teacher decisions about context. *Journal of Education Psychology, 73,* 129–141.

Fullan, M. (1993). *Change forces: Probing the depths of educational reform.* Bristol, PA: Falmer.

Fullan, M., & Stiegelbauer, S. (1991). *The new meaning of educational reform.* New York: Teachers College Press.

Gamoran, A., & Hannigan, E. C. (2000). Algebra for everyone: Benefits of college-preparatory mathematics for students with diverse abilities in early secondary school. *Educational Evaluation and Policy Analysis, 22,* 241–254.

Gehring, J. (2001, May). Not enough girls. *Education Week, 20*(35), 18–19.

Goldenberg, C., & Gallimore, R. (1991). Local knowledge, research, knowledge, and educational change: A case study of early Spanish reading improvement. *Educational Researcher, 20*(8), 2–14.

Goodlad, J. I., & Keating, P. (Eds.). (1990). *Access to knowledge: An agenda for our nation's schools.* New York: The College Board.

Grant, C. A., & Sleeter, C. E. (1988). Race, class and gender and abandoned dreams. *Teachers College Record, 90*(1), 19–40.

Haberman, M. (1991). The pedagogy of poverty versus good teaching. *Phi Delta Kappan, 73*(4), 290–294.

Hart, P. J., & Germaine-Watts, J. (1996). Foreword. In R. S. Johnson, *Setting our sights: Measuring equity in school change* (pp. 1–7). Los Angeles: The Achievement Council.

Hart, P. J., & Jacobi, M. (1992). *From gatekeeper to advocate.* New York: The College Board.

Haycock, K. (1998). Good teaching matters a lot. *Thinking K-16, 3*(2), 4–13.

Haycock, K. (2001). New frontiers for a new century: A national overview. *Thinking K-16, 5*(2), 1–2.

Haycock, K., Jerald, C., & Huang, S. (2001). Closing the gap: Done in a decade. *Thinking K-16, 5*(2), 3–21.

Haycock, K., & Navarro, S. (1988). *Unfinished business: Fulfilling our children's promise.* Los Angeles: The Achievement Council.

Henderson, A. T., Marburger, C. L., & Ooms, T. (1989). *Beyond the bake sale: An educator's guide to working with parents.* Columbia, MD: The Committee for Citizens in Education.

Hilliard, A., III. (1991). Do we have the will to educate all children? *Educational Leadership, 49*(1), 31–36.

Howard, J. (1991). *Getting smart: The social construction of intelligence.* Lexington, MA: Efficacy Institute.

Irvine, J. J. (1990). *Black students and school failure: Policies, practices, and prescriptions.* New York: Greenwood Press.

Johnson, R. S. (1996a). *Setting our sights: Measuring equity in school change.* Los Angeles: The Achievement Council.

Johnson, R. S. (1996b). Understanding the need for restructuring. In L. I. Rendon & R. O. Hope (Eds.), *Educating a new majority: Transforming America's educational system for diversity* (pp. 121–148). San Francisco: Jossey-Bass.

Johnson, S. T. (1995). Myths and realities: African Americans and the measurement of human abilities [Special issue]. *Journal of Negro Education, 64*(3).

Johnston, R. C. (2001). Central office is critical bridge to help schools. *Education Week, 20*(25), 1, 18–19.

Johnston, W. B., & Packer, A. H. (1987). *Workforce 2000: Work and workers for the 21st century.* Indianapolis, IN: Hudson Institute.

Jones, F. (2000). Educational leadership in a diverse society: Toward a tradition of empowerment and emancipation. *Journal of the California Association of Professors of Educational Administration, 12*(1), 175–186.

Jones, V. (1994). *Lessons from the Equity 2000 Educational Reform Model.* New York: The College Board.

Jones, V. C. (2001). *Effective policies and practices that have increased the academic performance of African American students: Culturally relevant and responsive education.* Paper presented at the conference Closing the Achievement Gap, Los Angeles, CA.

Jones, V. X. (1999). *Academic tracking: Systemically under educating African American, Latino and poor students American style.* Unpublished manuscript.

Kahle, J. B., Meece, J., & Scantlebury, K. (2000). Urban African-American middle school science students: Does standards-based teaching make a difference? *Journal of Research in Science Teaching, 37,* 1019–1041.

Kain, J. F., & Singleton, K. (1996, May/June). Equality of educational opportunity revisited. *New England Economic Review,* 109.

Kim, J. J., Crasco, L. M., Smith, R. B., Johnson, G., Karantonis, A., & Leavitt, D. J. (2001). *Academic excellence for all students: Their accomplishments in science and mathematics* (USI Evaluative Study, funded by the National Science Foundation). Norwood, MA: Systemic Research.

Kozol, T. (1990). *Savage inequalities.* Santa Monica, CA: RAND.

Ladson-Billings, G. (1994). *The dreamkeepers: Successful teachers of African American children.* San Francisco: Jossey-Bass.

Leinhardt, G. (1983). Overlap: Testing whether it is taught. In B. F. Madaus (Ed.), *The courts, validity, and minimum competency testing* (pp. 153–170). Boston: Kluwer-Nijhoff.

Leinhardt, G., & Seewald, A. (1981). Overlap: What's tested, what's taught. *Journal of Educational Measurement, 18*(2), 85–96.

Leitman, R., Bins, K., & Unni, A. (1995). Uninformed decisions: A survey of children and parents about math and science. *NACME, 5*(1), 1–9.

LeMahieu, P., & Leinhardt, F. (1985). Overlap: Influencing what's taught, a process model of teachers' content selection. *Journal of Classroom Interactions, 21*(1), 2–11.

Little, J. W., & McLaughlin, M. W. (1993). *Teachers' work: Individuals, colleagues, and contexts.* New York: Teachers College Press.

Maeroff, C. I. (1993). Building teams to rebuild schools. *Phi Delta Kappan, 74,* 512–519.

Mathematical Sciences Education Board & National Research Council. (1993). *Measuring what counts: A conceptual guide for mathematics assessment.* Washington, DC: National Academy Press.

McDonnell, L., Burstein, L., Catterall, J., Ormseth, T., & Moody, D. (1990). *Discovering what schools really teach: Designing improved coursework indicators.* Santa Monica, CA: RAND.

McGill-Franzen, A., & Allington, R. L. (1993). Flunk 'em or get them classified: The contamination of primary grade accountability data. *Educational Researcher, 22*(1), 19–22.

McLaughlin, R. (1996). *The evaluation food chain: The evaluation forum proceedings*. Providence, RI: New England Desegregation Assistance Center Press, Brown University.

Mickelson, R. A. (2001). Subverting Swann: First- and second-generation segregation in the Charlotte-Mecklenburg schools. *American Educational Research Journal, 38*(2), 215–252.

National Association of Educational Progress. (1992). *Trends in academic progress*. Washington, DC: Author.

National Center for Education Statistics. (1995). *Vocational course taking and achievement: An analysis of high school transcripts and 1990 NAEP assessment schools*. Washington, DC: U.S. Department of Education.

National Center for Education Statistics. (2000). *NAEP trends in academic achievement*. Washington, DC: U.S. Department of Education.

National Center for Education Statistics & U.S. Department of Education. (1993). *The condition of education 1993*. Washington, DC: U.S. Government Printing Office.

National Coalition of Educational Equity Advocates. (1994). *Educate America: A call for equity in school reform*. Chevy Chase, MD: The Mid-Atlantic Equity Consortium.

National Commission on Teaching and America's Future. (1996). *What matters most: Teaching for America's future*. New York: Author.

National Commission on the High School Senior Year. (2001). *Final report: Raising our sights: No high school senior left behind*. Princeton, NJ: Woodrow Wilson National Fellowship Foundation.

National Education Commission on Time and Learning. (1994). *Prisoners of time*. Washington, DC: U.S. Government Printing Office.

New York ACORN Schools Office. (1996). *Secret apartheid: A report on racial discrimination against black and Latino parents and children in the New York City public schools*. New York: Association of Community Organizations for Reform Now.

Nicholau, S., & Ramos, C. (1990). *Together is better: Building strong partnerships between schools and Hispanic parents*. New York: Hispanic Policy Development Project.

Nichols, B. W., & Singer, K. P. (2000). Developing data mentors. *Educational Leadership, 57*(5), 34–37.

Oakes, J. (1985). *Keeping track: How schools structure inequality*. New Haven, CT: Yale University Press.

Office of Education Research and Improvement. (1994). *What do student grades mean? Differences across schools* (Education Research Report). Washington, DC: U.S. Department of Education.

Ogbu, J. U., & Matute-Bianchi, M. E. (1990). Understanding sociocultural factors: Knowledge, identity, and school adjustment. In *Beyond language: Social and cultural factors in schooling language minority students* (pp. 73–142; developed by the Bilingual Education Office, California State Department of Education, Sacramento, California). Los Angeles: California State University, Los Angeles, Evaluation, Dissemination and Assessment Center.

Olsen, L. (1996). Moving the dialogue with data. *California Perspectives, 5*, 48–61.

Olsen, L., Chang, H., De La Rosa Salazar, D., De Leong, C., McCall Perez, Z., McLain, G., & Raffel, L. (1994). *The unfinished journey: Restructuring schools in a diverse society*. San Francisco: California Tomorrow.

Olsen, L., & Jaramillo, A. (1999). *Turning the tides of exclusion: A guide for educators and advocates for immigrant students.* Oakland, CA: California Tomorrow.

Olson, L. (2001, January 11). Balancing act: Finding the right mix. *Education Week, 20*(17), 13–21.

Parker, L. (1993). Acquiring and using resources. In P. B. Forsyth & M. Tollerico (Eds.), *City schools: Leading the way.* Newbury Park, CA: Corwin.

Pelavin, S. H., & Kane, M. (1990). *Changing the odds: Factors increasing access to college.* New York: The College Board.

Persell, C. H. (1977). *Education and inequality.* New York: The Free Press.

Principals Exchange. (2001a). *Numbers of students on "grade level": Comparison of grade point averages and SAT/9 performance, school evaluation report.* Whittier, CA: Author.

Principals Exchange. (2001b). [Unpublished documents]. Whittier, CA: Author.

Reich, R. B. (1991). *The work of nations.* New York: Knopf.

Rice, R., & Walsh, C. E. (1996). Equity at risk: The problem with state and federal education reform efforts. In C. E. Walsh (Ed.), *Education reform and social changes: Multicultural voices, struggles and visions.* Mahwah, NJ: Lawrence Erlbaum.

Rosenholtz, S. J. (1991). *Teachers' workplace: The social organization of schools.* New York: Teachers College Press.

Saavedra, E. (1996). Teacher study groups: Contexts for transformative learning and action. *Theory Into Practice, 35,* 271–277.

Sandham, J. L. (2001a, May). Driven data. *Education Week, 20*(17), 62–63.

Sandham, J. L. (2001b, January 11). Parent power. *Education Week, 20*(17), 60–61.

Sandham, J. L. (2001c, January 11). The personal touch. *Education Week, 20*(17), 66–67.

Scoon Reid, K. (2001). Racial disparities. *Education Week, 20*(35), 16–17.

Sergiovanni, T. J. (2001). *The principalship.* Needham Heights, MA: Allyn & Bacon.

Shavelson, R., & Stern, P. (1981). Research on teachers' pedagogical thoughts, judgments, decisions, and behaviors. *Review of Educational Research, 5*(4), 275–277.

Singham, M. (1998, September). The canary in the mine: The achievement gap between black and white students. *Phi Delta Kappan, 80*(1), 8–15.

Sleeter, C. E. (1991). *Empowering through multicultural education.* Albany: State University of New York Press.

Spring, J. (2000). *American education.* White Plains, NY: Longman.

Stevens, F. (1993). *Opportunity to learn: Issues of equity for poor and minority students.* Washington, DC: National Center for Education Statistics.

Stevenson, H., & Stigler, J. (1992). *The learning gap: Why our schools are failing and what can we learn from Japanese and Chinese education.* New York: Summit Books.

Stout, R. T. (1993). Establishing the mission, vision and goals. In P. B. Forsyth & M. Tollerico (Eds.), *City schools: Leading the way* (pp. 287–318). Newbury Park, CA: Corwin.

Swasey, M. (1996–1997, Winter). School shock. *Rethinking Schools,* 5–6.

Tewell, K. J. (1995). Despair at the central office. *Educational Leadership, 52*(7), 65–68.

Tuckman, B. W. (1965). Developmental sequence in small groups. *Psychological Bulletin, 63*(6), 384–399.

Valverde, G. A., & Schmidt, W. H. (1998, Winter). Refocusing U.S. math and science education: International comparison of schooling hold important lessons for improving student achievement. *Issues in Science & Technology*, 1–7.

Viadero, D. (2000, March). Lags in minority achievement defy traditional explanations. *Education Week, 19*(19), 18–22.

Wheelock, A. (1992). *Crossing the tracks: How "untracking" can save American schools.* New York: The New Press.

Wiley, D. (1990). *Opportunity to learn: A briefing for the Advisory Council on Education Statistics.* Washington, DC: National Center for Education Statistics.

Winfield, L. F. (1986). Teacher beliefs toward academically at-risk students in inner city urban schools. *Urban Review, 18*, 253–268.

Winfield, L. (1987). Teachers' estimates of test content covered in class and first-grade students' reading achievement. *Elementary School Journal, 87*(4), 438–445.

Winfield, L. F., Johnson, R. S., & Manning, J. B. (1993). Managing instructional diversity. In P. B. Forsyth & M. Tollerico (Eds.), *City schools: Leading the way* (pp. 97–130). Newbury Park, CA: Corwin.

Winfield, L. F., & Woodard, M. D. (1994). Assessment, equity, and diversity in reforming America's schools. *Educational Policy, 8*(1), 3–27.

Yoon, B., Burstein, L., Gold, K., Chen, Z., & Kim, K. (1990). *Validating teachers' reports of content coverage: An example from secondary school mathematics.* Paper presented at the annual meeting of National Council on Measurement in Education, Boston, MA.

Index

CORWIN
PRESS

The Corwin Press logo—a raven striding across an open book—represents the happy union of courage and learning. We are a professional-level publisher of books and journals for K-12 educators, and we are committed to creating and providing resources that embody these qualities. Corwin's motto is "Success for All Learners."